Rick.
S|

Reykjavík

CONTENTS

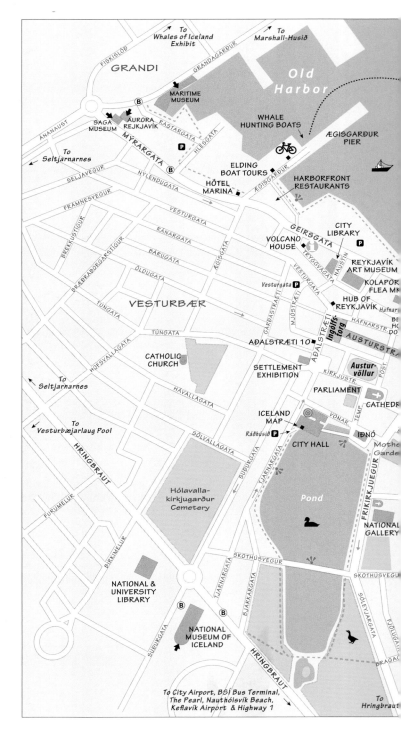

Reykjavík Center

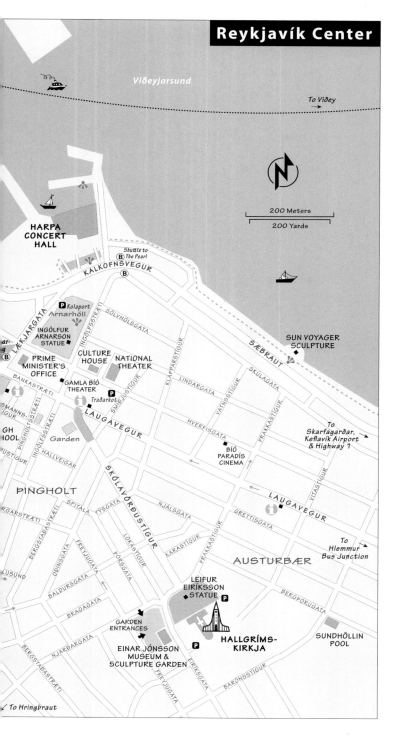

Viðeyjarsund

To Viðey

200 Meters
200 Yards

HARPA
CONCERT
HALL

Shuttle to
The Pearl

KALKOFNSVEGUR

Ⓑ

LÆKJARGATA

Ⓟ Kolaport
Arnarhóll

INGÓLFUR
ARNARSON
STATUE

SÖLVHÓLSGATA

INGÓLFSSTRÆTI

SUN VOYAGER
SCULPTURE

SÆBRAUT

Ⓑ

PRIME
MINISTER'S
OFFICE

CULTURE
HOUSE

NATIONAL
THEATER

KLAPPARSTÍGUR

BANKASTRÆTI

GAMLA BÍÓ
THEATER

LINDARGATA

SKÚLAGATA

SMIÐJUSTÍGUR

VATNSSTÍGUR

…MANNS-
…TÍGUR

Ⓟ
Traðarkot

LAUGAVEGUR

HVERFISGATA

FRAKKASTÍGUR

GH
…HOOL

INGÓLFSSTRÆTI

ÞINGHOLTSSTRÆTI

Garden

HALLVEIGAR

To
Skarfagarðar,
Keflavík Airport
& Highway 1

…USTIGUR

SKÓLAVÖRÐUSTÍGUR

BÍÓ
PARADÍS
CINEMA

ÞINGHOLT

SPÍTALA…

TÝSGATA

NJÁLSGATA

GRETTISGATA

LAUGAVEGUR

VITASTÍGUR

RGARSTRÆTI

BERGSTAÐA…STRÆTI

FREYJUGATA

ÓÐINSGATA

LOKASTÍGUR

ÞÓRSGATA

KÁRASTÍGUR

FRAKKASTÍGUR

To
Hlemmur
Bus Junction

…LUSUND

BALDURSGATA

AUSTURBÆR

BRAGAGATA

LEIFUR
EIRÍKSSON
STATUE Ⓟ

BERGÞÓRUGATA

BERGSTAÐASTRÆTI

NJARÐARGATA

GARDEN
ENTRANCES

EINAR JÓNSSON
MUSEUM &
SCULPTURE GARDEN

Ⓟ

HALLGRÍMS-
KIRKJA

EIRÍKSGATA

FREYJUGATA

BARÓNSSTÍGUR

SUNDHÖLLIN
POOL

To Hringbraut

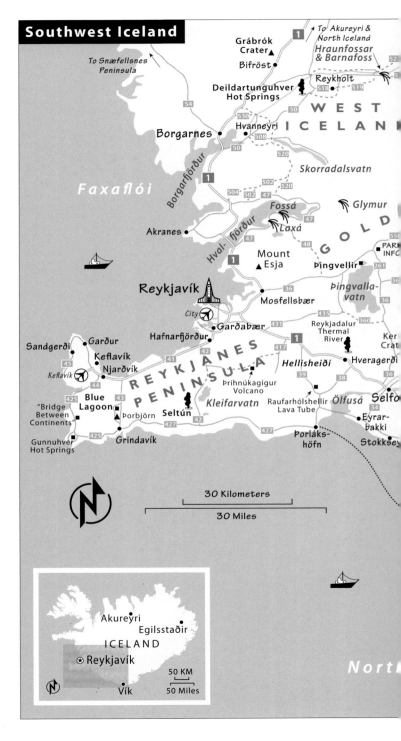

Southwest Iceland

To Akureyri &
North Iceland

Grábrók
Crater▲

Hraunfossar
& Barnafoss

To Snæfellsnes
Peninsula

Bifröst ●

Deildartunguhver
Hot Springs

Reykholt

W E S T

I C E L A N

Borgarnes ●

Hvanneyri

Faxaflói

Skorradalsvatn

Fossá

Glymur

Akranes ●

Laxá

G O L D

PARK
INFO

Mount
▲ Esja

Þingvellir ■

Þingvalla-
vatn

Reykjavík

Mosfellsbær

Reykjadalur
Thermal
River

Ker
Crat

City ✈

Garðabær

Hafnarfjörður

R E Y K J A N E S

Hveragerði

Sandgerði

Garður

Keflavík

Njarðvík

Hellisheiði

Ölfusá

Selfo

P E N I N S U L A

Keflavík ✈

Þríhnúkagígur
Volcano

"Bridge
Between
Continents"

Blue
Lagoon

Þorbjörn ▲

Kleifarvatn

Raufarhólshellir
Lava Tube

Seltún

Eyrar-
bakki

Gunnuhver
Hot Springs

Grindavík

Þorláks-
höfn

Stokkse

N

30 Kilometers

30 Miles

Akureyri

Egilsstaðir

I C E L A N D

⊛ Reykjavík

50 KM

50 Miles

Vík

N

Nort

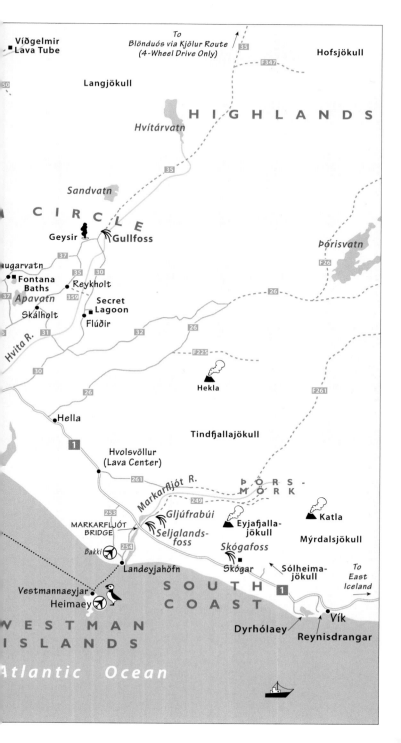

INTRODUCTION

This Snapshot guide, excerpted from my guidebook *Rick Steves Iceland*, introduces you to Iceland's capital city, Reykjavík. Its colorful, pedestrian-friendly downtown has fine museums, a stroll-worthy harbor, and a dozen thermal swimming pools, perfect for a rejuvenating soak among Icelanders. The capital's restaurants are surprisingly good, and its nightlife scene is legendary.

Iceland's natural splendors are what attract most visitors, but Icelanders are also worth getting to know. They have a gentle spirit and a can-do frontier attitude. They're also whip-smart (Icelandic scholars were the first to write down the legends and histories of the early Scandinavian people—collectively called "the sagas"). Enjoy meeting the easygoing Icelanders; in this little country, everyone's on a first-name basis.

Reykjavík is also the natural jumping-off point for exploring Iceland's dramatic countryside. It's an easy hop from Reykjavík inland to the Golden Circle route, studded with natural and historical attractions (from geysers to thundering waterfalls), or south to the legendary Blue Lagoon thermal baths (on the Reykjanes Peninsula, near the international airport at Keflavík). Excursions can take you beyond Reykjavík to a host of Icelandic experiences.

Iceland's countryside is famously spectacular. While it's hard to have a bad time here, it's easy to underestimate the notoriously changeable weather, blow through too much money, or waste time by not making a sensible plan. But if you equip yourself with good information (this book) and expect to travel smart, you will.

To help you have the best trip possible, I've included the following topics in this book:

• **Planning Your Time,** with advice on how to make the most of your limited time

• **Orientation,** including tourist information (abbreviated as TI), tips on public transportation, local tour options, and helpful hints

Sights with ratings:

▲▲▲—Don't miss

▲▲—Try hard to see

▲—Worthwhile if you can make it

No rating—Worth knowing about

• **Sleeping** and **Eating,** with good-value recommendations in every price range

• **Connections,** with tips on buses and driving

Practicalities, near the end of this book, has information on money, staying connected, hotel reservations, transportation, and other helpful hints.

It's my hope that this guide will make your trip more meaningful and rewarding. Traveling like a temporary local, you'll get the absolute most out of every mile, minute, and dollar.

Góða ferð! Happy travels!

Rick Steves

REYKJAVÍK

REYKJAVÍK

Reykjavík, the tiny capital of a remote island-nation, is unexpectedly cosmopolitan, with an artistic, bohemian flair. It lacks world-class sights, yet manages to surprise and delight even those who use the city mostly as a home base for exploring Iceland's natural wonders.

The city's downtown streets are lined with creative restaurants, quirky art galleries, rollicking bars serving everything from craft beer to designer cocktails, and shops selling stuffed puffins, local knitwear, and Gore-Tex parkas.

Reykjavík is a colorful enclave in a stark landscape: It seems every wall serves as a canvas for a vibrant street-art mural, and each corner is occupied by a cozy, art-strewn, stay-awhile café. In the old town center, colorful timber-frame houses clad in corrugated metal sheets huddle together amid a sprinkling of landmarks—such as the striking Hallgrímskirkja church, which crowns the town's highest point.

Like the rest of the country, Reykjavík has old roots. Viking Age farmers settled here in the ninth century. Until the 1750s, this area remained nothing more than a sprawling farm. As towns started to form in Iceland, Reykjavík emerged as the country's capital. Today, the capital region is a small city, home to two out of every three Icelanders—a population similar to that of Berkeley, California, or Fargo, North Dakota. The northernmost capital city on earth—which straddles the European and American hemispheres—feels more New World than Old.

With the recent tourism boom, these days Icelanders tend to work, live, and shop in the suburbs, and make fun of Reykjavík's downtown core with all its "puffin shops" sell-ing souvenirs. But that doesn't mean you should avoid downtown: Visitors find just about everything they need in this small, walkable zone. You can take in the vibe of this pithy city in a leisurely two-hour stroll, and it's an enjoyable place to simply hang out. While museums aren't a priority here, those seeking sights can eas-ily fill a day or two.

Step into Hallgrímskirkja's serene church interior. Learn about this little nation's proud history at the National Museum and the Maritime Museum, and about the city's humble Viking Age roots at the Settlement Exhibition—built around the surviving walls of a 10th-century longhouse. Art lovers can visit a half-dozen galleries highlighting Icelandic artists (early-20th-century sculptor Einar Jónsson is tops). Naturalists can go on a whale-watching cruise, or ride a ferry to an island. Modern architecture fans can ogle the award-winning Harpa concert hall, then walk along the shoreline to the iconic *Sun Voyager* sculpture.

Or head out to the suburbs to see the Pearl, the domed build-ing designed to check off many Icelandic targets in one go—with exhibits on whales, puffins, glaciers, volcanoes, and the northern lights, plus panoramic city views.

Plenty of family-friendly activities—open-air museum, zoo, botanic garden—are just beyond the city center. To recharge, the capital area has plenty of relaxing—and very local—thermal swim-ming pools.

But don't focus too much on Reykjavík. Instead, use the city as a springboard for Iceland's glorious countryside sights, taking advantage of its accommodations, great restaurants, and lively nightlife. Even on a longer visit, drivers may prefer sleeping at a distance, dropping into town only for occasional sightseeing, stroll-ing, and dining. To save money and have a more local experience, consider sleeping in suburban Reykjavík—which has fewer hotels, but ample Airbnb options.

REYKJAVÍK

Greater Reykjavík

Faxaflói

Lundey

Akurey   Engey   Viðey   Geldinganes

Grotta   IMAGINE PEACE
                                            TOWER
Seltjarnarnes   Örfirisey   *Old*   SKARFAGARÐAR
        SUÐURSTRÖND   *Harbor*   CRUISE
                                                           TERMINAL
                        HARPA
                                    LAUGARVEGUR 41   GRAY LINE
SELTJARNARNES   ■ ZOO   BUS
POOL   TERMINAL
            See Reykjavik maps
    SHORELINE   R e y k j a v í k
    STROLL   BSÍ BUS
                    TERMINAL   49   MIKLABRAUT
Skerjafjörður   *Reykjavík* THE   BÚSTAÐAVEGUR   49   VESTURLANDS-
                    City   PEARL
                                                          SLEDDING
                        Nauthólsvík 40   HILL   ■ B #16
                        Beach   ÁRBÆJARSAFN
BESSASTAÐIR   KÓPAVOGS ■ B   OPEN-AIR
(PRESIDENT'S   POOL   Kópavogur   41   FOLK MUSEUM
RESIDENCE)
ÁLFTANES   FÍFUHVAMMSVEGUR   ■ MJÓDD
POOL   ■ B   STRÆTÓ BUS
                                SMÁRALIND   TERMINAL
Hliðsnes   SHOPPING   413
                                MALL
                                Garðabær
                    See detail map   VÍFILSSTAÐAVEGUR   410
                        40
    Hafnarfjörður   41   Vífilsstaða-
                                             vatn
                                    ■ IKEA
                    #1 B
                        VIKING
                        VILLAGE
    STRAUMSVÍK   To Keflavík #1
    ALUMINUM   Airport &   B
    PLANT   Blue Lagoon 41   To Íshestar
                    ÁSVALLALAUG   Horse Farm
                    POOL

PLANNING YOUR TIME

On a short visit, savor Reykjavík's strolling ambience in the morning and evening, maybe drop into one or two sights early or late, and use your precious daytime hours to tour sights in the countryside (see the Beyond Reykjavík chapter for an overview of your options). My self-guided Reykjavík Walk offers a helpful town ori-

entation (and crash course on Iceland) that can be done at any time of day or night.

On a longer trip—or in winter (when countryside options are limited)—Reykjavík warrants more time. The following schedule is designed to fill two full days in Reykjavík itself. With less time, mix and match from these options. My plan ignores weather—in practice, let the weather dictate your itinerary. If it's blowing hard

REYKJAVÍK

and drizzling, prioritize indoor sights. When the weather's good, get outside.

Day 1: Start with my self-guided walk around downtown, and (if the line's not too long) ride up the tower of Hallgrímskirkja church. Find a nice lunch in the Laugavegur/Skólavörðustígur area. Walk down to the *Sun Voyager* sculpture for a photo op, then follow the shoreline to the Harpa concert hall (peek in the lobby, and stop by the box office to survey entertainment options). Follow the moored boats around to the Old Harbor, where you can comparison-shop whale watching and other boat tours for tomorrow. Then continue along the harbor to the Grandi area, where you can drop into your choice of exhibits: Whales of Iceland, Saga Museum, Maritime Museum, Aurora Reykjavík, or FlyOver Iceland. Return to the downtown area for dinner and after-hours strolling. Before or after dinner, unwind with the Icelanders in one of Reykjavík's thermal swimming pools.

Day 2: Begin your day at the Settlement Exhibition. If that compact exhibit whets your appetite for Icelandic history, take a walk along the Pond (the city's little lake) to the National Museum. After lunch, take your pick of activities: boat trip (either whale or puffin watching, or simply a ride out to Viðey Island); suburban sights, including the Pearl (with its many high-tech exhibits, and a grand city view), the sights in Laugardalur (botanic garden, zoo), and/or Árbær Open-Air Museum; or explore the city's many art museums. Consider another dip in a thermal pool before enjoying a food tour or dinner in the center.

If you're in town on a weekend, squeeze in a visit to the Kolaportið flea market, downtown.

Orientation to Reykjavík

Reykjavík's population is about 125,000, but the entire capital region stretches to about 216,000. The compact core of Reykjavík radiates out from the main walking street, which changes names from Austurstræti to Bankastræti to Laugavegur as it cuts through the city. You can walk from one end of downtown Reykjavík (Ingólfstorg square) to the other (the bus junction Hlemmur) in about 20 minutes. Just northwest of downtown is  the mostly postindustrial Old Harbor zone, with excursion boats, salty restaurants, and a few sights.

Greater Reykjavík is made up of six towns. Hafnarfjörður

("harbor fjord"), to the south, has its own history, harbor, and downtown core. Kópavogur and Garðabær, between Reykjavík and Hafnarfjörður, are 20th-century suburbs. Mosfellsbær, once a rural farming district along the road running north from Reykjavík, has turned into a sizable town of its own. And Seltjarnarnes is a posh enclave at the end of the Reykjavík peninsula. While I haven't recommended specific hotels or restaurants in these neighborhoods (except in Hafnarfjörður), finding an affordable Airbnb in one of these areas can provide a local home base.

TOURIST INFORMATION

Reykjavík has four tourist information offices (TIs), called **What's On,** sprinkled along the main east-west tourist axis, from Laugavegur to the Old Harbor (see the "Reykjavík Walk" map). Each offers mostly the same services (including baggage storage, excursions, and tour bookings) and has similar hours (generally daily 9:00-20:00, shorter hours Sun and in winter, tel. 551-3600, www.whatson.is). You'll find offices at Laugavegur 54, Laugavegur 5, Bankastræti 2 (set back from the street, closed Sun), and in the Volcano House at Tryggvagata 11. Bus passes are only available at the Bankastræti location; this location also has a **Safe Travel** counter, which offers advice about driving, weather, and other concerns while on the road or out in the backcountry (www.safetravel.is). There's also a lounge with tables where you can sit and enjoy free coffee while you ponder your options.

The TI's free and helpful monthly entertainment guide, *What's On,* is distributed at their offices and at hotels.

Alternatively, **Visit Reykjavík,** the city-run TI, offers info online at www.visitreykjavik.is.

The *Reykjavík Grapevine,* a free informative English-language paper and website, provides a roundup of sightseeing hours, music listings, helpful restaurant reviews, and fun insights into local life (www.grapevine.is). The local blog IHeartReykjavik.net also has helpful insights about both the capital region and all of Iceland.

Sightseeing Pass: The **Reykjavík City Card** may make sense for busy museum sightseers on a longer stay, but is not worth it for a short visit. It covers bus transport, city-run museums, Reykjavík swimming pools, and some other attractions (24 hours-3,900 ISK, 48 hours-5,500 ISK, 72 hours-6,700 ISK; sold at participating museums, TIs, hotels and hostels, and at City Hall; www.citycard.is).

ARRIVAL IN REYKJAVÍK

International flights use Keflavík Airport, a 45-minute drive from downtown Reykjavík (the Reykjavík City Airport is for domestic flights). For information on getting between Keflavík and down-

REYKJAVÍK

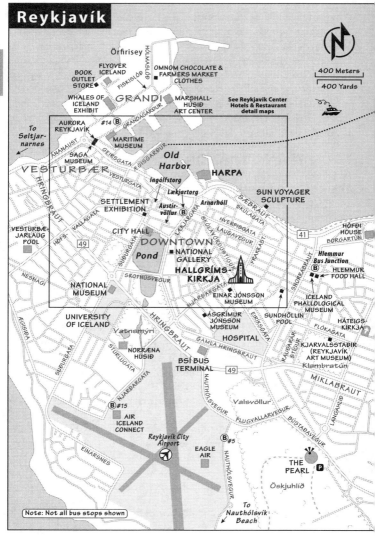

town Reykjavík, and for getting to other destinations around Iceland, see "Reykjavík Connections" at the end of this chapter.

HELPFUL HINTS

Money: Remember, you'll use credit cards more than cash in Iceland. If you do need cash, several big banks downtown have ATMs. The downtown branch of Landsbankinn at Austurstræti 11 is convenient and along my self-guided walk.

Useful Bus App: If you'll be using public buses, use the **Strætó**

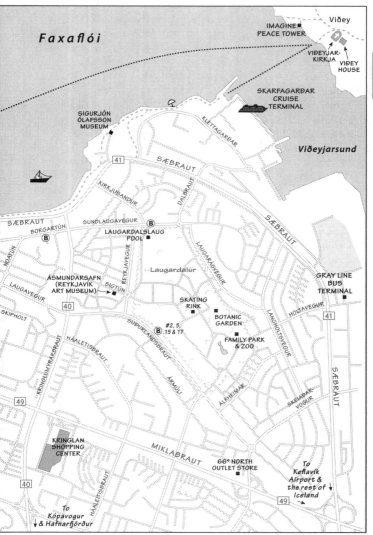

app to avoid having to carry exact bus fare. Download the app, then change the default language to English under "Settings." At the prompt to enter your mobile number, include "+1" for the US country code. You'll receive a PIN number on your mobile phone—once you enter the PIN, you can enter your credit card details to buy bus tickets. The app also has a real-time route planner, which lets you track your bus to be confident of your stop.

Pharmacy: Downtown pharmacies are at Austurstræti 19 (Mon-

Fri 9:00-18:00, Sat 11:00-16:00, closed Sun, tel. 552-4045, www.lyfja.is) and Laugavegur 46 (Mon-Fri 9:00-19:00, Sat 10:00-16:00, closed Sun, tel. 414-4646, http://islandsapotek. business.site). For a pharmacy with longer hours, try Lyfja Granda in Grandi at Fiskislóð 3 (tel. 512-3770) or, farther out, the Lyfja at Smáratorg 1, under the Læknavakt after-hours medical service near the Smáralind shopping mall (tel. 564-5600).

Laundry: A handy full-service laundry, **Úðafoss,** is located just off Laugavegur at Vitastígur 13. They promise same-day wash/ dry/fold service if you drop off before 11:00, otherwise it's next-day service (Mon-Fri 8:00-18:00, closed Sat-Sun, tel. 551-2301). The downtown **Laundromat Café** has four self-serve washers and dryers in its basement (long hours daily, Austurstræti 9, tel. 587-7555). It's also a popular comfort-food restaurant (described later in this chapter)—turning your chore into a fun night out.

Baggage Storage: All What's On TIs offer baggage storage for 1,000 ISK/bag per day—just be sure to note the closing time.

Bike Rental: For quality bikes, **Reykjavík Bike Tours** rents from its location on the pier in the Old Harbor (3,500 ISK/4 hours, 4,900 ISK/24 hours; in summer daily 9:00-17:00, in winter by appointment; Ægisgarður 7, mobile 694-8956, www. icelandbike.com). They also run tours (see "Tours in Reykjavík," later).

Taxis: The two long-established companies are **Hreyfill** (tel. 588-5522, www.hreyfill.is) and **BSR** (tel. 561-0000, www. taxireykjavik.is). Both offer flat rates to Keflavík Airport. For early-morning rides, call the evening before to reserve. Icelanders usually order taxis by phone, but there are a few taxi stands downtown and at major transportation hubs. In general, though, taxis are expensive—even a short ride in Reykjavík will cost 2,000 ISK—so use them only when there's no better option (cabbies expect payment by credit card but not a tip). Ride services such as Uber and Lyft don't operate in Reykjavík.

Online Translation Tips: A few of the websites I list in this chapter are in Icelandic only. To view them in English, use Google's Chrome browser (for automatic translation) or paste the URL into the translation window at Translate.google.com. When searching for Icelandic words on a website, omit all the accent marks and use *th, d,* and *ae* instead of *þ, ð,* and *æ.*

GETTING AROUND
By Car
North Americans will feel at home in Reykjavík, as it's largely a

car city. If you'll be renting a car to explore the countryside, you may want to keep it for part of your time in Reykjavík. Several important sights are outside of downtown (where parking is generally free and easy).

That said, you don't need a car to enjoy your visit. And if you're staying in the center (inside the street called Hringbraut) and visiting only downtown sights, a car can be a headache. If you plan to have your own wheels in town, consider looking for accommodations with free parking a little outside the center.

Parking: Downtown, on-street parking is metered (Mon-Fri 9:00-18:00, Sat 10:00-16:00; free outside these times). Pay with credit cards or coins at machines (look for the white and blue "P" sign), and display your ticket on the windshield. Parking in the P1 zone is the most expensive (370 ISK/hour); parking in P2 through P4 costs about 190 ISK/hour. You can prepay for an entire day, so even if overnighting in the center, you don't have to worry about returning to feed the meter. Check along Garðastræti and its side streets, just a couple of blocks above Ingólfstorg. A few coin-only parking meters may still survive.

There are several small public parking garages downtown (check up-to-the-minute availability at www.bilastaedasjodur. is/#bilahusin). The following all charge 240 ISK for the first hour, then 120 ISK/hour after that, and are open daily 7:00-24:00. The Traðarkot garage at Hverfisgata 20 is the best option and close to the end point of my Reykjavík Walk. Progressively closer in, but typically full on weekdays, are the Kolaport garage, near the Harpa concert hall at Kalkofnsvegur 1; the Ráðhúsið garage, underneath City Hall at Tjarnargata 11; and—closest to my Reykjavík Walk's starting point—the Vesturgata garage at Vesturgata 7 (on the corner with Mjóstræti). Another very central choice is the private garage at the Hafnartorg building (enter on Steinbryggja, from the main harborfront road Geirsgata).

You can also park just outside downtown in a neighborhood with free on-street parking, such as behind Hallgrímskirkja church or near the BSÍ bus terminal. A free parking lot is along Eiríksgata at the top of the hill by Hallgrímskirkja church, but it's often full. There's also plenty of free parking in the Grandi box-store zone to the far side of the Old Harbor.

By Public Transportation

Greater Reykjavík has a decent bus *(strætó)* system. In this late-rising city, buses run from about 6:30 on weekdays, 8:00 on Saturdays, and 10:00 on Sundays, with last departures between 23:00 and 24:00. Service is sparse on evenings and weekends, when most buses only run every half-hour.

Bus routes intersect at several key points, notably Hlemmur,

Reykjavík at a Glance

▲▲▲Thermal Swimming Pools Bathe with the locals at more than a dozen naturally heated municipal pools. See page 64.

▲▲Laugavegur Eastern stretch of Reykjavík's main drag, a delight to stroll any time of day. See page 42.

▲▲Hallgrímskirkja Iconic Guðjón Samúelsson-designed Lutheran church, with crushed-volcanic-rock exterior, serene and austere interior, and bell tower with sweeping views. **Hours:** Daily 9:00-21:00, tower until 20:30; Oct-April until 17:00, tower until 16:30. See page 43.

▲▲Einar Jónsson Museum and Garden Talented sculptor's house and studio, with free back garden decorated with his works. **Hours:** Tue-Sun 10:00-17:00, closed Mon. See page 44.

▲▲National Museum of Iceland Well-curated Icelandic artifacts that illustrate the nation's history. **Hours:** Daily 10:00-17:00, mid-Sept-April closed Mon. See page 45.

▲▲Harpa Boldly modern harborfront concert hall, with a fun-to-explore lobby and regular schedule of cultural events. **Hours:** Lobby open daily 9:00-22:00. See page 49.

▲▲The Pearl (Perlan) Domed building in the suburbs with fine views over Reykjavík's skyline and the Wonders of Iceland exhibit. **Hours:** Daily 9:00-22:00. See page 58.

▲The Settlement Exhibition Modern museum showcasing the actual ruins of a millennium-old Viking Age longhouse. **Hours:** Daily 9:00-18:00. See page 38.

at the eastern end of Laugavegur, Reykjavík's downtown shopping street; Lækjartorg, at the western end of Laugavegur; Mjódd, in the eastern Reykjavík suburbs; and Fjörður, in the town of Hafnarfjörður. The English journey planner at Straeto.is makes using the system easy, and recognizes addresses without Icelandic characters (you can omit all the accent marks and use *th, d,* and *ae* instead of *þ, ð,* and *æ*). To get help from a real person, call 540-2700.

You can pay for the bus in cash (470 ISK), but few do this, and drivers don't give change. Instead, buy a pass, a shareable perforated strip of paper tickets, or use the Strætó app (described in "Helpful Hints," earlier; one-day pass-1,800 ISK; three-day pass-4,200 ISK; 20 tickets-9,100 ISK and more than most visitors will need).

▲**Kolaportið Flea Market** Lively market hall just off the Old Harbor, with fun food section. **Hours:** Sat-Sun 11:00-17:00. See page 39.

▲*Sun Voyager (Sólfar)* Modern harborfront sculpture by Jón Gunnar Árnason evoking Iceland's earliest settlers. See page 48.

▲**Old Harbor** Modern harbor with waterfront eateries and sightseeing cruises. See page 50.

▲**Aurora Reykjavík** Modest but enjoyable exhibit on the northern lights, starring a mesmerizing film of the aurora borealis. **Hours:** Daily 9:00-21:00. See page 53.

▲**Whales of Iceland** Pricey exhibit with life-size models of the gentle giants in Icelandic waters. **Hours:** Daily 10:00-17:00. See page 56.

▲**FlyOver Iceland** Stunning virtual flight over the country in a simulator, capturing all the senses of the landscape. **Hours:** Daily 9:00-21:00. See page 57.

▲**Viðey Island** An easy ferry ride to a smattering of attractions, including the John Lennon Imagine Peace Tower (lit in fall). Ferries depart daily in season from the Old Harbor (none off-season) and Skarfagarðar (off-season Sat-Sun only). See page 60.

▲**Árbær Open-Air Museum** Collection of old buildings in the suburbs, offering a glimpse of traditional lifestyles. **Hours:** Daily 10:00-17:00, Sept-May 13:00-17:00. See page 62.

Buses are also covered by the Reykjavík City Card (described earlier).

Tickets and passes are sold at 10-11 convenience stores, the TI at Bankastræti 2, most swimming pools, information desks at the Kringlan and Smáralind shopping malls, and at the Mjódd bus junction (but not from bus drivers). Without a pass, ask the driver for a free transfer slip if you need to change buses.

Tours in Reykjavík

While you'll see bus tours advertised in Reykjavík, I wouldn't take one. The city is easy and enjoyable by foot and lends itself to walking tours.

Walking Tours

CityWalk is a group of young, fun-loving locals who give chatty two-hour walks of the town center at least three times a day (in season). The cost: whatever you think it's worth. Tours start in front of the parliament building. While my self-guided town walk covers more standard information on essentially the same route, these walks fill the time with fun local insights (mobile 787-7779, www.citywalk.is, citywalk@citywalk.is). Their website explains other options, like a Walk the Crash tour with journalist/historian Magnús Sveinn Helgason, who gives the inside story of the 2008 financial crash (magnus@citywalk.is).

Funky Iceland runs a variety of tours with an irreverent spirit, including a Reykjavík Highlights Walk (7,000 ISK, 2.5 hours, daily at 14:00); a Funky History Walk that includes lunch (6,000 ISK, 2.5 hours, daily at 10:30); and a Funky Food and Beer Walk (14,000 ISK, includes 5 craft beers and stops at 5 restaurants, 3 hours, nightly at 17:00). Get details, learn about their other tours, and book ahead on their website (www.funkyiceland.is).

Food Tours

To learn more about Icelandic cuisine and cooking—from traditional dishes to modern interpretations—you can take a three- to four-hour guided walk with stops at a half-dozen local eateries. Show up with an appetite, as it amounts to a big mobile feast.

Wake Up Reykjavík Food Tour (www.wakeupreykjavik.com) and **Your Friend in Reykjavík** each offer good food tours for around 14,000 ISK. Your Friend in Reykjavík's tour mixes local history, fun, and classic traditional dishes (smoked puffin, lamb soup, hot dog, shark, whale, *skyr;* daily at 11:00, 13:00, and 17:00, RS%—use code "RICKSTEVES" for 10 percent discount, 2-12 people, mobile 655-4040, www.yourfriendinreykjavik.com). **Funky Iceland,** listed above, does a similar food tour.

Bike Tours

Reykjavík Bike Tours takes you on a 2.5-hour, fairly flat guided bike tour that starts on the Old Harbor pier and does a circuit through downtown and all the way over to the university and residential areas on the other side of the peninsula. This is a nice way to get to know more of the city than the downtown core (7,500 ISK, mid-May-Sept daily at 10:00, confirm times in advance, Ægisgarður 7, mobile 694-8956, www.icelandbike.com, Stefan Valsson).

Private Guides

I Heart Reykjavík, run by Auður and Hrannar, offers private walking tours (2.5 hours, 35,000 ISK, tel. 511-5522, www.iheartreykjavik.net, hello@iheartreykjavik.net). **Guðrún Helga**

Sigurðardóttir, another good local guide, charges $390 USD for a half-day ($700 with car for 5.5 hours in and around Reykjavík, mobile 891-7074, www.privateguideiniceland.is, ghs@ mountainclimbing.is). **City Walk** and **Reykjavík Bike Tours** (see earlier listings) also offer private walks for roughly the same cost.

Reykjavík Walk

This self-guided walk, rated ▲▲▲, introduces the highlights of downtown Reykjavík, as well as some slices of local life, in about two hours. While a few indoor sights may be closed early or late, the walk can be done at any time—allowing you to fit it in before or after your day trips. The walk starts at one of Reykjavík's central squares, Ingólfstorg, and finishes at Hallgrím-

skirkja, the big, landmark church on the hill. As Reykjavík is likely your first stop in Iceland, I've designed this walk as a crash course not only for the city, but for the whole country—introducing you to names, customs, stories, and themes that will come in handy from here to the Eastfjords.

• *Begin on the modern, sunken square called...*

❶ Ingólfstorg (Ingólfur's Square)

While this somewhat dreary square isn't much to look at, it packs a lot of history and myth. Ingólfstorg is named for Ingólfur Arnarson who—according to the Icelandic sagas—settled at Reykjavík in 874. You can think of him as Iceland's version of the Pilgrims.

In the middle of the square, look for the two nondescript **stone pillars** (one of them marked *874*). These recall the much-told legend about Ingólfur: As he sighted the southeast coast of Iceland, he followed an old Scandinavian custom and threw the two carved wooden pillars from his "high seat" (belonging to the head of the household) overboard—vowing to establish his farm wherever they washed ashore. In the meantime, he set up a temporary settlement on the South Coast and sent two of his slaves on a scavenger hunt all over the island. Three years later (in 874), they discovered the pillars here. Ingólfur called this place Reykjavík, meaning "Smoky Bay"—likely for the thermal vapor he saw venting nearby.

While the details of this story are a mix of fact and legend (see the "Sagas of the Icelanders 101" sidebar in this chapter), archaeologists confirm that the original Reykjavík farm was just a few steps

REYKJAVÍK

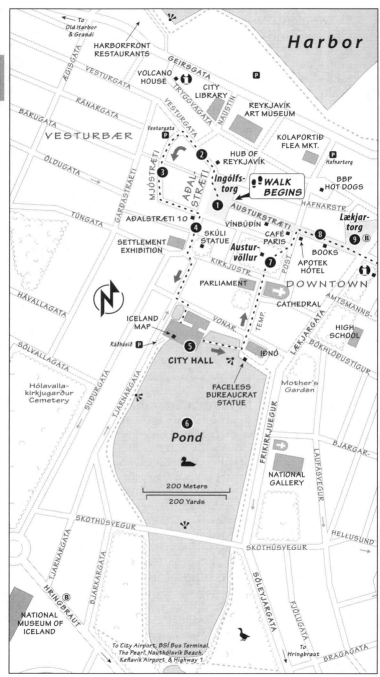

REYKJAVÍK

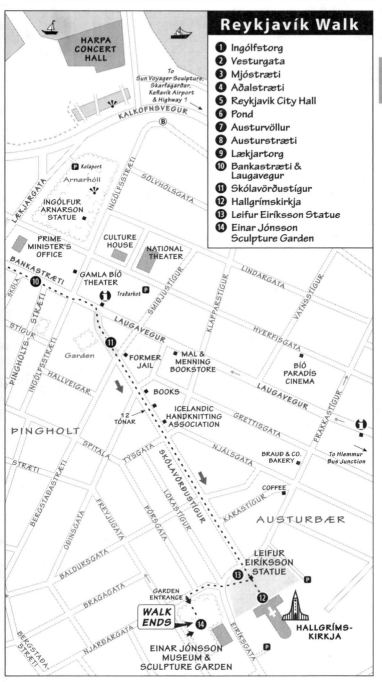

Reykjavík Walk

1. Ingólfstorg
2. Vesturgata
3. Mjóstræti
4. Aðalstræti
5. Reykjavik City Hall
6. Pond
7. Austurvöllur
8. Austurstræti
9. Lækjartorg
10. Bankastræti & Laugavegur
11. Skólavörðustígur
12. Hallgrímskirkja
13. Leifur Eiríksson Statue
14. Einar Jónsson Sculpture Garden

from where you're standing. And for most of its history, Reykjavík remained nothing more than a farm—set between the sea and a pond a few hundred yards inland (we'll go there in a few minutes). But in the 18th century, Reykjavík gradually emerged as the country's dominant town and the logical seat of Iceland's government.

Ingólfstorg was not an open space until 1944, when a big hotel that used to stand here burned down. The lot was left vacant and became a seedy hangout where Reykjavík teens would drink, smoke, and do other things they didn't want their parents to know about. Locals called it Hallærisplan (which means, roughly, "Messed-Up Square"). Only in 1993 was it cleaned up, redesigned, and respectably renamed. Today, this square is designed for skateboarders, and hosts outdoor concerts and performances in summer. Lining the square are cafés and fast-food joints where you can pick up a hot dog, a slice of pizza, a toasted sub sandwich, or an ice cream (or even a decadent *bragðarefur*—a giant cup of soft serve with mix-ins, like a supersized McFlurry).

The big, glass-fronted, **eight-story building** that dominates the square represents the latest chapter in Reykjavík's story: its recent tourism boom. Long the

headquarters of Iceland's biggest newspaper, those offices recently moved out to the suburbs, and the building is now a hotel. A generation ago, downtown Reykjavík was mostly offices, government institutions, cheap housing, and lots of students. But with the flood of tourism over the last decade, most of these have been replaced by hotels, bars, restaurants, shops, and tour operators; the number of Icelanders who actually live downtown has dropped sharply.

• *Let's take a little loop through the back streets. Facing that big building, angle to the right and walk to the end of the square. The street leaving the square is...*

❷ Vesturgata, Reykjavík's Original Shoreline

This lovely lane (literally "West Street") is lined with colorful buildings from the early 20th century. The **yellow building** (today the Restaurant Reykjavík) was once the base of the town pier, back when the waterfront came all the way up to this point. The entry to the pier ran under the building's tower (beneath the round window). In 1874, when the king of Denmark visited Iceland, his fleet anchored in the harbor, and he came ashore on a little boat right here. Around 1910, land reclamation created the modern harborfront zone, just beyond the yellow building. Today, this so-called Old Harbor area has some appealing sights (see page 50).

In the sidewalk immediately in front of the yellow building, notice the brass plaque marking the **"hub of Reykjavík"**—both the symbolic gateway to the city and the spot from where the city's address numbers radiate.

Around the left side of the yellow building, you can spot faint remains of the **original wharf,** and a little tidal pool that's still connected underground to the harbor (for a better look, cross partway over the little footbridge and look down). Several recommended restaurants are on or near this square (see "Eating in Reykjavík," later).

• *Now continue along Vesturgata. Just after the bright red building on the left corner, turn left onto...*

❸ Mjóstræti, Back-Streets Reykjavík

Even in the bustling downtown of Iceland's capital, you're never more than a block or two away from a sleepy residential area. Stroll a couple of blocks along Mjóstræti ("Narrow Street"), appreciating some slices of Reykjavík life.

As you walk along Mjóstræti, notice, by a bench, one of Reykjavík's distinctive **fire hydrants**—painted in garish, McDonald's-esque red and yellow. Residents embrace these cheery hydrants, some embellished with faces, as a sort of local symbol.

Moving on, you'll see houses sided with vertical **corrugated iron** (despite the name, it's usually steel, galvanized with zinc).

Since the late 19th century, corrugated metal sheets have been widely used for siding and roofing in Iceland. Many cover older wooden walls. Wood, which needed to be imported on this treeless island, didn't do well when exposed to the harsh weather. Corrugated iron, meanwhile, stands up well to the punishing wind and sideways rain, it doesn't burn, it's easy to maintain, it's cheap and easy to transport to Iceland, and can dress up renovated old houses as well as new ones. Many locals prefer to use brightly saturated hues, perhaps to help cheer them through the gloomy winters. Around town, you may also notice a few houses

REYKJAVÍK

with boring gray metal: Newer siding needs to weather for a few years to get rough enough for primer and paint to adhere.

As you stroll, notice lots of **propped-open windows.** Icelanders mostly heat their homes with geothermal hot water—harnessing the substantial natural power of their volcanic island. There are radiators in every room, but typically no central thermostat. Heating costs are low, so when things get too warm or stuffy indoors, Icelanders just open the window to create a cross-breeze. For tourists, opening a window also helps vent the sulfur smell that accompanies the city's scalding-hot tap water, which is piped in directly from boreholes in the countryside. (Residents are used to the smell and don't even notice.)

Another way Icelanders use all that hot water is to heat **swimming pools.** Every Iceland town has a municipal thermal pool complex where locals swim laps, relax, and socialize—particularly appealing in the cold and dreary winter months. These basically feel like your hometown swimming pool...except the water is delightfully warm-to-hot year-round. Tourists are welcome to join in the fun, and many find it the most local-feeling experience they have in Iceland. (For more about visiting pools, see "Experiences in and near Reykjavík," later.)

Any **cats** roaming around? Reykjavík has a relaxed, small-town vibe, and people tend to let their cats wander free by day. Watch for clever little cat doors built into windows and doors. You won't see many dogs, though; until 1984 they were banned in the city for health reasons, and condo owners still need permission from their neighbors to keep a dog.

• *After another block, Mjóstræti dead-ends into someone's driveway. Turn left on Brattagata and head downhill. You'll pop out back at the bottom of Ingólfstorg square, on...*

❹ Aðalstræti, Reykjavík's First Street

While today it feels more like an alley, this "Main Street" (as its name means) was Reykjavík's first thoroughfare.

The **one-story black house** on your right (at Aðalstræti 10) was originally built around 1760 for the textile industry. The current version is a complete rebuild (only the location of the walls is original), but faithful to the original style. The hand pump across the street (under the arcade) is a reminder that,  until 1910, locals used pumps like this one as their sole source of drinking water.

Turn right down Aðalstræti. A few doors down on the right is the Hótel Reykjavík Centrum. When this hotel was built in 2001, workers unearthed the ruins of a 10th-century Scandinavian longhouse—part of the original Reykjavík farm. Today it's the excellent **Settlement Exhibition,** where you can step down into the cellar and walk around the ancient structure (enter at the corner; museum described later, under "Sights in Reykjavík").

Opposite the hotel, a statue of **Skúli Magnússon** stands in a small square with a few trees. Skúli was an Enlightenment-era entrepreneur whose enterprises seeded settlement at Reykjavík in the mid-1700s—finally transforming it from a farm into a real town, and setting the stage for its eventual capital status. While Ingólfur may have settled in Reykjavík, Skúli put it on the map. The little square was the village cemetery until 1838.

• *Directly in front of Skúli is a lane called Tjarnargata (between two yellow houses). Follow this for a long block to Vonarstræti, where you'll see, on your left, a large, modern concrete building with a curved roof and a mossy pond in front. This is the...*

❺ Reykjavík City Hall (Ráðhús Reykjavíkur)

Enter the blocky, curved-roofed, concrete-and-glass building using the door at the inner corner of the fountain (Mon-Fri 8:00-18:00, Sat from 10:00, Sun from 12:00, free WCs and free smartphone charging kiosk). The city council meets upstairs, but most city offices are outside the center, and this "City Hall" is more of a ceremonial hall for the city's residents. Its ground-floor space, normally open to the public, is rented out for concerts, exhibitions, and other cultural events.

A huge wooden **relief map of Iceland** is sometimes displayed in front of the large windows overlooking the little lake known as the Pond. The towns on the map are not labeled, but it's easy to find Reykjavík and the Reykjanes Peninsula: Look for the airport. Pick out the island's major landforms: Fjords ruffle the coastline in the northwest (the Westfjords), the east coast (the Eastfjords), and the far north (Skagafjörður and Eyjafjörður, flanking the mountainous Tröllaskagi—"Troll Peninsula"). Glacier-covered volcanic peaks loom ominously above the South Coast, while the desolate Highlands cover the middle of the country. Trace your own route through Iceland; spotting the roads and towns around the country is absorbing. Topographic maps help you identify fjords, mountains, and rivers.

• *Exit the building to the left from where you entered, and walk across the pedestrian bridge that runs along...*

⑥ The Pond (Tjörnin)

This miniature lake feels just right for this small capital of a small country. On sunny days, parents bring small children to feed the ducks and swans that live in the Pond. In the winter, if the temperatures drop to a safe range (generally several days a year), snow on the Pond is cleared away to make a skating rink. It's a pleasant one-mile walk all the way around.

At the far end of the pedestrian bridge, you're greeted by a quirky statue of a **faceless bureaucrat.** The period building next to him is Iðnó, Reykjavík's old theater, which now houses a café.

Gaze out to the far end of the Pond, where you'll see some of the **University of Iceland** buildings (that's the science center with the curved glass roof). The country's oldest and largest university, with a total enrollment of around 13,000, was founded in 1911. Before that, students had to go abroad for college (mostly to Denmark)...a reminder of just how recently this country came into its own.

Farther right, rising a couple of stories above the rooftops, is the brown tower of the recommended **National Museum,** where a thoughtfully explained collection of artifacts tells the story of Ice-

REYKJAVÍK

land (described under "Sights in Reykjavík"). Along the right side of the Pond are fine homes built by wealthy families a century ago.

On the left of the Pond is the historic **Free Church of Reykjavík,** a Lutheran congregation that broke from the state church over a difference in social issues.

• *Standing next to the "faceless bureaucrat," turn your back to the Pond, cross the street, and walk straight up Templarasund. You'll arrive at a lovely little park with a big statue in the middle. Stand by the statue and get oriented to...*

➐ Austurvöllur, Iceland's Parliament Square

Translated roughly as "Eastern Field," Austurvöllur is the political center of this small country. With your back to the statue, the

big, stone building facing the square is Iceland's parliament, the **Alþingi** (pronounced, roughly, "all-thingy"). While Icelanders like to call the Alþingi the "world's oldest parliament," this is an exaggeration. The Alþingi that met at Þingvellir in the centuries after settlement was very different from a modern democratic parliament. From about 1400 to 1800, it was an appeals court, not a legislature. Then there were 45 years when the Alþingi didn't meet at all. It was reestablished in Reykjavík, in a totally new and different form, in 1845. In 1874, Iceland received a constitution that gave the Alþingi real decision-making power—even though Iceland remained fully part of Denmark.

On the building's gable, notice the crowned *9*, which represents King Christian IX (the Danish ruler in 1881, when the building was erected). Engraved over four of the upstairs windows of the Alþingi, notice the mythical "four protectors of Iceland"—dragon, eagle, giant, and bull—which also appear on Iceland's coat of arms and many Icelandic coins. (As if to drive home Iceland's closeness to the sea, the flipsides of the coins feature cod, dolphins, crab, and lumpfish.) Imagine Iceland when this was built, in 1881, its people so excited to have at least some self-rule. One of the poorest countries in 19th-century Europe, it's said that this single building cost a third of the entire country's national income.

There are no public tours of the Alþingi, but if parliament is in session visitors are welcome to sit in the gallery (the 63-member parliament is on vacation June-mid-Sept; otherwise confirm session times at www.althingi.is—typically Mon and Wed at 15:00, Tue at 13:30, Thu and sometimes Fri at 10:30). The gallery entrance is around the back of the building, by a fine little walled garden that's open to the public.

Now turn your attention to the statue on the pillar: **Jón Sigurðsson** (1811-1879) was the 19th-century scholar and politician who successfully advocated for Iceland's increased autonomy under the Danish crown. Jón spent most of his life in Denmark, where he politely but forcefully pressed the case for freer trade and a constitution that would reduce the king's power. At the time, many other Europeans were agitating for the same kinds of things, and often took up arms. But Icelanders achieved their goals without firing a shot—thanks largely to the articulate persistence of this one man. The parliament building was finished just a couple of years after Jón's death. In Jón's honor, his birthday—June 17—became Iceland's National Day.

Look around the **square.** Early each summer new turf is laid and flower beds are filled in preparation for National Day ceremonies and speeches. But it was quite a different scene in the winter of 2008-2009: Thousands of Icelanders gathered here to demand the government's resignation in the wake of the country's financial collapse. Protesters banged pots and pans with wooden spoons, and pelted politicians with eggs and tomatoes (hence the protest's nickname, the "Kitchenware Revolution"). New elections were called, and the prime minister was censured for failing in his responsibilities. Ólafur Þór Hauksson—a small-town cop who became the unyielding special prosecutor for financial crimes—emerged as something of an international folk hero. A good number of bankers were tried, convicted, and in a few cases jailed for their role in the crisis.

Then, in spring 2016, thousands came to this square again after it was revealed that Iceland's then-prime minister had kept some of his considerable family wealth in an offshore account in Panama. Again, new elections were called.

To the left of the Alþingi is Reykjavík's **Lutheran Cathedral** (Dómkirkjan; generally open Mon-Fri 10:00-15:00, closed Sat-Sun except for services, occasional concerts—look for posters, www.domkirkjan.is). Surprisingly small, it was built in the 1790s and expanded in the 1840s. The city now has larger churches, but the cathedral is still regularly used for weddings, funerals, and the opening of parliament. If you

go inside, you'll find a beautifully tranquil interior, with an upstairs gallery and finely painted ceiling. The centerpiece—directly in front of the main altar—is a marble baptismal font by renowned

19th-century Danish sculptor Bertel Thorvaldsen, whose father was Icelandic.

At the right end of the Alþingi, notice the **statue of a strong woman** on a pillar: Ingibjörg H. Bjarnason (1867-1941), who was elected Iceland's first female member of parliament in 1922. Iceland has an impressive tradition of honoring women's rights. On October 24, 1975, 90 percent of Icelandic women went on strike to drive home their importance to society. The country ground to a halt. (Icelandic men—who very quickly learned their lesson—gave the protest the tongue-in-cheek nickname "The Long Friday," which is also what Icelanders call Good Friday.) In 1980, Iceland became the first modern, democratic nation to elect a female head of state, when single mother Vigdís Finn-

bogadóttir became president. She served for four terms (16 years) and remains a beloved figure today.

Facing the Bjarnason statue, at the corner of the park, notice the chunk of rock split in half by **"The Black Cone."** This monument to civil disobedience was placed here (somewhat controversially) in 2012—when memories of those 2009 protests were still fresh and, for some, painful.

• *Exit the square behind Jón Sigurðsson's left shoulder, and go one short block up the street called Pósthússtræti ("Post Office Street"). Pause at the intersection with Austurstræti ("Eastern Street"), in front of Apotek Hótel.*

❽ Austurstræti, Reykjavík's Main Street

Reykjavík's main drag begins about a block to your left (at Ingólfs-torg, where we started our walk) and continues about a mile to your right, changing names as it runs through town.

Looking straight ahead, on your right is the red former **post office** building. Across the street on the left, the old-meets-new building is **Landsbankinn,** founded as Iceland's national bank in 1886. It was privatized around 2000, failed spectacularly in 2008, and then continued operations under a slightly altered name. Past that, at the end of the block, you'll see a white, boxy building that houses the **Kolaportið flea market** on weekends—a fun browse, even for nonshoppers (see page 39).

Tucked away kitty-corner from the flea market (just down this street and on the right, a block away but not quite visible from here) is Reykjavík's most famous **hot dog stand.** (You can side trip

there now, or come back later.) It's been serving weenies to an enthusiastic local following since 1937. In 2004, Bill Clinton was in Reykjavík to speak at a UNICEF event. When the proprietor of this stand offered him a free frankfurter, Clinton—a notorious connoisseur of junk food—couldn't say no. Camera shutters clicked...and suddenly, eating at Bæjarins Beztu Pylsur—"The City's Best Sausages"—became *the* thing to do when visiting Reykjavík. Now people stand in long lines to shell out 600 ISK for what is, by any honest assessment, a fairly average weenie. On the street corner by the stand, you can fill up your water bottle for free at the red dispenser.

Back on Austurstræti, look up at the Art Deco-style facade of the **Apotek Hótel.** This was designed by Guðjón Samúelsson, Iceland's best-known 20th-century architect, who's responsible for many of the major landmarks around town—including his masterpiece church, Hallgrímskirkja.

Facing the hotel, across the street, is **Café Paris,** an old standby. Look up at the relief on the pediment-like gable, from the 1920s, which shows an imagined scene from the settlement of the country: An established settler—standing in front of his pack animals—shakes hands with a new arrival, whose crew is taking down the mast of his longship. While you may sometimes hear the word "Viking" used to describe those early Icelandic settlers, that's not quite right. They were contemporaries (and actually relatives) of the Vikings, but had a different modus operandi: Rather than pillage, plunder, and rape, the first Icelanders were mostly farmers in search of good grazing land.

Now look up the street past Café Paris (back toward Ingólfstorg). On the left side of the street (next to the English pub), notice **Vínbúðin**—one of the unobtrusive state-run liquor stores. Only weak beer can be bought at supermarkets; every other kind of alcohol can be purchased only here. While nationalized liquor stores are fairly standard in Nordic countries, Iceland has at times taken a particularly hard line against alcohol. From 1915 all the way until 1989—in an attempt to curtail everyone's favorite, cheap "gateway drug"—beer with an alcohol content over 2.25 percent was illegal. Icelanders compensated by mixing spirits—which were, oddly, perfectly legal—with light beer, creating a super-alcoholic faux-brew. Today, as if making up for lost time, Iceland has a vibrant microbrew culture (see recommendations, including many within a few steps of this walk, on page 76). Also look for the Icelandic firewater called *brennivín*. In another anti-alcohol crusade, originally the *brennivín* bottle came with a health warning in the form of a black skull. While that's long gone, today the drink still carries the tongue-in-cheek nickname "Black Death" *(svartidauði)*. Pop in to survey the liquor store if you like. The only cheap way to try the interesting array of local beers is to buy them here—a fun, affordable cultural experience. Single cans and bottles cost about 300 ISK each.

From Café Paris, turn right and walk up Austurstræti. After a few steps, on your right, look for one of the city center's three main **bookstores** (this one is run by Eymundsson—Iceland's answer to Barnes & Noble). Books are clearly valued here: A high percentage of Icelanders are published authors, and every Icelandic living room has shelves of books on display. Books also play a key role in Christmas gift exchanges: The Iceland publishers' association mails a catalog of the year's new releases each fall, just in time for holiday shopping lists.

Just past the bookstore, notice "The Hot Dog Stand"...taking full advantage of its prime location to hijack hungry tourists looking for the famous place around the corner.

• *Across the street from the bookstore is a 10-11 convenience store, useful for bus tickets or a bus pass. (But it's much more expensive for groceries.) At the end of the street, you'll emerge into a square fronting a busy street. Stop here to survey the scene.*

❾ Lækjartorg (Creek Square)

This square and the adjacent, busy street (Lækjargata) are named for a creek *(lækur)* that ran from the Pond (to your right) down to the sea (to your left) in Reykjavík's early days. It still flows, but was buried in an underground culvert more than a century ago.

Look across the street at the white stone building with the five upstairs windows. As Reykjavík grew in the mid-1700s, the first building constructed of materials more permanent than turf or timber was not a church or palace but a prison, built across the creek from the village center. Today it's the **office of Iceland's prime**

Icelandic Names:
From Magnússon to Gunnarsdóttir

Traditionally, Icelanders' last names were patronymics, formed from the father's name plus "son" or "dóttir." So if you meet a man named Gunnar Magnússon, you know his father's name was Magnús. If Gunnar has a son Jón, he'll be named Jón Gunnarsson. A daughter María will be María Gunnarsdóttir. Get it? (This system was the norm all over Scandinavia until just a few hundred years ago.) Women keep their name at marriage.

Around 1900, fashions changed, and Icelanders started to assume family names and pass them down from generation to generation, like we do in the US. Then the pendulum swung back: In 1925, family names were banned as un-Icelandic, but people who had already taken one were allowed to keep it. (You may run into a few of these today.) Things went so far that for a few decades, immigrants who wanted to take up Icelandic citizenship had to abandon their foreign surname and choose an Icelandic patronymic (this requirement was abolished only in the 1980s). Today, with immigration rising, and many marriages between Icelandic women and immigrant men, family names are on the increase in Iceland again.

These days, Icelanders can choose to form their children's last name from either parent's first name. So, if Gunnar and Katrín have a son, they could give him the last name Katrínarson. But the country's Personal Names Committee still controls what first names parents can give their children (from a list of 3,500 autho-

minister. The *no parking* sign out front indicates the spot reserved for the prime minister.

But no matter how high you rise in Icelandic society, you're called by your first name—so President Guðni Jóhannesson is known to Icelanders simply as "Guðni." That's why, in this book, I'm on a first-name basis even with big-name historic Icelanders. This isn't necessarily because Icelanders are more casual than the norm—it's because of the unique way they form their last names. (For more on this tradition, see the "Icelandic Names" sidebar, above.)

Flanking the prime minister's office are two streets: **Banka-stræti** (on the right) runs uphill for a couple of blocks, and then changes its name to Laugavegur. This has long been the main rized names). While this seems oppressive, it's largely a grammatical concern—to ensure that names will work within the structure of the Icelandic language. Recently, politicians have moved to abolish the committee. Stay tuned.

All Icelanders address each other by first names, which may seem strangely informal. But in Icelandic, using a person's full first name actually has a ceremonial ring to it. Most Icelanders go by a nickname among family and friends, so Magnús's old school-mates probably call him "Maggi." But strangers wouldn't dare call him anything less than Magnús. There's no real equivalent of "Mr." or "Ms." in Icelandic.

It's traditional for Icelandic parents to reveal their children's names only when the child is christened (usually a few weeks after birth, but the law lets them wait for up to six months). Many parents choose the name before the birth, but still follow custom and keep it a secret. Others appreciate the chance to get to know their child before deciding. In the meantime, parents use nicknames for their baby, like "The Short One."

What children do get within minutes of birth is a 10-digit identification number, based on their birth date, which follows them through life. This number, called the *kennitala,* is almost like an alternative name, and Icelanders use it very openly and casually to identify themselves to schools, banks, or the power company. Anyone can look up anyone else's ID number and address. This shocks Americans, who are used to keeping their Social Security number secret. Despite—or perhaps because of—this openness, identity theft in Iceland is practically unknown.

By the way, many Icelandic first names are comically hard for tourists to pronounce, something locals have fun with. (And locals in the tourist trade generally have an easy-to-remember nickname.)

downtown shopping street; we'll head up this way soon. **Hverfisgata** (on the left), a more heavily trafficked commercial street, is where city buses run on their way between the two main bus stops downtown: Lækjartorg (where you're standing) and Hlemmur (just under a mile to the east).

On the hill to the left of Hverfisgata are many government offices, including Iceland's supreme court, ministry of finance, and central bank.

Cross the busy street. Before you head straight uphill on Bankastræti, look back on your left by the harbor. The dark, glassy, boxy building is called **Harpa**—Reykjavík's concert hall and conference center. Don't trek out to Harpa now; at the end of this walk, you can head to Harpa to enter the hall's futuristic lobby for a good look at its multicolored windows.

• *Now, walk uphill on Bankastræti (passing the prime minister's office on your left).*

⑩ Bankastræti/Laugavegur, More of Reykjavík's Main Drag

By the end of the 19th century, Reykjavík had expanded, and most people lived on this side of the town's little creek. This stretch became the city's main shopping and business street. Today, most locals shop at malls and in the suburbs, and services along Laugavegur are geared toward tourists.

A half-block up on your left, notice another old stone building (marked with the *Stella* sign). This was Iceland's first bank building, built in 1882, which gave Bankastræti its name. To the right, tucked back from the street, is one of three TIs sprinkled along the main drag (generally daily 9:00-20:00, shorter hours Sun and in winter).

Continuing up Bankastræti, notice the moveable **traffic barriers** (including some shaped like bicycles). In the summer, some stretches of this street are closed to cars to promote strolling.

Keep your eye out—both along this main strip, and in the residential side streets—for big **street-art murals.** This isn't eyesore

graffiti, but quite the opposite: Locals have found that if you supply a blank canvas, it'll be tagged. But if you decorate it yourself, taggers leave it alone. So government and private property owners commission murals like these. Many of the most renowned Icelandic street artists are women. The back lanes are even more highly decorated than the main streets we're seeing on this walk—be sure to explore later.

After two short blocks, pause at the lively intersection where Skólavörðustígur splits off to the right (dead-ending at Hallgrímskirkja, crowning the bluff). This is also where the street changes names to **Laugavegur** (roughly LOY-ga-VEH-grr, Hot Springs Road)—once the walking route for those going to do their laundry in the Laugardalur hot springs east of downtown. We won't walk the length of Laugavegur right now, but you'll certainly find plenty of excuses to explore it while you're in town—many of the city's best restaurants, shops, and bars are on or within a few steps of this street. About 10 minutes' walk away, at Laugavegur's far end, is Hlemmur, the main city bus junction (with a trendy food hall and the Phallological Museum—see "Sights in Reykjavík," later). While the entire drag is commercialized, the farther you go up Laugavegur, the less it feels like a tourist circus.

• *From here, dogleg right and head uphill on the rainbow-painted street toward the distant church steeple. This street is called...*

⓫ Skólavörðustígur Street

This street (SKO-la-vur-thu-STEE-grr, "School Cairn Lane") leads up to Hallgrímskirkja church. The street got its name from

a pile of rocks that Reykjavík schoolchildren set up long ago atop the hill, near where the church is now. Like Laugavegur, this street is lined with cafés, restaurants, and bookstores. As it's a bit less congested, and capped with a lovely church steeple, this street is a favorite place to stroll in Reykjavík.

Just a few steps up Skólavörðustígur at #4 (on the right), notice the tiny gap between the buildings. From the gate, peek discreetly into an adorable, private little **garden** facing a bright red house—a tranquil parallel world to the bustle just a few steps away. Many downtown blocks have an interior garden, shared among the surrounding houses. Sometimes, like here, little houses are tucked behind other houses. This was a good way to increase the capacity of your lot in this city of chronic housing shortages (and loosely enforced building regulations).

Back on Skólavörðustígur, continue a block uphill. A few steps up on the left is **Mokka Café.** The first place in town to do fancy Italian-style coffee (since 1958), it's long been a writers' hangout and retains its old atmosphere. Farther up on the left, you'll see another **old stone building.** It looks a bit like the historic jail we saw earlier—and yes, it's another former jail, built in 1874 (after the city had expanded, and this area was just outside town). This remained in use until summer 2016. Run your fingers over the chunky, volcanic rock in the building's facade.

Just past the jail, also on the left, the boxy three-story building at #11 was a bank until the financial crisis, and now houses a branch of the Eymundsson bookstore chain.

While the lower end of the street is dominated by big, glitzy shops (like Geysir, with modern Icelandic fashion, or the venerable Rammagerðin handicraft shop), as you continue uphill the shops become smaller, more characteristic boutiques. Ceramic and jewelry shops—often with a small workshop in the back—are popular along here. At #15 (on the left), 12 Tónar is Reykjavík's most beloved music store, specializing in Icelandic tunes. Browsers can listen in their sampling lounge and enjoy a free cup of coffee. A few doors up at #19 (with the metal balcony) is the Handknitting Association of Iceland's shop, a co-op where you can browse expensive but top-quality handmade Icelandic sweaters and other woolens. For more recommendations, see "Shopping in Reykjavík," later.

• *The last couple of blocks on the street are increasingly residential. It's fun to explore the side streets in this neighborhood, where you'll find more corrugated metal siding, propped-open windows, street art, hidden gardens, and cats. But for now, continue straight uphill until you run right into...*

⓬ Hallgrímskirkja Lutheran Church

After Reykjavík's Catholic minority built their church atop the hill west of downtown in 1929, Lutheran state church leaders felt they needed to keep up. They hired the same well-known architect, Guðjón Samúelsson, and commissioned him to build a taller, bigger response on the higher hill to the east of downtown. His distinctive Hallgrímskirkja (HAHTL-greems-KEER-kyah) was designed in the 1930s, with construction beginning in 1945, but was not completed until the 1980s. On New Year's Eve, this square is where locals gather to watch fireworks.

Exterior: The basalt-column motif soaring skyward on the facade recalls Iceland's volcanic origins—and evokes the cliffs you'll see around the country. In the winter, as you look up from Skólavörðustígur, light shining out through the windows makes the top of the 250-foot tower glow like a giant jack-o'-lantern.

Guðjón Samúelsson (1887-1950)—an Icelander who trained in Denmark—was Iceland's most influential architect. Arriving back home after finishing his studies in 1919, he was hired as the government's in-house building designer—a plum post that he kept until his death. These were good years for architects, as Iceland urbanized and the availability of concrete opened up new design possibilities. Guðjón's favored aesthetic was the functionalist style typical of the 1920s and 1930s. He attempted to forge a distinctly Icelandic architectural style...and, because he designed so many buildings here, you might say he succeeded. In Reykjavík alone, he designed this church, the main university building, the original National Hospital building, the National Theater, the Sundhöllin swimming pool, the Apotek Hótel we saw earlier, and the Hótel Borg across the square from the parliament building.

Hallgrímskirkja is named for the 17th-century Icelandic poet Hallgrímur Pétursson, who wrote a well-known series of 50 hymns retelling the story of the Passion of Christ.

Interior: Step inside (free, daily 9:00-21:00, Oct-April until 17:00). Temporary art installations fill the entry foyer. Strolling

down the church's dramatically austere nave, you're immersed in a sleek space culminating in classically Gothic pointed arches—with virtually no adornments. The glass is clear, not stained, and the main altar is a simple table. Notice how the ends of the pews echo the stair-step steeple outside.

Turn around and face the massive organ, which was "crowdfunded" in 1991; people paid to sponsor individual pipes. (To the right of the door you came in, notice the collection box shaped like an organ pipe—donations for the instrument's upkeep.) The church is a popular venue for organ and choral concerts (look for posters, and see page 73). If the organist is practicing (most likely in the morning), sit down and enjoy a little musical break.

Notice that the pews are reversible—the seat backs can be flipped over to face the organ. Not only is this in keeping with Lutheranism—where the most important aspects of worship are the sermon (pulpit) and the music (organ)—but it's also very practical. In smaller towns, you can't have both a church and a concert hall—so one building has to do double-duty.

Before leaving, consider riding the elevator (plus 33 steps) to the top of the **tower,** with a fine view over the rooftops (1,000 ISK, daily 9:00-20:30, Oct-April until 16:30). If there's a long line for the small elevator, consider coming back in the evening.

• *Head back outside. Prominently displayed in front of the church is a...*

⓲ Leifur Eiríksson Statue

Known as Leif Erikson (c. 970-1020) to Americans, this Viking Age explorer was—if we can trust the sagas—the first European

REYKJAVÍK

to set foot on the American continent. The sagas weave a colorful tale of Leifur's outlaw-family lineage and his clan's explorations. His grandfather, Þorvaldur Ásvaldsson, was exiled from Norway to Iceland, and his father, Eiríkur Þorvaldsson (Erik the Red), was in turn exiled from Iceland—establishing the first settlements on Greenland. Leifur carried on farther west, seeking a mysterious land that had been spotted by another Nordic sailor when he was blown off course.

Around five centuries before Christopher Columbus, Leifur and his crew landed in the New World, very possibly at L'Anse aux Meadows, in today's Newfoundland, where there are ruins of a Viking Age complex. Norsemen may have established more settlements in this area—which they called *Vínland* (meaning either "Land of Wine" or "Land of Meadows") for its relatively lush climate—but if so, they did not last. On his way home, according to the sagas, Leifur rescued the crew of another ship that had been stranded on a small island, and after that he was dubbed "Leifur Heppni" (Leif the Lucky). The US government donated this statue to mark the Alþingi's 1,000th anniversary in 1930. The inscription delicately acknowledges Leifur as the "discoverer of Vínland"—but not of America.

If it's summertime, in the park flanking Leif the Lucky, look for three types of **flowers** that grow abundantly in this otherwise inhospitable land: the vivid purple Nootka lupine (from Alaska, introduced to Iceland in the mid-20th century to combat erosion); bright yellow European gorse, an alpine shrub with a pungent herbal fragrance in the early summer; and...dandelions. All three are considered weeds in much of the world, but most Icelanders don't remove them. As one local explained, "We're just happy when *anything* grows here."

• *We'll finish our walk with one more hidden sight. With the church at your back, turn left and head toward the bunker-like mansion. You'll curl around the right side of this building, passing a fun little metal cutout that lines up perfectly with the jagged roofline of the church—turn around and try it. Just past the cutout, watch for a gate on the left and enter the...*

⓮ Einar Jónsson Sculpture Garden

Of Iceland's notable artists, Einar Jónsson (1874-1954) was one of the first and most significant. After studying in Copenhagen and Rome, Einar made his name working in big European capitals. But, like so many Icelanders, after half a lifetime of living abroad he felt drawn back to his homeland. Einar struck a deal with the Alþingi (much like the sculptor Gustav Vigeland did in Oslo): If they built him a mansion and studio, he'd move back to Reykjavík and bequeath all that he produced to the city. He designed and built this house back when this was a naked, largely uninhabited hilltop (not even the church was built yet), seeding what has become a desirable neighborhood.

Linger over the 26 bronze works in the sculpture garden (free to enter, open late). Einar's statues—with universal human

themes—are taut with tension and angst. Einar was a fearful man, yet also very spiritual; his work suggests glimmers of hope in frightening times. You'll see motifs from Norse mythology and references to Iceland's "hidden people" (elves and the like). The men are mighty warriors, and the women (whose faces are modeled after Einar's wife, Anna) are protectors. Einar and Anna lived in a small, cozy, wood-paneled penthouse apartment at the top of the building's tower. To learn more about Einar, see some plaster casts of his work, and walk through his apartment, you can pay to enter the building (today the **Einar Jónsson Museum**— described on page 44, entrance facing the church).

• *Our walk is over. Both of the two downtown shopping streets— Skólavörðustígur and Laugavegur—are lined with eating options. To quickly get down to Laugavegur (and the Hlemmur bus junction), head down Frakkastígur, which runs to the left as you face the church from the top of Skólavörðustígur; on your way to the main drag, you'll pass several good places to take a break—including top-end coffee shop Reykjavík Roasters, and the "destination" bakery Brauð & Co (other options are described later, under "Eating in Reykjavík").*

If you follow Frakkastígur down to Laugavegur, then cross it and continue straight downhill through an uninviting condo zone (near the recommended Kex Hostel café, a block to the right down Skúlagata), you can cross a busy street to reach the city's iconic Sun Voyager *sculpture. From here, it's an easy five-minute walk (with the water on your right) to the Harpa concert hall. The Old Harbor zone is just beyond.*

Sights in Reykjavík

In addition to its fine state- and city-run museums, Reykjavík has an assortment of pricey private museums (including Whales of Iceland, Saga Museum, Aurora Reykjavík, and the Phallological

REYKJAVÍK

Museum). You might expect these to be tourist traps, but (while expensive) they're thoughtfully presented.

DOWNTOWN REYKJAVÍK
Near Parliament and Laugavegur

These sights are all within a short walk of the city's main artery. They're listed roughly from west to east.

▲The Settlement Exhibition (Landnámssýningin)

During downtown construction work in 2001, archaeologists discovered the remains of a 10th-century longhouse from the original Reykjavík farmstead. These ruins were carefully preserved, and a small, modern, well-presented museum was built around them. This is the most accessible (and most central) place in Reykjavík to learn about Iceland's earliest history.

Some of the oldest building remains here were covered by tephra material from a volcanic eruption; carbon dating has narrowed the time of the eruption to AD 871...give or take a couple of years. (That's why you see "Reykjavík 871±2" around town.) It's worth paying admission to see what's left of the old Viking Age house and the modern, well-presented exhibits that surround it.

Cost and Hours: 1,700 ISK, covered by Reykjavík City Card, free for kids 17 and younger, daily 9:00-18:00, Aðalstræti 16, tel. 411-6370, www.settlementexhibition.is.

Tours: Admission includes an audioguide (ask for it) and a guided 45-minute tour in English—worth planning your visit around (June-Aug Mon-Fri at 11:00, no tours on weekends or off-season).

Visiting the Museum: You'll descend to cellar level and walk around the stone-and-turf wall that survives from the 65-by-26-foot longhouse. A circle of high-tech exhibits on the surrounding walls explains the site. You'll learn how Scandinavians first settled the Reykjavík area a little before a volcanic eruption that took place around AD 871. This house dates from later (around 930) and may have belonged to the grandson of Reykjavík's semi-legendary founder, Ingólfur Arnarson (famous for throwing carved pillars overboard to select a building site). The house of a fairly prosperous farmer, it held an extended family of about 10 people. It had a sod roof and a big hearth in the middle. The house was abandoned after only a few decades—around AD 1000— perhaps due to damage from a spring that still runs beneath it. Exhibits explain the landscape, flora, and fauna of this area in that era, suggesting why it was an attractive place to establish a farm. You'll see actual items excavated here: a spindle whorl with runic inscriptions, and primitive tools such as keys, fishhooks, arrowheads, and ax heads. A model and a virtual, interactive reconstruction of the longhouse further illustrate the lifestyles of these earliest Icelanders.

▲Kolaportið Flea Market

Reykjavík's flea market, open only on weekends, takes up the dingy ground floor of the old customs building. While you'll see plenty

of tourists, the market is still aimed largely at locals. It's fun to rummage through the stalls of used books and music, clothing (including knockoff Icelandic sweaters), and collectibles.

Cost and Hours: Free entry, open Sat-Sun 11:00-17:00, closed Mon-Fri, closed or varying hours on major holiday weekends, Tryggvagata 19, tel. 562-5030, www.kolaportid. is.

Visiting the Market: The food section serves as a crash course in Icelandic eats. Several stalls offer free samples. Look for the different kinds of smoked fish: *silungur* is trout, *bleikja* is arctic char, and *lax* is salmon. If you're a bit bolder, there's *harðfiskur* (air-dried, skinless white fish that's been pounded flat—eaten as a snack with butter), crunchy fish chips, or dried seaweed (which might be labeled *hollustusnakk*—"health snack"). And if you're even more daring, you can buy a tiny 200-ISK tub containing cubes of the notorious fermented shark, *hákarl* (you'll never eat more than this amount, and the rare restaurant that serves it charges much more). Occasionally you may be offered a free sample of *hákarl*—which is ideal, since you'd never want to buy more.

Also look for other unusual Icelandic eats: horsemeat and horse sausage, and in summer, seabird eggs (typically from guillemots or other *svartfuglar*—birds in the auk family, which also includes puffins and murres). Look in the freezers for cod *(þorskur),* haddock *(ýsa),* and plaice *(rauðspretta),* which are all Icelandic, as well as Asian imports such as pangasius (catfish), mussels, and squid. To cleanse your palate, grab some samples at the bakery counter (they might have a layer cake with frosting or jam), or taste-test the many different varieties of chocolate-covered licorice.

REYKJAVÍK

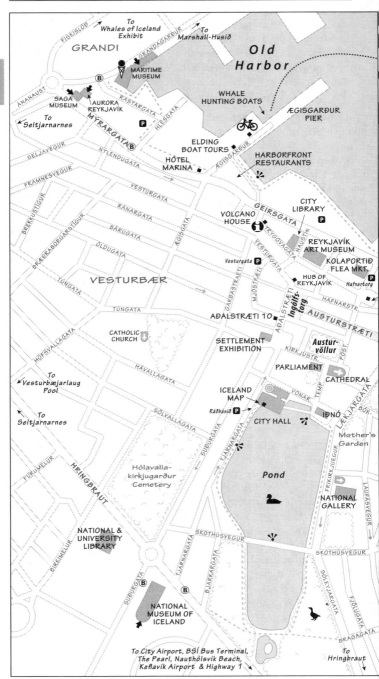

REYKJAVÍK

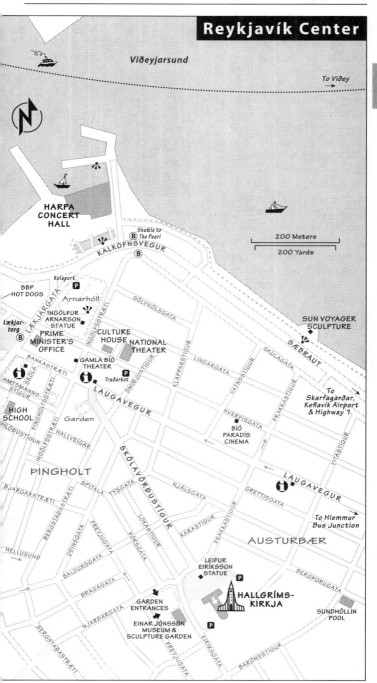

Culture House (Safnahúsið)

Built in 1909 to house Iceland's National Museum, and later home to the National Library, today this stately building holds the downtown branch of the National Museum. It hosts mostly temporary exhibits with well-described historic artifacts arranged by theme.

The collection's highlight is a display of 14 manuscripts of the *Jónsbók*—the law code imposed on Iceland by Norway in the late 1200s, and named "Jón's Book" after the man who compiled it. The earliest is the priceless *Skarðsbók* from 1363, an illuminated manuscript painstakingly written on vellum (calfskin). As the original Icelandic saga manuscripts are not on public view, this is as close as you'll get to seeing pages from that era. It's a very big deal to Icelanders.

Cost and Hours: 2,000 ISK, covered by Reykjavík City Card, includes admission to National Museum, daily 10:00-17:00, closed Mon off-season, Hverfisgata 15, tel. 530-2210, www.culturehouse.is.

Tours: The audioguide (which you can rent, or browse on your phone using the free Wi-Fi) is worthwhile for history buffs.

▲▲Laugavegur, Reykjavík's Main Drag

The city's main walking street is a delight to stroll—particularly its eastern stretch, Laugavegur. While far from "local" (you'll

rarely spot an Icelander here who doesn't work in the tourist trade), it's enjoyable to wander and browse, with characteristic old houses, vivid street art, tempting cafés and bars, and—yes—plenty of touristy puffin shops. Many visitors wind up doing several laps up and down Laugavegur, picking out new details with each pass. I've described a short stretch of Laugavegur on my self-guided "Reykjavík Walk," and listed several businesses along here in the Eating, Shopping, and Entertainment sections.

Icelandic Phallological Museum (Hið Íslenzka Reðasafn)

This gimmicky museum near the Hlemmur bus junction (at the far end of Laugavegur) is a one-room collection of preserved animal penises that can be seen in 15 minutes, plus various depictions of phalluses in folk art. It's impossible to describe (or visit) this place without juvenile jokes, so here goes: You'll see more wieners than you can shake a stick at—preserved, pickled peckers floating in jars of yellow liquid. You'll see a seal's schlong, a wolf's wang, a zebra's zipper trout, a fox's frankfurter, a giraffe's gherkin, a dog's dong, a badger's baloney pony, a squirrel's schwanz, a coyote's crankshaft, a horse's hardware, a reindeer's rod, and lots of whale willies. If you can't get through this description without giggling, maybe you should visit. If you're about to set down this book and write me an angry letter...don't.

Cost and Hours: 1,700 ISK, daily 10:00-18:00, Laugavegur 116, tel. 561-6663, www.phallus.is.

Hallgrímskirkja Area

This hilltop zone is marked by the prominent tower of Reykjavík's landmark church.

▲▲Hallgrímskirkja Lutheran Church

Reykjavík's most recognizable icon is the stairstep gable of this fine, modern church, designed in the 1930s by state architect

Guðjón Samúelsson. It boasts a sleek interior and a tower with grand views. For more on the church, see my "Reykjavík Walk," earlier. In the summer, there are regular performances on its booming organ (see "Entertainment in Reykjavík," later).

For a fine photo op, view the church from atop the steps of the Einar Jónsson Museum across the street.

Cost and Hours: Church—free; tower—1,000 ISK, 100 ISK for kids under 15. Church open 9:00-21:00, tower until 20:30; Oct-April church until 17:00, tower until 16:30. The church sometimes closes for special events. Tel. 510-1000, www.hallgrimskirkja.is.

Tower: The 250-foot-tall tower offers a commanding view of the city. A six-person elevator takes you up to the belfry, where you can look down on the city's colorful roofs amidst the clang of the church bells (cover your ears at :00 and :30 past the hour). Straight ahead, look down over the colorful roofs lining Skólavörðustígur street, which stretches toward the harbor. In the distance, if it's clear, you may see the snow-capped Snæfellsjökull peak at the end of the Snæfellsnes Peninsula, 50 miles away. The closer mountain, looming to the right, is the 3,000-foot Mount Esja, a popular destination for local hikers. And to the right, the island you see is Viðey, reachable on an easy cruise (see page 60). Ponder that well over half of Iceland's population lives in view of this church. Lines for the elevator can be long—if there's a crowd, swing back later in the day.

▲▲Einar Jónsson Museum and Garden (Listasafn Einars Jónssonar)

The former home of gifted sculptor Einar Jónsson (1874-1954)—facing Hallgrímskirkja church—has a free sculpture garden out back (described in "Reykjavík Walk," earlier). For a more intimate look at the artist, tour the museum (entrance at the front, facing the church). Inside, you'll see his home, and several large- and small-scale plaster casts for Einar bronzes that decorate the city.

Cost and Hours: 1,000 ISK, Tue-Sun 10:00-17:00, closed Mon; English-language info sheets available; Eiríksgata 3, tel. 551-3797, www.lej.is.

Visiting the Museum: Stepping into the grand **entry hall,** immediately on your right is *Outlaws* (*Útlagar,* 1901). This break-

through work, completed while Einar was a student in Denmark, is one of his trademark pieces. It depicts a convicted man who takes his wife's lifeless body to a cemetery before escaping with his child to live in the Highlands. (As many original Icelandic settlers were themselves outlaws—exiled from Norway—this theme is particularly poignant.) Just beyond that, *Dawn* (*Dögun,* 1906) illustrates a scene from an Icelandic folk tale, in which a girl tricks a troll by keeping him talking until the sun rises. He sweeps her up in his arm at the very moment the sun freezes him in stone, and he shakes his fist defiantly.

In the red room, down the spiral staircase, the striking *Rest* (*Hvíld,* completed in 1935) is an eerie, oversized bust of a young man whose face is half-covered by reptilian basalt columns. Beneath his chin stands a sculptor leaning against a giant hammer, taking a break. This recalls the notion (dating back to Michelangelo) that the sculpture already exists within the stone; it's the artist's job to chip away and reveal it. In *The Spell Broken* (*Úr Álögum,* completed 1927), a St. George-like knight—protectively cradling a woman—slays a dragon by driving his sword through its head. In the green room, the evocative *Remorse* (*Samviskubit,* completed 1947) shows a man tormented by tiny, conscience-like beings. One holds his eyes open, the other recites a litany of wrongdoings in his ear, and both ensure he can't escape whatever's wracking him with guilt.

For a peek at the life of the artist himself, climb the tight spiral staircase to the top floor to see the intimate **apartment** that Einar and his wife Anna shared—a cozy, human-scale contrast to the beefy building and Einar's dynamic works.

Beyond the Pond
▲▲National Museum of Iceland (Þjóðminjasafnið)
The National Museum presents a thoughtful and manageable look at the history of this island nation, making excellent use of artifacts and a top-notch audioguide that brings meaning to the exhibits. The collection is well laid out and strikes just the right balance, presenting enough information to satisfy those with a reasonable attention span while not going overboard. There's also a pleasant café and a classy gift shop.

Cost and Hours: 2,000 ISK, covered by Reykjavík City Card, includes admission to Culture House; daily 10:00-17:00, mid-Sept-April closed Mon; Suðurgata 41, tel. 530-2200, www.thjodminjasafn.is.

Tours: You can rent an audioguide for 500 ISK—or download it for free via the museum's Wi-Fi.

Getting There: The museum is near the far end of the Pond, a pleasant 10-minute walk from City Hall along Tjarnargata; you can also take bus #1, #3, #6, or #12 to the Háskóli Íslands stop. If walking between the harbor area and the museum, you can short-cut along Garðastræti and through Hólavallakirkjugarður, the city's oldest cemetery.

Visiting the Museum: The permanent exhibit fills the two long floors upstairs, telling the story of Iceland. The exhibit is loosely chronological and well-explained in English.

From the ticket desk, head upstairs to begin. You'll see a few objects from the Settlement Age, including candle holders and gorgeous, oversized brass "dome brooches." Much of this floor is dominated by medieval church art, created after the island's conversion to Christianity around 1000. The darkened room in the center displays vestments, statues, altar tapestries, and bells that were all imported from Europe—a reminder that early Icelanders were hardworking frontier farmers who had to order their luxury goods from "back east." Two locally made exceptions are wooden panels

from a c. 1100 *Judgment Day* painting, and a carved crucifix from c. 1200. Nearby, examine the exquisite wood-carved door from the church in Valþjófsstaður (in eastern Iceland), illustrating the story of a knight who slew a dragon to save a lion. Like many precious Icelandic objects, this door was taken to Denmark for safekeeping; the Danish government returned it in the 1930s, as part of a gift to Iceland in honor of the millennial celebration of the Alþingi.

Near the end of this floor, look for Guðbrandur's Bible—the first-ever Bible in Icelandic (1584). The Protestant Reformation, which began in Europe, also spread to Iceland, and to this day, the majority of Icelanders are Lutheran. The landing at the far end of the hall quickly covers the period of Danish rule and has an exhibit on the church in Iceland.

The exhibit continues upstairs, covering the 17th century through the present. Look for the drinking horn by Brynjólfur Jónsson, painstakingly carved with Bible scenes (1598). Following the Reformation, the Danish king also headed the Lutheran Church of Iceland, giving him tremendous power. While absolute rule by the king limited his subjects' freedom, it spurred efficiency and economic progress. Exhibits explain how, in 1703, Iceland conducted the world's first census that recorded every person's name (allowing us to know with precision that, in that year, Iceland

was home to 50,358 people—99 percent of them farmers and farm workers).

Other exhibits explain how Danes maintained a monopoly on trade in Iceland. Starting around 1750, first the Enlightenment and then the wave of nationalism and democracy that swept Europe also reached these shores—with diverse effects, from the reconstitution of the Alþingi in 1845, to the creation of an Icelandic national costume by a local artist in 1860 (Sigurður Guðmundsson's *skautbúningur*). Meanwhile, the humble people of Iceland toiled along on chilly, smelly

farms in the countryside—peer inside a typical farmhouse living room (called a *baðstofa*). They also lived off the sea—fishing from basic, small, open rowing/sailing boats, like the one on display, all the way up to the advent of motorized vessels.

Soon Iceland was primed for self-rule, and you'll see the desk of the man who worked hardest to make it happen: Jón Sigurðsson, who loudly agitated in Copenhagen for a national constitution and an end to the trade monopoly. Nearby, look for "The Blue and White"—an early, unofficial Icelandic flag (missing the current red cross). In 1913, a young Icelander flew the flag from his small boat in Reykjavík harbor, until a Danish coast guard ship seized the "unauthorized" colors. Furious Icelanders demanded that the issue

be resolved, and it eventually caught the attention of the Danish king—who agreed that Iceland deserved its own banner. Viewing tests from a distance showed that the blue-and-white flag was too easy to confuse with Sweden's, so the red cross was added. The flag was made official in 1915. Iceland became a sovereign state in 1918, and a fully independent republic in 1944.

The exhibit finishes with a look at modern Iceland. Look for the giant, white trawl wire cutters—a weapon used in the "Cod Wars" between Iceland and the UK (1958-1976), when the two countries squabbled over fishing rights (rather than torpedoing each other, they cut fishing nets). Finally, an airport conveyor belt displays various trappings of modern Icelandic life.

REYKJAVÍK'S ART MUSEUMS

This small community has a busy arts scene, and the six local museums described next proudly show off Iceland's 20th-century artists. Iceland's artistic tradition goes back only a century or so; most Icelandic artists (even today) traveled abroad to get a solid education. The Reykjavík City Card covers all six branches, but I wouldn't dedicate much time here: These museums have a hard time competing with all the nearby natural beauty and interesting history.

National Gallery of Iceland (Listasafn Íslands)

The National Gallery has three branches, each with separate costs and hours (you can get a 2,000 ISK combo-ticket that covers all three). The **main branch** is near the Pond, with five gallery spaces showing off a continually changing selection of pieces from their permanent collection of mainly modern Icelandic artists. They also have a few international pieces—including works by Picasso and Munch—but these are not always on display (2,000 ISK, daily 10:00-17:00, off-season Tue-Sun from 11:00, closed Mon; café, Fríkirkjuvegur 7, www.listasafn.is).

The **Ásgrímur Jónsson Collection** highlights a rotating selection of works by this early-20th-century painter who specialized in Impressionistic landscapes of his homeland, dynamic illustrations of the sagas, and some later Expressionistic Munch-like pieces (1,000 ISK, daily 13:00-17:00; in his former home at Bergstaða-stræti 74—a few blocks southeast of the main branch and Pond).

The **Sigurjón Ólafsson Museum** showcases the heavily stylized, sometimes abstract works of this mid-20th-century sculptor, who studied under both Einar Jónsson and Ásgrímur Jónsson (1,000 ISK, daily 13:00-17:00; northeast of downtown near the Skarfagarðar cruise terminal, at Laugarnestangi 17).

Reykjavík Art Museum (Listasafn Reykjavíkur)

This institution has three branches, each with changing exhibits focusing on modern art (for the latest lineup, see www.artmuseum.is). The **Hafnarhus main branch,** right downtown and near the Kolaportið flea market at Tryggvagata 17, has an eclectic range of temporary exhibits, and sometimes highlights works by Pop artist Erró—Iceland's answer to Roy Lichtenstein. The **Kjarvalsstaðir** branch exhibits some works by idiosyncratic modern painter Jóhannes Sveinsson Kjarval, who blended Icelandic landscapes with abstract and surreal flourishes (it's a 10-minute walk south of the Hlemmur bus junction, in the Klambratún park at Flókagata 24). And the **Ásmundarsafn** branch, in the eastern neighborhood of Laugardalur, highlights work by the mid-20th-century, mostly abstract, Miró-like sculptor Ásmundur Sveinsson, displayed in his architecturally striking former home (on Sigtún, near the corner of Reykjavegur).

Cost and Hours: All three museums are covered by an 1,800-ISK ticket for 24 hours, covered by the Reykjavík City Card, and open daily 10:00-17:00. The main branch stays open until 22:00 on Thu, and Ásmundarsafn has shorter hours off-season (13:00-17:00; www.artmuseum.is).

ALONG THE WATERFRONT

These sights are spread along a lengthy stretch of the city waterfront. I've listed them roughly from east to west.

Just Below the Main Drag

These sights are just downhill from Bankastræti/Laugavegur streets.

▲Sun Voyager (Sólfar)

This popular outdoor stainless-steel sculpture is shaped like an old Viking boat, pointing northwest in the direction of the setting sun in summer. This ode to the sun is a good place to watch the sea, take a selfie, and ponder the promise of undiscovered territory

that brought Scandinavians to Iceland more than a thousand years ago—and the impulses that pushed them farther west, to Greenland and Canada. The sculpture, by Icelandic artist Jón Gunnar Árnason, is a few blocks along the shore past Harpa, at the base of Frakkastígur street, about a five-minute walk below Laugavegur; drivers on the westbound waterfront highway will find a handy pullout right at the sculpture.

▲▲Harpa Concert Hall

One of Reykjavík's newest landmarks, this cutting-edge performing arts and conference center almost feels too big for such a small

city. That's because the ambitious building was conceived during Iceland's banking mania. When the crash came in 2008, construction had already begun. (Some cynics proposed that it be left half-built, as a monument to the greed and excess of unbridled capitalism.) By the time Harpa was opened in 2011, the hall was hemorrhaging money and was kept alive thanks only to huge subsidies (which some Icelanders felt would be better spent elsewhere). Despite the woes, Reykjavík wound up with a fine performance space, and the city is growing into it. In 2013, the building (designed by the Danish Henning Larsen firm) won the EU's prestigious Mies van der Rohe Award—achieving the goal of putting Iceland on the world architectural map. And in 2019, a once-shelved plan for a massive new residential and commercial quarter next to it was finally under construction.

Harpa's honeycombed facade, designed by Danish-born Icelandic artist Ólafur Elíasson, is the most-loved part of the building: In summer the windowpanes reflect the light in patterns, and in winter they're illuminated in pretty colors. The choice of location, parroting the harborside opera house cliché that started in Sydney, unfortunately separates Harpa from the rest of downtown across a busy four-lane road. But photographers drool over the building, and find lots of great angles to shoot. Don't miss the view from the far end of the pier that extends to the right of the building; from there, the facade is reflected in the harbor along with sailboats.

Be sure to step inside, where you're bathed in the light of those many windows. The dominant interior materials are black concrete and red wood, evoking the volcanic eruptions that have shaped Iceland. To enjoy the building's full effect, catch a performance (see options under "Entertainment in Reykjavík," later) or take a tour.

Cost and Hours: Lobby free to enter, daily 9:00-22:00; box office open daily 12:00-18:00; café and gift shops, tel. 528-5000, www.harpa.is.

Tours: In summer, a 30-minute guided tour for 1,750 ISK runs hourly 11:00-16:00. Some tours include a musical performance in the concert hall in an exclusive viewing area. For a brisk intro to Iceland's natural and human diversity, watch *Iceland in a Box,* an immersive video projected on four walls (1,500 ISK, every half-hour daily 10:00-17:30, 15 minutes).

Old Harbor Area

Reykjavík's Old Harbor—about a 10-minute walk west of Harpa—isn't a creaky, shiplap time capsule, but an industrial-feeling port. Tucked around the busy berths and piers are a few seafood restaurants, kiosks selling boat trips, and (at the far end) a smattering of museums. To get here, walk out from downtown (10 minutes), or take bus #14 to the Mýrargata stop.

▲Exploring the Harbor

To get your bearings at the harbor, stand on the seaward side of the turquoise-colored sheds (which house some recommended restaurants) and face the bobbing boats. This "old" harbor was built only in the 1910s, on reclaimed land. (For much of its history—back when Reykjavík was a farm, then a small town—there was good anchorage, but no real harbor.) Today, heavy traffic has moved to the newer container terminal farther along the peninsula. The harbor serves a mixture of excursion boats, small craft, the coast guard (notice the hulking gray ships with red-and-blue trim), and a few fishing trawlers that bring their catch to processing plants. A single small cruise ship can also moor in the harbor (larger ones use the cruise terminal farther out of town).

On your left is the Ægisgarður pier, lined with ticket offices for several whale-watching tours (described next), as well as bike tours. On your right, across the harbor, you can see the angular, glass facade of the Harpa concert hall. And the dramatic mountain rising up straight ahead is Esja—six miles away and 3,000 feet high.

Stroll out to the end of the **Ægisgarður pier** to comparison-shop excursion boats, and to get a good look at the hodgepodge of vessels that call this harbor home. At the beginning of the pier, an anti-whaling organization would love to talk you out of sampling whale meat. At the far end (on the left), you'll see part of Iceland's whale-hunting fleet moored (look for the black-and-white boats called *Hvalur 8* and *Hvalur 9*)—an odd juxtaposition with the whale-watching industry all around you.

Back at the base of the pier, in front of Hótel Marina, is a slip where boats are hauled up to be painted (one of the remaining vestiges of the maritime industry here). To extend your visit to the nearby Grandi area—with several sightseeing attractions and eateries—simply follow the footpath between the harborfront and Hótel Marina. For more on this area, see "Grandi," later.

Whale Watching and Other Boat Trips

Whale watching out in Faxaflói bay is a popular Reykjavík activity. While it can be enjoyable to get out on the water—and catching a glimpse of a whale is undoubtedly exciting—it's a substantial investment of time and money, particularly given that you may see nothing at all. Before deciding to go on a whale-watching cruise, read the description on page 173. As an alternative to a pricey whale-focused trip, consider a faster and cheaper boat trip—such as to the island of Viðey (see later). And if you want to be assured of seeing "whales"—very up-close—you may prefer a visit to the Whales of Iceland exhibit, a short walk away (described later, under "Grandi"). If you're traveling around Iceland, be aware there are also whale-watching opportunities in the north, in the Akureyri area and in Húsavík.

The many boat-tour companies with ticket booths along the Old Harbor's Ægisgarður pier are fiercely competitive, offering much the same experience. For the latest prices, schedules, and details, check each company's website, look for brochures locally, or stop by the sales kiosks. The most established outfit is **Elding** ("Lightning," described later); others in-

clude **Whale Safari** (www.whalesafari.is), **Special Tours** (www.specialtours.is), and **Ambassador** (www.ambassador.is). While Elding is typically the most all-around reliable choice, check the latest online reviews to survey the pros and cons of each one. For comparison's sake, I've outlined Elding's offerings here. Prices are typically a bit cheaper if you prebook directly online, where you'll usually find special offers.

Whale Watching: The **classic** whale-watching trip is three hours and runs daily all year, weather permitting (from 6/day mid-June-Aug to 1/day Dec-Jan; adults 11,000 ISK, children 7-15 pay half-price, children under 7 free; Ægisgarður 5, tel. 519-5000, www.elding.is). You'll pay about double for a **"premium"** option on a "RIB"—a rigid inflatable boat that also includes a high-speed zip across the waves. You'll be issued a warm coverall and goggles for this two-hour thrill ride (22,000 ISK, April-Oct only).

Other Boat Trips: Elding and their competitors also run other seasonal boat trips. The **puffin-watching** cruise (May-mid-Aug only) is shorter (1 hour) and cheaper (6,500 ISK adults) than whale watching—so if you're most interested in riding a boat, it's a reasonable alternative. Cheaper still is Elding's 20-minute ferry service to **Viðey Island** (1,600 ISK round-trip, 2/day, mid-May-Sept only; for more on what to do on the island, see page 60). In the early winter (early Oct-early Dec), when the **Imagine Peace Tower** on Viðey Island is illuminated, Elding offers a two-hour cruise for a closer look (8,500 ISK). Anglers enjoy the **sea-angling** trips (3 hours trying your luck catching cod, haddock, mackerel, and catfish, with an on-board grill party at the end, May-mid-Sept only, 15,000 ISK). And in the dark months, you can take a two-hour, late-evening cruise in hopes of viewing the **northern lights** from the water (11,000 ISK, Sept-mid-April at 21:00 or 22:00).

Volcano House

This attraction, a block off the Old Harbor, is just a small theater that shows two volcano videos—it's 50 minutes of fire and fury (including clips of Iceland's most famous recent eruptions: the Westman Islands in 1973, which swallowed up part of the town of Heimaey; and Eyjafjallajökull in 2010, which halted European air traffic). The movies are interesting, particularly if you're not getting beyond Reykjavík and are curious about Iceland's famous volcanoes, but it's pricey. The building also contains a branch of the What's On TI, which has a display of volcanic rocks, crystals, and other stones.

Cost and Hours: 1,790 ISK, daily 9:00-22:00, showings on the hour starting at 10:00, last film begins at 21:00, Tryggvagata 11, tel. 555-1900, www.volcanohouse.is.

Grandi

The long, broad peninsula that juts out beyond the far end of the
Old Harbor is an up-and-coming district called Grandi. This former sandbar, built up with landfill, is an odd assortment: A spread-
out strip of old warehouses and new big-box stores, but with a lively
little waterfront zone (along Grandagarður) where you'll find some
excellent eateries, and several sights (which I've listed in the order
you'll approach them, if walking from the Old Harbor). At the far
tip of the peninsula—a 15-minute walk or short drive away—is
a trendy little cultural zone, anchored by the Marshall-húsið arts
center.

Saga Museum

The Saga Museum is your best bet for an experience focused on
the stories of the early Norsemen who turned Iceland's wilderness
into a European community (even the National Museum covers the
sagas only tangentially). This place does a valiant job of telescoping
the sagas into an educational 35 minutes. The included audioguide
takes you on a 17-stop tour of Iceland's Settlement Age, through 17
mannequin scenes—each one rooted in textual evidence from the
sagas. While the audioguide is academic enough that it might bore
younger or less interested visitors, a treat for kids of all ages awaits
at the end: a chance to dress up in Viking garb for a photo.

Cost and Hours: 2,200 ISK, 800 ISK for kids 6-12, includes
audioguide, daily 10:00-18:00, Grandagarður 2, mobile 694-3096,
www.sagamuseum.is.

▲Aurora Reykjavík: The Northern Lights Center

Many visitors come to Iceland and spend lots of time and money
failing to see the northern lights. But this little museum offers a
sure-fire, no-risk solution. You'll walk through some sparse exhibits, including one on legends and superstitions that attempted to
explain these once-mysterious dancing lights. Then you'll learn a
bit about the science of the phenomenon. But the main attraction is
a lounge-like theater playing an extremely soothing 38-minute wi-
descreen film on a loop, featuring time-lapse footage of the aurora
borealis at points around Iceland, photographed over eight years of
cold nights. In the gift shop, enjoy a free coffee, then slip on a pair
of virtual-reality goggles and spin around in a chair, tracking the
lights as they flutter through the sky. (For more on the northern
lights, and how to see them yourself, see the Icelandic Experiences
chapter.) Note: If you're heading out to the Pearl, consider spending less to watch the excellent 20-minute Áróra planetarium show
there instead (described later).

Cost and Hours: 1,800 ISK, daily 9:00-21:00, Grandagarður
2, mobile 780-4500, www.aurorareykjavik.is.

Sagas of the Icelanders 101

As with tales of Beowulf, King Arthur, and Robin Hood, scholars

don't know how much of the Icelandic sagas are historically based and how much are fictionalized. But all agree that the sagas are an essential resource for understanding both Iceland's history and the cultural heritage it shares with mainland Scandinavia.

Icelanders have strong narrative traditions. Before they had a written language, legends and laws were passed down orally. With Christianity around AD 1000 came the Latin alphabet, which Icelandic scribes used to document their history, writing mostly in their own language.

These historical narratives, known collectively as "the sagas," were written on precious vellum (calfskin) mainly in the 13th and 14th centuries. It was the Icelanders who first wrote down the dynamic stories of the early Norsemen—from myths of Norse gods like Óðinn (Odin) and Þórr (Thor) to early histories of Scandinavian warriors and kings. Like the epic poems of the ancient Greeks, the sagas provide a cultural foundation for the Nordic people, stretching all the way through history to the present.

Here's a simplified overview of some of the most famous or influential sagas and other early writings:

The **Book of Settlements** *(Landnámabók)*—not strictly a "saga"—documents the earliest ninth- and tenth-century settlers in Iceland. This chronicle tells the story of Hrafna-Flóki (the Raven) Vilgerðarson, who followed a bird to Iceland after he'd been blown off course on his way to the Faroe Islands; and the story of Ingólfur Arnarson, who threw two carved pillars overboard and built his settlement where they washed up (Reykjavík). Remarkably, the Book of Settlements lists more than 400 different families, where each one settled, their family tree, and vivid stories of what they encountered here. The much shorter **Book of Icelanders** *(Íslendingabók),* written by Ari Fróði ("the Wise") Þorgilsson in the early 12th century, gives a concise summary of the history of Iceland up to Ari's own time, including the establishment of the Icelandic Commonwealth and the conversion to Christianity.

The **Saga of Erik the Red** *(Eiríks saga rauða)* and the **Saga of the Greenlanders** *(Grænlendinga saga),* known together as "the

Vínland sagas," tell of how Eiríkur rauði ("the Red") Þorvaldsson (950-c. 1003)—banished from Norway, then Iceland—founded a Norse settlement in Greenland; and how his son, Leifur Heppni ("the Lucky") Eiríksson, explored what we now know as North America.

Egill's Saga *(Egils saga Skallagrímssonar)* tells the story of Egill Skallagrímsson (c. 904-c. 995). Egill is a fascinatingly complex figure: Swarthy and ugly, he was both a fearsome champion warrior and a tender-souled poet. When he was just seven years old, after losing a game, a furious Egill buried his ax in the head of his opponent—claiming his first of many victims. And yet, Egill composed his first poem at the tender age of three, and went on to author some of the loveliest verse in Icelandic literature (after two of his children died, Egill composed the heartbreaking "Lament for My Sons"). Egill's Saga tells of his tortured relationship with his equally short-tempered father, Skalla-Grímur ("Grímur the Bald"); his friendship and rivalry with his dashing brother, Þórólfr; his relationship with his foster sister, turned-sister-in-law, turned wife, Ásgerður; his run-ins with the powerful witch Gunnhildur; and his clashes with his nemesis, King Harald Fairhair of Norway.

Njál's Saga *(Brennu-Njáls saga)* tells the story of wise Njáll Þorgeirsson and his best friend, the gallant Gunnar Hámundarson. Things take a tragic turn—as they always do in the sagas—as early Iceland's penchant for escalating blood feuds spirals out of control, culminating in several tragic deaths. (Spoiler: The protagonist is also known as Brennu-Njáll—"Burning Njáll.")

Icelanders also recorded mythic histories much older than the settlement of Iceland. **Völsunga Saga,** which may have roots in the fifth-century conquests of Attila the Hun, is a sprawling, epic tale of the Völsung clan, including Sigurðr Fáfnisbani ("Slayer of the dragon Fáfnir"), which has inspired artists from Richard Wagner to J. R. R. Tolkien. The two Eddas—the anonymous **Poetic Edda** and Snorri Sturluson's **Prose Edda**—contain ancient poetry that records the myths of the Germanic pagan religion.

Snorri Sturluson (1179-1241)—who also wrote **Heimskringla,** the history of the Norwegian kings—was himself a dynamic figure whose life is described in **Sturlunga Saga.**

For a hefty (and I mean hefty) sample of some of the better-known sagas, pick up *The Sagas of the Icelanders,* a good, brick-like English translation edited by Robert Kellogg. If you're headed to Snæfellsnes, you can enhance your time there by reading some of the many sagas specific to that area.

Reykjavík Maritime Museum (Sjóminjasafnið í Reykjavík)

This exhibit covers Reykjavík's connection to the sea, tracing its history from remote farm to bustling capital—partly thanks to its role as a fishing, shipping, and maritime center. You'll see plenty of well-described artifacts telling the story of the seafood industry and the evolution of the harbor, models of fishing vessels, and vintage fish-processing machinery. You'll learn why stockfish (naturally dried in the cold Reykjavík wind) was so important on early voyages, how boats gradually evolved from rowing and sailing to industrial trawlers, and how radios and navigational technology improved over time.

Cost and Hours: 1,700 ISK, daily 10:00-17:00, Grandagarður 8, tel. 411-6300, www.borgarsogusafn.is.

▲Whales of Iceland

Tucked unassumingly in a box-store zone a five-minute walk beyond the museum strip, this attraction fills a cavernous warehouse with life-size models hanging from the ceiling of the whales found in the waters around Iceland. The models are impressively detailed, bathed in a shimmering blue light, and painted on Styrofoam.

Cost and Hours: 2,900 ISK, 1,500 ISK for kids ages 7-14, free for kids under 7, includes audioguide, daily 10:00-17:00, Fiskislóð 23, tel. 571-0077, www.whalesoficeland.is.

Getting There: The exhibit is a little tricky to find. From the Maritime Museum and recommended Grandi restaurants along Grandagarður, walk to the end of the first long, white-and-turquoise warehouse building with eateries and boutiques, then turn left on Grunnslóð and walk one long block. You can also take bus #14 to the Grunnslóð stop, or drive (free parking right in front).

Visiting the Museum: Get the included audioguide and, as you walk one species at a time, enjoy the serious 30-minute education on these amazing creatures—all with the additional audio backdrop of gleeful children around you.

Begin with the smaller marine mammals: dolphin, narwhal, orca. Then step into a vast space to ogle the majestic giants: pilot whale, humpback whale, sei whale, bowhead whale, minke whale (the one you'll see on local menus—fittingly suspended above the museum café), *Moby Dick*-style sperm whale, and the largest specimen, the blue whale—which can grow up to 110 feet long and (they say) has a tongue as big as an elephant. While this is very expensive considering the brief amount of time most visitors spend here, it's legitimately educational and scratches your Icelandic-whale itch.

▲FlyOver Iceland

A block beyond Whales of Iceland, this attraction offers a thrilling virtual flight over stunning Icelandic scenery. You'll be strapped into a flight simulator, then lifted off your feet toward a big wrap-around screen, where you'll have the sensation of soaring over Iceland's volcanoes, coastline, farmlands, and islands. You'll be spritzed by "clouds" and smell the flowers and the sulfur. (It's very similar to the popular "Soarin'" attraction at Walt Disney theme parks.) The whole experience lasts about 30 minutes, including 20 minutes of setup and a nine-minute "flight." While it's quite expensive—and the "Icelandic history" lessons that precede the ride are silly (lacking the substance of other Reykjavík attractions)—as a thrill ride, it's pretty thrilling. (If you're prone to motion sickness, give it a miss.)

Cost and Hours: 4,000 ISK, 2,000 ISK for kids 12 and under, daily 9:00-21:00, Fiskislóð 43, www.flyovericeland.com.

Marshall-húsið Art Center

Filling a converted fish factory at the far tip of the pier (and of interest mainly to art lovers with a car), this arts center hosts several galleries. The big draw is the gallery of Ólafur Elíasson, the renowned Icelandic artist who was born in Denmark and keeps a (private) studio upstairs here. Ólafur—who helped design Reykjavík's Harpa concert hall—specializes in large-scale, multimedia pieces that combine technical precision with intangible elements like light, water, wind, temperature, and movement. The building also has two other artist-run gallery spaces (The Living Art Museum, www.nylo.is; and Kling & Bang, www.this.is/klingogbang) and La Primavera, an appealing **$$$** café/restaurant facing the harbor (generally same hours as galleries, tel. 519-7766).

Cost and Hours: All galleries are free, Tue-Sun 12:00-18:00, Thu until 21:00, closed Mon, Grandagarður 20, bus #14 to Fiskislóð stop.

Nearby: This far tip of Grandi has attracted some trendy businesses. Across the street in a nondescript warehouse zone, you'll find the flagship store of the Farmers Market brand—called **Farmers & Friends**—with updated Icelandic fashion (open daily, www.farmersmarket.is; city-center branch described later, under "Shopping in Reykjavík"), and **Omnom,** a boutique chocolate factory (closed Sun, www.omnomchocolate.com).

OUTSIDE THE CENTER

You'll need a car, a bus, or a boat to reach the sights in this section. Driving is quick and a breeze, and parking is free and easy at all these sights.

Just South of Downtown
▲▲The Pearl (Perlan)

This attraction, housed in the city's former water-storage tanks, ticks off several sightseeing boxes at once: a fine view of the city skyline; engaging high-tech ex-

hibits extolling Iceland's abundant natural wonders; and a top-floor café, also with a stunning view. Seemingly designed to keep tourists happy in bad weather, it's well done and worth the short drive. A visit here is a great primer before you head out to the Golden Circle or Ring Road—or a satisfying substitute if you're only visiting Reykjavík. It's pricey, but even if you skip the museum, the views from the café are worth the short detour.

Cost and Hours: Museum and view deck—3,990 ISK, 1,950 ISK for kids 6-15; museum, view deck, and Áróra planetarium show—4,490 ISK, 2,450 ISK for kids; view deck only—890 ISK; daily 9:00-22:00, last entry one hour before closing, www.perlanmuseum.is.

Seeing the Pearl for Free: It's free to see the basement photo exhibit, and to enjoy the top-floor café, shop, and view from inside. To go outside to the view deck, however, you'll need to pay.

Getting There: For drivers, the Pearl is 100 yards off highway 40, the main drag into town; there's a big, free parking lot. If you're without a car, you can catch an hourly shuttle bus from the Harpa concert hall (typically leaves Harpa at the top of the hour, and the Pearl at the bottom of the hour; 890 ISK for the shuttle also includes the view deck, or your shuttle fare can be applied to a ticket for the exhibits).

Visiting the Pearl: Read the descriptions below before you enter to decide which ticket you want. If there's a line, look for the ticket machines.

The **Wonders of Iceland exhibit** features a variety of informative displays about Iceland's unique environment. The curators have cleverly designed interactive displays to satisfy your curiosity about this volatile island. The volcano exhibit—nearly as good as the Lava Center on the South Coast—vividly teaches about Iceland's cracked-eggshell pastiche of tectonic plates. In the atrium stands a towering re-creation of the Látrabjarg seabird wall of the Westf-jords; aim the binoculars to learn about the many species that call Iceland home. Nearby is a small whale-watching exhibit and the entrance to the ice cave—an artificial, 300-foot-long cave actually made of ice brought in from a glacier, designed to teach chilly visi-tors how glaciers hold clues to a thou-sand years of history (such as stripes of ash from various volcanic eruptions). At 15°F, the ice cave is a frigid highlight for many (don't worry—they provide jackets). Climbing up through the ice cave, you reach an exhibit on glaciers, with a 180-degree immersive video screen that lets you "stand on top" of Iceland's biggest glacier, plus poignant time-lapse videos of the world's great glaciers receding. Also on this floor is a detailed exhibit about aquatic creatures that live in Iceland's seas and rivers.

The 20-minute **Áróra planetari-um show** explains the northern lights with a sweeping after-dark tour of Icelandic landmarks. With eye-popping visual effects and an engaging mix of science and folklore, it offers a thrilling intro-duction to the aurora borealis for summertime visitors (or disap-pointed wintertime cloudy-day visitors) who won't have the chance to see it in person. It plays on the ground floor on the half-hour, usually in English (confirm at the desk).

After touring the museum, climb to the top floor for the dome and the **view.** Under the dome on the top floor is **$$ Kaffitár café,** with a short menu of good food, as well as the posh **$$$$ Út Í Bláinn** ("Out in the Blue"), serving pricey modern Icelandic food. One floor down is a branch of the Rammagerðin gift shop (free to ogle the view from its windows), and the door to a 360-degree panorama of the city and surrounding countryside, well-explained by orientation tables. From here, Reykjavík lines up on its hilltop around the spire of the Hallgrímskirkja church, while in the op-posite direction, you'll see the downtown airport that connects the capital to far-flung Icelandic outposts.

Nearby: Around the Pearl is the forested **Öskjuhlíð** hill, with walking paths, WWII ruins (signboards explain them), many rab-bits, the temple for Iceland's revived pagan religion (the "first Norse temple built here in a thousand years," www.asatru.is), and a large cemetery (Fossvogskirkjugarður).

Southwest of Downtown
Seaside Stroll

For a break from sightseeing (if the weather's nice), join the locals for a stroll along the paths on the south side of the Reykjavík peninsula. There are plenty of diversions and good places for a picnic, especially at low tide, when you can walk down onto the rocks and sand. Start near the streets called Ægisíða and Faxaskjól (take bus #11; see the "Greater Reykjavík" map at the beginning of this chapter).

Northeast of Downtown
▲Viðey Island

On a nice day, spend an afternoon enjoying the views of the sea and the mountains from this island a few hundred yards offshore. It's a relaxing escape from the crowds in the city, though it takes a little work to reach. But, it gets you into the Icelandic outdoors inexpensively and without a trip out of town. Viðey's rich bird life is readily evident—watch your step—and bird-watchers may spot golden plovers, godwits, snipe, greylag geese, and oystercatchers. The island also has an interesting history that dates back to the 10th century. An Augustine monastery stood on Viðey during the Middle Ages, and during the early to mid-20th century, the island was home to a bustling port.

Getting There: You have two options for reaching Viðey (schedules below). From the Old Harbor in the city center, Elding runs a direct but infrequent ferry (2/day, mid-May-Sept only, 20 minutes). Or—for a more frequent and much shorter connection—go to the Skarfagarðar ferry dock, right next to Reykjavík's cruise-ship terminal, where a small passenger ferry makes a five-minute crossing to the island (take bus #16 from the Hlemmur bus junction—look for the stop hidden behind the white building with the red, peaked roof—and ride six stops to Skarfagarðar). Drivers park for free by the Skarfagarðar dock. Grab a free island map on board the ferry.

Cost and Hours: The ferry is 1,600 ISK round-trip from either the Old Harbor or Skarfagarðar, and is covered by the Reykjavík City Card; sights on the island are free. You have the option of cruising to the island from one harbor and returning to another, if you wish. Ferries from the Old Harbor leave daily mid-May-Sept at 11:50 and 14:50 (none off-season); last return from island at 17:30. Hourly ferries from Skarfagarðar leave mid-May-Sept daily 10:15-17:15, last return from island at 18:30; Oct-mid-May Sat-Sun only 13:15, 14:15, and 15:15, last return from island at 16:30. Ferry info tel. 519-5000, www.elding.is.

Visiting the Island: Above the island's dock, the large, restored **house** from the 1750s is the oldest in the capital area. It was originally built for Iceland's Danish governor, but he chose to live in Reykjavík instead. Inside is a modest **$** café, a free exhibit about the island, and a free WC. Next door, look into the small, traditional church, which is almost as old (from the 1760s).

From where you land, you can stroll to either end of the island in about 25 minutes. To the left, the west part of the island is empty grassland except for a series of columnar basalt statues by American sculptor Richard Serra. To the right, the road through the east part of the island leads to an **abandoned village** that, in the 1920s, had a port almost as important as Reykjavík's. You can enter the old village school (its last class was in 1941) to view a photo exhibit on the island's history—and use the WC.

A five-minute walk to the left of the café is the **Imagine Peace Tower**—paid for by Yoko Ono, the widow of murdered Beatle John Lennon. The cylindrical white pedestal, inscribed with "Imagine Peace" in several languages, launches a powerful vertical pillar of light each year from October 9, Lennon's birthday, until December 8, the day he died (www.imaginepeacetower.com).

In Laugardalur, East of Downtown

Though modest by international standards, the Laugardalur (LOY-gar-DA-lurr) valley makes a pleasant outing on a nice day and lets you hang out with Icelandic families and their kids. You pay to enter the zoo and amusement area (the adjacent botanic garden is free). A lovely café in the gardens serves meals, and there's also an indoor ice rink. Nearby are the big, excellent Laugardalslaug swimming pool (described later) and the Reykjavík Art Museum's Ásmundarsafn branch (see listing, earlier).

Getting There: Take bus #2, #5, #15, or #17 to the Laugardalshöll stop and walk 10 minutes downhill to the parking lot and entrance.

Family Park and Zoo (Fjölskyldu- og Húsdýragarðurinn)

The park and zoo combines animal exhibits, amusement-park rides, and a giant playground area. You'll see Icelandic farm animals—pigs, cows, horses, sheep—plus a seal pool, birds, reindeer, rabbits, and a small aquarium. The website lists feeding times (click on "Program"). The park is open all year, but in winter it's a bit desolate, especially on weekdays, and most rides are closed.

Quick Icelandic horse rides for little kids are offered year-round (Sat-Sun at 14:00). If you're hungry, you can grab a meal at the nondescript café, or stop by one of the hot-dog or ice-cream stands and enjoy a picnic at the outdoor tables with grills.

Cost and Hours: 1,900 ISK, covered by Reykjavík City Card, less for kids; rides cost about 250-750 ISK, or buy a day pass for 2,300 ISK, free parking; daily 10:00-18:00, mid-Aug-May until 17:00; Múlavegur 2, 411-5900, www.mu.is (yes, that's the Icelandic word for "moo").

Botanic Garden (Grasagarður)

Next to the Family Park and Zoo, the city-run botanic garden showcases local trees, herbs, flowers, and other plants. Dotted with ponds and small white bridges, it's a soothing place for a stroll. And buried in the garden is the excellent **$$ Flóran café** (described later, under "Eating in Reykjavík"), which makes a visit worthwhile even on a rainy day (free, daily 10:00-22:00, Oct-April until 15:00, tel. 411-8650, www.grasagardur.is).

Nearby: Follow the parkland five minutes downhill from the gardens (past the ponds and bridges) to an open grassy area. Here you can see the remains of the washing troughs and channels where city residents used to do their laundry in hot spring water, all the way up to the 1970s. Outdoor posters tell the story, and give you a feel for how fast the country has modernized.

Ice Rink (Skautahöllin)

Next to the parking lot for the zoo and gardens is the city's indoor ice rink with public skating most afternoons—a useful bad-weather option (entry including skate rental-1,500 ISK, less for kids; closes for several weeks in summer, confirm current hours on website; Múlavegur 1, tel. 588-9705, www.skautaholl.is).

FARTHER EAST OF REYKJAVÍK

The Árbær Open-Air Museum is just on the outskirts of town, while the **Halldór Laxness House** is farther east, roughly on the way to or from the Golden Circle loop. If you're efficient, you may be able to squeeze one of these into your Golden Circle day trip. Or you can consider these as easy side-trips from the capital—each is about a 30-minute drive from downtown.

▲Árbær Open-Air Museum (Árbæjarsafn)

Reykjavík's open-air museum is a modest collection of old buildings and farm animals—meant to help visitors envision Icelandic life in the 1800s. Homes hold period furnishings and reward those with the patience to poke around and ask questions; while everything is described in English, exhibits seem designed for Icelandic families. At the far edge of the property, the four attached houses (one with a

sod roof) are the only ones that were originally located here; walking through them, you can see how each successive generation added its own wing. The grounds—tucked next to a subdivision, with a highway rumbling along the horizon—are underwhelming, especially if you've visited the lush open-air museums elsewhere in northern Europe. But the exhibits compensate.

Try to time your visit to coincide with the 13:00 hour-long guided tour (included in admission). In the weeks before Christmas, the museum opens with a holiday spirit on Sundays from 13:00 to 17:00.

Cost and Hours: 1,700 ISK, covered by Reykjavík City Card, free for kids under 17. Museum open daily 10:00-17:00, Sept-May 13:00-17:00. Café (waffles and snacks) open June-Aug daily 11:00-17:00 and on the Sundays before Christmas. Kistuhylur 4, tel. 411-6300, www.borgarsogusafn.is.

Getting There: The museum is at the end of the street called Kistuhylur, just off busy highway 49. The easiest bus connection from downtown is #16 from Hlemmur to the Strengur/Laxakvísl stop.

Nearby: Very close to the open-air museum is one of the capital region's best neighborhood swimming pools, **Árbæjarlaug** (described later). If you're considering trying this Icelandic custom, bring your swimsuit and go for a dip after your museum visit.

Halldór Laxness House (Gljúfrasteinn)

Iceland's most famous author, Nobel Prize winner Halldór Laxness (1902-1998), lived in a house called Gljúfrasteinn ("Canyonstone"). The house has been preserved as a museum; an audioguide explains each room. The backyard borders on a rushing stream.

Cost and Hours: 1,200 ISK, daily 9:00-17:00; shorter hours off-season and closed Mon; Nov-March closed Sat-Mon; tel. 586-8066, www.gljufrasteinn.is.

Getting There: It's one of the last houses on the right as you drive up the Mosfellsdalur valley on highway 36, about 25 minutes from downtown Reykjavík. You can easily combine Laxness's house with a visit to Þingvellir, but doing the house plus the whole Golden Circle in a day is too much.

Background: Born in Reykjavík, Halldór Guðjónsson was the eldest son of parents who started life poor. His father worked in road construction, and bought a farm at Laxnes in Mosfellsdalur when Halldór was three. Halldór grew up in the valley and started to write as a teenager. Like many Icelanders of his time, he took a surname (based on the farm where he grew up) instead of using his traditional patronymic. In the 1920s and 1930s he traveled in Europe and America, and converted to Catholicism. In 1945, he settled at Gljúfrasteinn, close to where he grew up, with his second wife. Here he lived comfortably, but not lavishly.

Over his lifetime, Laxness wrote more than a dozen novels, some brilliant...and others barely readable. *Independent People* (in Icelandic, *Sjálfstætt fólk*) is the best known. He also wrote short stories, plays, poetry, travel books, memoirs, and other nonfiction. In his writing, Laxness concerned himself strongly with social justice and the struggles of working people. Icelanders on the political right forbade their children to read his books, and cringed when he received the Nobel Prize; those on the political left loved him and felt he told the truth. In the end, no one could deny that he was a gifted writer and a person of insight and compassion.

Experiences in and near Reykjavík

▲▲▲Thermal Swimming Pools

The vast majority of tourists head straight for the Blue Lagoon, but never consider diving into Iceland's many thermal swimming pools. That's a shame, because—while they lack the atmospheric lava-rock landscape and opaque water—these pools are more authentic and local...and they're much cheaper. They offer a relaxing way to unwind from a busy day of sightseeing, and warm you up in cold weather. You can still visit the Blue Lagoon, but consider complementing it with a swim in a community pool.

There are more than a dozen pools to choose from in the greater Reykjavík area, each one run by the local municipality. The more recently built pools in the suburbs are typically more spacious, with more elaborate waterslides and at least one weatherproof indoor pool—making them well worth a short drive or bus ride. Of the ones I list below, only the first two are within walking distance of downtown. (If doing day trips by car, swing by a pool for a relaxing dip at the end of a long day.) Any Icelander you ask will have a favorite pool and can rattle off its advantages and disadvantages. The recommended pools below are definite winners.

How to Visit: As they're designed for Icelanders, these pools do come with some special etiquette and can be intimidating to outsiders. Read the "Thermal Waters" section on page 170, and you'll have a smooth, comfortable visit.

Cost: Pools in Reykjavík charge 1,000 ISK. The pools in Seltjarnarnes and Hafnarfjörður provide the same experience for a little less—950 and 600 ISK, respectively. In Reykjavík, a shareable 10-entry ticket costs 4,650 ISK, which saves money with only five entries (for example, a couple visiting three times). These are adult rates—kids get in for less. You can bring your own towel, or rent one for 600 ISK; swimsuits are also available for rent or sale.

Hours: On weekdays, most swimming pools in the capital area open early in the morning (before 7:00) and stay open until 22:00. On weekends, pools open a little later (around 8:00 or 9:00) and may close earlier in the evening (often 18:00 or even earlier)—confirm hours online at www.reykjavik.is/en/swimming-pools. Note that most pools close on national holidays. Pools are most crowded after work and school, in the late afternoon; during the day, it's mostly kids and retirees.

▲▲Sundhöllin

Reykjavík's oldest swimming pool—designed by state architect Guðjón Samúelsson in 1937—is the only one within the downtown zone. Parts of the complex retain a classic, antique feel, though the newer outdoor section (from 2017) feels modern and engaging. For nondrivers, the central location makes it an easy choice for sampling a thermal pool. From the windows by the ticket desk, look down over the outdoor section, with city sprawl beyond. From here, the old-fashioned, tiled men's changing rooms are to the left along with a couple of hot pools and a sauna. To the right are both women's changing rooms and additional ones for men, and a variety of pools to choose from. The two sections—indoor and outdoor—are connected by a staircase or elevator; if you enter near one section, don't miss the other (Barónsstígur 45a, 5-minute walk from Hlemmur bus junction or Hallgrímskirkja, limited free street parking in front, tel. 411-5350).

▲Vesturbæjarlaug

This compact 1960s-era pool, in a somewhat posh neighborhood near the university, is a good all-around choice for those staying downtown (20-minute walk, or take bus #11, #13, or #15). While nothing fancy, it offers a look at a typical suburban pool; it's close enough to the center to catch a few tourists, but has a predominantly neighborhood feel. It's outdoor-only, with a  small lap pool, a wading area, hot pots, a steam room, and a sauna (corner of Hofsvallagata and Melhagi, free parking in front or on the street nearby, tel. 411-5150).

Nearby: The burger/hot dog stand immediately in front of the pool is a local favorite. For something classier, the recommended Kaffihús Vesturbæjar café is across the street. And next door is a branch of the delicious Brauð & Co bakery. After your soak and meal, you can explore the neighborhood—a mellow coastal walk is just a couple of blocks away.

▲▲Árbæjarlaug

Farther from the center, this complex wins for nicest modern design (from the 1990s)—and may be the most appealing all-around choice. A soaring glass dome covers its small indoor section, from which you can swim right outside to an interconnected series of pools, including a lap pool, large warm pool with bubbles and waterfalls, modest water slide, several hot pools, and a steam bath. While there's a lot of variety, it's compact and manageable, and looks out over a wooded valley with the sprawl of Reykjavík on the horizon (Fylkisvegur 9, tel. 411-5200). It's a 20-minute drive from downtown, or take bus #5 or #16 to the Fylkisvegur stop. Árbæjarlaug is just off highway 1—convenient for those coming back from Golden Circle or South Coast day trips. It's also handy to combine with a visit to the nearby Árbær Open-Air Museum.

▲Laugardalslaug

The country's largest pool is a bit industrial-feeling and long in the tooth, but it's big enough to offer a wide variety of entertaining options. As you step out of the locker room, the left side is all business (including a pool of seawater that's pumped in from the coastline) and the right side is all fun (with a thrilling waterslide tower). A short bus ride east of the center, Laugardalslaug is next to the official Reykjavík youth hostel and sports complex. It's a good option if you're staying nearby, if you want to go swimming late on a weekend evening, or on major holidays like Christmas or New Year's Day, when it's typically the only pool open (Sundlaugavegur 30, bus #14 to Laugardalslaug stop, big free parking lot on Reykjavegur just before the pool complex, tel. 411-5100).

▲Sundlaug Seltjarnarnes

This small, cozy residential pool is frequented mainly by locals (10-minute drive or bus ride from the center on #11, or a 40-minute walk). It's outdoor-only, and has easy parking, nice views, a modest water slide, and a cozy wading and lounging area (on Suðurströnd in Seltjarnarnes; bus #11 to Íþróttamiðstöð Seltjarnarness stop, tel. 561-1551, www.seltjarnarnes.is).

▲Ásvallalaug

The best indoor pool in the capital area, and arguably the best family pool overall, is on the outskirts of Hafnarfjörður (the bedroom community south of Reykjavík, which you'll drive through on the way in from the airport). From downtown Reykjavík, it's a 20-minute drive or a long 45 minutes by direct city bus. Opened in 2008, it has a full-size lap pool, a large wading pool, a large and shallow family pool, a good water slide, and hot pools; the only outdoor facilities are two small hot pools. It's a great bad-weather destination with a big parking lot (Ásvellir 2, Hafnarfjörður, bus #1 to Ásvallalaug stop, tel. 512-4050, www.hafnarfjordur.is). You could stop in downtown Hafnarfjörður to eat afterward (see recommendations later in this chapter), or drive to the cheap cafeteria at IKEA, which is on the way back to Reykjavík.

Heated Beach: Nauthólsvík

Nauthólsvík, maintained by the city of Reykjavík, is an artificial beach *(ylströnd)* in a sheltered part of the shoreline, where you can bathe in an area heated with excess geothermal water from the city's heating system. This can be fun on a nice summer day, although you'll find better facilities and services at the regular pools (free, possible charge for changing facilities; daily 10:00-19:00, limited hours and 650 ISK charge mid-Aug–mid-May, off Nauthólsvegur, bus #5 to Nauthóll/HR stop, free parking, or walk from here to the Pearl, tel. 511-6630, www.nautholsvik.is).

Also Consider...

Lágafellslaug, a large, new pool in the town of Mosfellsbær (about 9 miles northeast of downtown Reykjavík), has a small indoor section. It's convenient if driving between Reykjavík and the Golden Circle (Þingvellir) or the north (toward Akureyri; Lækjarhlíð 1a, Mosfellsbær, mobile 617-6080, www.mosfellsbaer.is).

Álftaneslaug, with a high waterslide and the country's only wave pool, is in the formerly separate town of Álftanes (on the peninsula due south of Reykjavík). This pool cost so much to build that the town went bankrupt and merged with neighboring Garðabær (Breiðmýri, Garðabær, tel. 550-2350, www.gardabaer.is).

Sundlaug Kópavogs, an older pool in the town of Kópavogur, is handy for those staying nearby (Borgarholtsbraut, Kópavogur, tel. 570-0470, www.kopavogur.is).

More Experiences

The following activities are described in more detail in the Icelandic Experiences chapter.

Horseback Riding

Several horse farms on the outskirts of Reykjavík run riding tours for tourists.

Volcanic Underground Tours

Two pricey subterranean excursions exploring Iceland's volcanic origins are close to Reykjavík. At the very expensive Þríhnúkagígur ("Inside the Volcano"), you're lowered 400 feet into a vast chamber inside a 4,000-year-old dormant volcano (4-6 hours including pickup from Reykjavík hotel). More affordable is **Raufarhólshellir** ("The Lava Tunnel"), where you are guided through a 5,000-year-old lava tube (1-hour basic tour, 3-4 hour "adventure" tour, about 45 minutes from Reykjavík). See page 166 for more info and other volcanic-exploration opportunities.

Shopping in Reykjavík

While you'll find plenty of shopping opportunities, don't expect any bargains: Iceland has almost no manufacturing industry of its own, so many items are imported and quite expensive. My shopping advice emphasizes items that are produced or at least designed in Iceland.

Store Hours: Most shops are open at least Mon-Fri 10:00-18:00; on Saturdays, many close earlier. Sundays are unpredictable—larger or tourist-oriented shops remain open, while others close. In general, touristy shops on the main shopping streets downtown (Laugavegur and Skólavörðustígur) have longer hours in the evening and on Sundays.

WHERE TO SHOP

Downtown Reykjavík seems designed for shoppers—you'll find plenty of temptations as you window-shop along the main drag, **Laugavegur.** Dozens of stores along here run the gamut from gaudy "puffin shops" to high-end craft and design boutiques; a few highlights are mentioned in the next section.

Don't be so mesmerized by Laugavegur that you miss **Skólavörðustígur,** the charming street leading up from Laugavegur to Hallgrímskirkja. It's lined with more authentic-feeling small boutiques. I've listed some of my favorites in the next section, but here's a quick rundown: Near the bottom are large branches of Geysir (fashion), Rammagerðin (top-end souvenirs), and Eymundsson (books). Farther up—especially

around the intersection with Týsgata—you'll find an enticing assortment of one-off boutiques, including the 12 Tónar record shop and the Handknitting Association of Iceland.

Jewelry is a popular item along here, including at **Orrifin** (with funky style, at #17A) and **Fríða** (#18). This street also specializes in ceramicists; look for **Stígur** (a collective showcasing the work of seven artists, at #17B) and **Kaolin** (at #5). It also has some eclectic fashion boutiques, such as **Yeoman** (at #22B). **Nikulásar-kot** features delicate, handmade dolls and ornaments infused with Icelandic folk culture (at #22). Many of these stores have their own little workshops attached, where you can watch artisans at work.

REYKJAVÍK

WHAT TO BUY
Sweaters and Other Icelandic Fashion

At the top of many shopping lists is a handmade Icelandic wool sweater *(lopapeysa)*. Knitting is a major pastime in this nation where

sheep outnumber people, and where hobbies get you through the dreary winter months. Traditional Icelandic designs—often with classy one- or two-tone patterns radiating from the neck—are both timeless and stylish. A good, handmade sweater starts at around $200; they tend to be bulky, so you'll need room in your luggage.

Classic Sweaters: The best place for a traditional sweater (as well as other knitwear and yarn) is the cozy little **Handknitting Association of Iceland** (Handprjónasambandið) shop; browse their website before you go (Mon-Fri 9:00-22:00, Sat until 18:00, Sun 10:00-18:00, Skólavörðustígur 19, tel. 552-1890, www.handknitted.is).

Secondhand Sweaters: For a quality sweater at a lower price (closer to $100-120), consider buying secondhand. For a big, well-stocked vintage clothing shop, stop by **Spúútnik** on the main drag (Laugavegur 28) or their second location, **Fatamarkaður** (at the Hlemmur bus junction, Laugavegur 126). Or, to support a good cause while you shop, the **Red Cross** charity shop has three very central locations (at Laugavegur 12B, Laugavegur 116, and Skólavörðustígur 12). Note that these places line up conveniently—allowing you to comparison-shop easily in about a 10-minute stroll along Laugavegur. There's also a **Salvation Army** (Hertex) branch at the corner of Garðastræti and Ránargata. You'll find plenty of sweaters at the **Kolaportið flea market**—but don't expect top quality there (Sat-Sun only, see listing on page 39).

Stylish Sweaters (and Other Fashion): Icelandic designers enjoy updating traditional sweater designs. **Farmers & Friends** has a full range of fashionable Farmers Market-brand clothes, including sweaters (www.farmersmarket.is). Their downtown outpost is at Laugavegur 37, while their flagship store is at the far end of the Old Harbor's Grandi pier (near the Marshall-húsið arts center) at

Hólmaslóð 2. **Geysir**—another modern Icelandic fashion designer with several branches downtown (including at Skólavörðustígur 7 and Skólavörðustígur 16, www.geysirshops.is)—also has contemporary sweater styles, as do various one-off boutiques along Laugavegur.

Other Clothes: 66°North, Iceland's best-known outerwear brand, is *the* place to buy waterproof shells and puffy vests. Two convenient locations are right on the main drag (Laugavegur 17 and Bankastræti 5). For a better deal, drivers can head to their suburban outlet store with deep discounts—typically about half off (buried in the back of the Skeifan shopping zone, Mon-Fri 9:00-18:00, Sat from 10:00, Sun from 12:00, Faxafen 12, bus #5 to Fen stop, tel. 535-6676, www.66north.is).

Icelandic Souvenirs

Visitors enjoy browsing for keepsakes emblazoned with the Icelandic flag, or an outline of the country. Other popular items include stuffed puffins, whales, cheesy Viking-themed trinkets, and polar bears (they don't live in Iceland, but every now and then, a stray bear drifts across from Greenland on an iceberg). Laugavegur and adjoining streets seem to specialize in tacky souvenir outlets; most of what you'll find is overpriced and made in China. Here are a few better options for more authentically Icelandic souvenirs.

Locally produced and inexpensive, edible souvenirs may be your best bet. **Icelandic candy** is unusual and hard to get outside of Iceland, but easily found at discount grocery stores (Bónus and Krónan), which are generally cheaper and have a better selection than the duty-free airport shops. Cooks on your shopping list might enjoy some of the wide variety of flavored **Icelandic sea salts** (including birch-smoked, seaweed, black lava, and arctic thyme).

Gift shops at the **National Museum** and the **Harpa** concert hall are a little more sophisticated than the norm (see listings in "Sights in Reykjavík").

Rammagerðin, a venerable, high-end boutique, offers extremely expensive but good-quality Icelandic handcrafts and design (www.rammagerdin.is). The main branch—with a row of taxidermy puffins looking out the window—is in the heart of the main shopping zone at Skólavörðustígur 12; other branches are just up the street at Skólavörðustígur 20, at Bankastræti 9, at the Pearl, and at the airport ("Iceland Gift Store").

Iceland, like other Nordic countries, has a knack for clean, eye-pleasing design. **Hrím Eldhús** has a fun selection of upscale kitchen gadgets and housewares—a mix of Icelandic and international (Laugavegur 32); their sister shop just up the street, **Hrím Hönnunarhús,** has a more eclectic selection (Laugavegur 25, www.hrim.is). Also check out **Epal Icelandic Design** (Laugavegur 70); and **Hjarta Reykjavík,** with colorful images of the city's cute houses (Laugavegur 30, www.hjartareykjavikur.com).

Bookstores

Some English-language books on Iceland are available much more cheaply back home; others are hard to find outside the country.

Mál og Menning, along Laugavegur, is Reykjavík's most enjoyable-to-browse bookstore. In the big atrium, tables are piled with intriguing choices, including many English books and travel guides, and there's a tiny café upstairs (Mon-Fri 9:00-22:00, Sat-Sun from 10:00, Laugavegur 18, tel. 580-5000, www.bmm.is).

Three downtown branches of **Eymundsson,** Iceland's answer to Barnes & Noble, are at Austurstræti 18, Skólavörðustígur 11, and Laugavegur 77 (similar hours to Mál og Menning, www.penninn.is).

Those with a car or bike can visit the **publishers' outlet store** in the Grandi neighborhood beyond the Old Harbor, which has a large selection of books, maps, and posters offered at a 15 percent discount (Mon-Fri 10:00-18:00, Sat 11:00-16:00, closed Sun, Fiskislóð 39, tel. 575-5636, www.forlagid.is).

Other Ideas

12 Tónar, downtown at Skólavörðustígur 15, is a local institution. Their shop specializes in Icelandic music, and they run their own label—making this a beloved outpost for indie music lovers. You're welcome to listen to whatever you like over a free cup of coffee (Mon-Sat 10:00-18:00, Sun from 12:00, www.12tonar.is).

Greater Reykjavík's two big **shopping malls** (Kringlan and Smáralind) are convenient for drivers and give you a nontouristy look at Icelandic commercial life.

Entertainment in Reykjavík

PERFORMANCES AT HARPA

Iceland's cutting-edge arts center (described earlier, under "Sights in Reykjavík") has several venues, big and small, that offer entertainment options every night of the year. Three serious musical ensembles are based at Harpa: the **Iceland Symphony Orchestra** (Sinfóníuhljómsveit Íslands, http://en.sinfonia.is), the **Icelandic Opera** (Íslenska Óperan, http://opera.is), and the **Reykjavík Big Band,** a large jazz ensemble (Stórsveit Reykja-

víkur, www.reykjavikbigband.com). All three regularly perform in the 1,800-seat main hall, called Eldborg. Harpa's smaller halls (200-1,100 seats) host many types of performances. Check the schedule for a chance to combine a show with a visit to the most architecturally exciting building in Iceland (box office open daily 12:00-18:00, often later during performances, http://en.harpa.is).

Among the shows at Harpa are likely to be the following tourist-oriented options (all designed for an English-speaking audience). While these may change, each one has been running for several years (though sometimes only in summer). All are entertaining and (aside from the first and last) designed to give visitors insights into Icelandic culture.

Reykjavík Classics is a daytime concert offering a 30-minute presentation of some "greatest hits" of classical music (Mozart, Beethoven, etc.) performed by a smaller ensemble from the symphony. As it's short and nearly always in the main hall, it's an affordable way to experience Harpa without investing too much time and money...but there's very little Icelandic about it (2,600-3,300 ISK, usually at 12:30, http://en.harpa.is).

Pearls of Icelandic Song presents a collection of traditional tunes sung by operatically trained soloists with piano accompaniment. The formal presentation of these informal songs may not be to everyone's taste, but it's authentically Icelandic (3,900 ISK, usually at 18:00 in the main hall, www.pearls.is).

Icelandic Sagas: The Greatest Hits is a frenetic two-person show that attempts to compress centuries of deep and complex Icelandic heritage into 75 minutes, with plenty of humor and costume changes. Though more entertaining than educational, you'll come away with a somewhat better appreciation for Iceland's history (4,900 ISK, usually at 19:30 in the Northern Lights Hall, www.icelandicsagas.com).

How to Become Icelandic in 60 Minutes is a breezy, irreverent, and sometimes naughty one-man comedy show that's a 15-step lesson on what it takes to live like a local on the "biggest little island in the world" (4,850 ISK, usually at 19:00 in the smaller Kaldalón, www.h2become.com).

Múlinn Jazz Club hosts weekly jazz performances in an intimate setting (2,500 ISK, typically Wed and Fri at 21:00, www. facebook.com/mulinnjazzclub).

OTHER PERFORMANCES

The Gamla Bíó theater—a classic old cinema in the heart of town—periodically presents **Saga Music 101.** A contemporary songwriter has written music designed to tell some of the saga stories with English lyrics (4,700 ISK, occasional Wed at 20:00, www. sagamusica.com). The theater hosts other performances, too (check www.gamlabio.is), and its recommended rooftop bar—Petersen Svítan—is a fine venue for a before- or after-show drink.

Various **churches** around Reykjavík present low-key concerts. The big, landmark Hallgrímskirkja offers concerts (mainly on their huge organ) about four times weekly in summer (late June-late Aug, as part of the "International Organ Summer"), and sporadically at other times of year (www.hallgrimskirkja.is). And the cathedral—the modest building next to the parliament, downtown—hosts occasional concerts in its intimate, lovely space (www.domkirkjan.is).

Movies: Bíó Paradís, a beloved art-house cinema just off the main drag downtown, shows international films in their original language with Icelandic subtitles, as well as Icelandic films with English subtitles. Locals kick off weekend revelry at their throwback film series every Friday night—camp classics, '80s movies, interactive screenings (like the *Rocky Horror Picture Show*), and so on. Their bar/café is a popular hangout. The movie lets out just as things get rolling outside (Hverfisgata 54, tel. 412-7711, www. bioparadis.is).

NIGHTLIFE

Reykjavík is renowned for its crazy nightlife. It's pretty simple: Just go downtown any Friday or Saturday night and hit your choice of bars and clubs. Typically, Icelanders come here only on weekends. Many young Icelanders drink at home first (less expensive) before heading downtown between 23:00 and midnight. Higher-end drinking places—hotel cocktail bars, craft-beer specialists, and the like—tend to close on the "early" side...which, in Reykjavík, means midnight on weeknights and 1:00 in the morning on weekends. Harder-partying places stay open until 3:00 or later.

I've recommended some well-established watering holes (see the "Reykjavík Center Restaurants" map, later)—but this scene

Icelandic Music

For centuries, there were few instruments in Iceland, and it was hard to organize an ensemble in a land with difficult travel and no towns or villages. What little music Icelanders had was mostly vocal, using simple melodies in minor keys and lyrics from old ballads and verses, sometimes accompanied by primitive string instruments. At Christmastime, Icelanders danced holding hands in a line while singing traditional verses. When the Pietist movement gained ground among Lutherans in the mid-1700s, music and dance were frowned upon.

But over time, that changed—especially in the 20th century, as Icelanders became wealthier and better tied into European culture. Young Icelanders started to take music lessons, sing in choirs, and play in bands, and both classical and popular music blossomed. Today, Icelanders love to sing along to local folk songs at birthdays or Christmas parties.

The best-known modern Icelandic musician is Björk Guð-mundsdóttir—known worldwide by her first name alone. Born in 1965 in Reykjavík to two politically active parents (her father was the head of the Icelandic electricians union for years), Björk sang in choirs as a child. She gained fame as the lead singer of the Sugarcubes, then struck out on her own in 1993. Björk is known for her eclectic musical style, unique voice (which strikes some ears as discordant), energetic performances, and avant-garde fashion sense (most famously, the swan-shaped dress she wore to the 2001 Oscars). Björk has also dabbled in acting, taking home the Cannes Best Actress prize for her lead performance in the 2000 Lars von Trier film *Dancer in the Dark.* While Björk's music

changes quickly. For a more timely take, pick up the latest issue of the *Reykjavík Grapevine* (or read it online at www.grapevine. is) to find what's in, what's on, and which bands or DJs are playing where. The *Grapevine* also publishes a list of best happy hours—good to know about in this pricey city.

If you want company, go on a **guided pub crawl** such as the one offered by CityWalk (2,500 ISK, Fri-Sat at 22:00, mobile 787-7779, www.citywalk.is).

Upscale Cocktails

These options are for those who'd prefer a more sophisticated scene, and don't mind investing in a pricey (2,000-2,500 ISK) but well-crafted cocktail in a memorable setting.

Sophisticated Art Deco Vibe: Right in the heart of town, **Apotek** fills the ground floor of a landmark hotel by renowned architect Guðjón Samúelsson. This stuffy place loves to brag about its many "best cocktails" awards and generous happy-hour deals (half-price drinks 15:00-18:00). More sedate than the rowdy party scene is not for everybody, her fans are devout. To get a taste for Björk, some of her early albums in Icelandic are available for free on YouTube and well worth listening to. Try *Gling-Gló* (roughly, "Ding Dong"), with accessible but typically idiosyncratic interpretations of jazz standards. Later in her career, Björk moved to England, but still spends a lot of time in Iceland.

Over the last decade or so, other Icelandic bands have become known internationally. Sigur Rós and, more recently, Of Monsters And Men specialize in soaring, bombastic soundscapes (fitting for their dramatic homeland) that often turn up in Hollywood epics. Singer-songwriter Ásgeir is attempting to become the next Icelander to break out in a big way.

Icelandic music fans may enjoy the Icelandic Museum of Rock 'n' Roll, a five-minute drive from Keflavík Airport (see page 126). The 2013 book *Blue Eyed Pop* is also good (buy it at the museum, or from the website of the author, Gunnar Lárus Hjálmarsson, better known as Dr. Gunni; http://blueeyedpopdotcom1.wordpress.com).

Two annual festivals showcase the latest in Icelandic pop music. Iceland Airwaves takes place in Reykjavík in late October/early November (www.icelandairwaves.is). Aldrei Fór Ég Suður (which loosely translates as "I never moved to Reykjavík") fills Ísafjörður, the largest town in the Westfjords, with young visitors for a few days at Easter (www.aldrei.is). There's also Eistnaflug, a heavy metal festival each July in the eastern town of Neskaupstaður (www.eistnaflug.is), and the famous Þjóðhátíð music festival in the Westman Islands (www.dalurinn.is).

all around it, this is a popular choice for a genteel drink. They also serve a full menu of food—including a decent lunch special—but better restaurants are nearby; come for the drinks and the ambience (daily 11:30-late, Austurstræti 16).

Rooftop Bars: To reach **Petersen Svítan** ("The Petersen Suite"), you'll slip through a side door next to the classic Gamla Bíó theater, then ride the elevator up to a rooftop deck. You can sit in the Old World interior, but the main draw is the large outdoor area, overlooking city rooftops—a delight on warm evenings. Don't miss the spiral stairs up to an even higher deck (open daily from 14:00, happy hour until 20:00, Ingólfsstræti 2a).

The recommended **Loft Hostel** runs a convivial rooftop bar perched above the Bankastræti action, with a city-view deck that's as much a draw for locals as visitors (daily until 23:00, happy hour 16:00-20:00, Bankastræti 7, take elevator to the fourth floor).

By the Harbor: Slippbarinn ("Dry Dock Bar") is one of the best places in town for quality, creative cocktails. The menu is vividly described and fun to peruse, with a few mainstays and lots of seasonal concoctions. A mellow hangout by day, at night it's a big, boisterous, and colorful party. It sprawls through the spacious, creative, industrial-mod lobby of the Icelandair Hótel Marina, right along the harborfront, facing the namesake dry dock (daily 11:30-late, also serves food, occasional DJs or live music, Mýrargata 2).

Craft Beer

Iceland has a burgeoning craft beer scene, including high-end bars where you can focus on sampling local brews. While some proudly feature Icelandic beer, most acknowledge the limits of local brewers and make a point to also offer a carefully curated range of imports. Most craft-beer bars have several taps and a chalkboard listing what's on today. Figure on paying 1,000-1,800 ISK for a pint.

Skúli Craft Bar, named for the statue of the original Reykjavík developer on the downtown square it faces, has a great section of Icelandic craft beers. The prices are high, but the glassy, modern, aboveground space feels inviting and attracts a few locals along with the tourists. At the bar—in front of an illuminated wall displaying bottles like trophies—you can choose between Icelandic brews (marked with red-and-blue stripes) and imports. They also have pleasant outdoor tables (Mon-Thu from 15:00, Fri-Sat from 14:00, Sun from 16:00, happy hour until 19:00, Aðalstræti 9, tel. 519-6455).

MicroBar fills a straightforward cellar with happy drinkers (mostly tourists, thanks to its main-drag location) enjoying an even wider selection of microbrews. They specialize in Icelandic beers—with 14 on tap, and more than 100 in bottles—and is the only craft beer place I saw that offers 5- or 10-beer sampler boards; this being Iceland, you'll pay dearly for each sip (daily from 16:00, happy hour 17:00-19:00, Vesturgata 2, mobile 865-8389).

Ölstofa Kormáks og Skjaldar ("Kormákur and Skjöldur's Tavern") is a nice hybrid of the beer-geek places mentioned earlier. Because it's tucked away from Laugavegur, it feels more local, with a *Cheers* vibe and a table often filled with regulars. While they do have taps and bottles from local brewers, their draft selection is limited (all from the same brewery, Borg Brugghús); visit for the atmosphere, not a deep dive into Icelandic brews (daily from 15:00, Vegamótastíg 4, tel. 552-4687).

Session Craft Bar pours mostly Icelandic microbrews from its 16 taps in a modern space, one floor above the tourist parade at the intersection of Laugavegur and Skólavörðustígur (daily from 12:00, Bankastræti 14, above the Subway sandwich shop, mobile 690-1938).

Lively Late-Night Bars

These places really get rolling late at night on weekends (though you're welcome to stop by earlier in the evening, when they can already be quite crowded on weekends). Come for Reykjavík's famous social weekend experience, not the drinks.

Kaffibarinn is a classic dive bar right in the center. It's a local institution that still attracts a largely Icelandic clientele. Filling an old house, it can feel crowded and gets pretty wild on weekends; for a mellower visit, check it out on a weeknight (daily from 15:00, good happy-hour deals before 20:00, live DJ at prime times, Bergstaðastræti 1, tel. 551-1588).

Right along the busiest stretch of Laugavegur, you can't miss **Lebowski Bar,** with neon lights, a Dude-Walter-and-Donny bowling theme, 16 versions of white Russians...and, one would assume, owners very nervous that the Coen Brothers' legal team will catch on. It's rollicking, rowdy, and popular with young Americans (open long hours daily and nightly, Laugavegur 20b, tel. 552-2300).

A block from Ingólfstorg toward the harbor is a cluster of rowdy, hole-in-the-wall bars for late-night revelry. **Húrra** is the all-around favorite, with a big dance floor and great DJs and live music (Tryggvagata 22, tel. 571-7101). **Paloma** is a late-late-late-night weekend option with a dance floor and a vaguely nautical vibe; it's bigger than most, so it feels less claustrophobic (Naustin 1, above The Dubliner). And **The Dubliner** is the city's most central Irish pub (daily from 12:00, Naustin 1, below the Paloma).

In addition, several of the places listed under "Eating in Reykjavík," later, can be good places to grab a drink, including the hipster café **Kaffi Vínyl** and **Kex Hostel.**

Sleeping in Reykjavík

Reykjavík is an expensive place to spend the night. With its spike in tourism, the city is bursting at the seams, demand is soaring, and lots of new places are opening up (or old places expanding) each year—some of them great, others not.

I've focused my listings on relatively established hotels offering good value. Given how pricey Reykjavík's hotels are (especially in the center), I'd also give guesthouses and private rentals (such as on Airbnb) a serious look; youth hostels are especially good for solo travelers. Real hotels are very expensive, especially in the center, and can easily cost $400 a night in summer. Guesthouses (figure $200 a night) and Airbnb (closer to $100 a night) give you more value for the money and a more local experience.

Whatever you do, book any accommodations well in advance, as the best places sell out early for the peak summer months, or if your trip coincides with a major holiday.

In Iceland, prices drop a lot if you are willing to share a bathroom. If a place has the option of a shared bathroom, I've noted

REYKJAVÍK

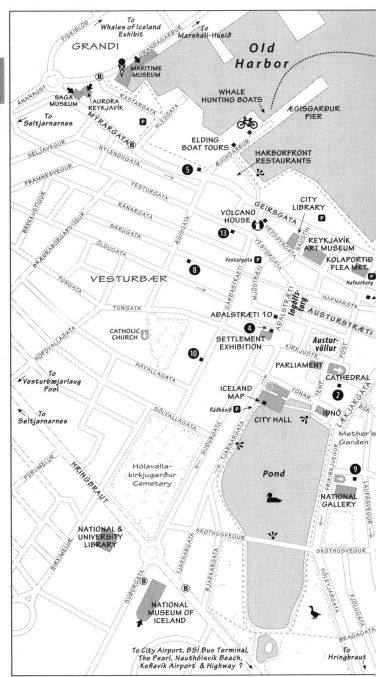

REYKJAVÍK

Reykjavík Center Hotels

1. The Reykjavík Residence Hotel
2. Hótel Kvosin
3. Hótel Óðinsvé
4. Hótel Reykjavík Centrum
5. Icelandair Hótel Marina
6. Guesthouse Galtafell
7. Guesthouse Sunna
8. Hótel Hilda
9. Castle House Apartments
10. Embassy Luxury Apartments
11. Nest Apartments
12. Kex Hostel
13. Downtown Hostel
14. Loft Hostel
15. Laundry

To Viðey

HARPA CONCERT HALL

Note: See also Reykjavik Hotels & Restaurants Outside the Center map

200 Meters

200 Yards

KALKOFNSVEGUR

Shuttle to The Pearl

BBP HOT DOGS

Kolaport

Arnarhóll

SÓLVHÓLSGATA

SUN VOYAGER SCULPTURE

INGÓLFUR ARNARSON STATUE

Lækjartorg

SÆBRAUT

PRIME MINISTER'S OFFICE

CULTURE HOUSE

NATIONAL THEATER

SKÚLAGATA

LINDARGATA

BANKASTRÆTI

GAMLA BÍÓ THEATER

Traðarkot

SMIÐJUSTÍGUR

KLAPPARSTÍGUR

VATNSSTÍGUR

FRAKKASTÍGUR

To Skarfagarðar, Keflavík Airport & Highway 1

AMTMANNS-STÍGUR

SKÓLA

LAUGAVEGUR

HVERFISGATA

HIGH SCHOOL

Garden

HLÖÐUSTÍGUR

HALLVEIGAR

BÍÓ PARADÍS CINEMA

PINGHOLT

BJARGARSTRÆTI

SPÍTALA

ÝSAGATA

NJÁLSGATA

GRETTISGATA

LAUGAVEGUR

BERGSTAÐASTRÆTI

FREYJUGATA

LOKASTÍGUR

KARLASTÍGUR

FRAKKASTÍGUR

YTASTÍGUR

To Hlemmur Bus Junction

HELLUSUND

ÓÐINSGATA

ÞÓRSGATA

AUSTURBÆR

BALDURSGATA

LEIFUR EIRÍKSSON STATUE

BERGÞÓRUGATA

BRAGAGATA

GARDEN ENTRANCES

HALLGRÍMS-KIRKJA

SUNDHÖLLIN POOL

NJARÐARGATA

EINAR JÓNSSON MUSEUM & SCULPTURE GARDEN

EIRÍKSGATA

BERGSTAÐASTRÆTI

BARÓNSSTÍGUR

that in the listing—a shared bath often knocks down the price considerably.

Without a car, stay downtown. It's more convenient for restaurants, nightlife, much of the worthwhile sightseeing, and bus-excursion pickups (though if noise is an issue, request a quiet room, as it can get loud on weekend nights). With a rental car, it can make better sense to stay outside the downtown core—where lodgings cost less and parking is easy. There are fewer hotels and guesthouses in the suburbs, but Airbnb and other rentals are abundant.

For car travelers, the outlying community of Hafnarfjörður is a nice compromise. It has its own little downtown core and quaint old houses, but free parking and less noise and traffic than Reykjavík. It's strategically situated for those driving to and from the airport, the Golden Circle, the Blue Lagoon, and the South Coast.

City buses run to every corner of the metropolitan area, although some parts are a long ride (with a transfer) from downtown. When scoping out a place to stay, check bus access by plugging the address into the journey planner at www.straeto.is and seeing how long it takes to get to the main downtown stops (Lækjartorg and Hlemmur).

I rank accommodations from $ budget to $$$$ splurge. To get the best deal, contact small hotels and guesthouses directly by phone or email. If you go direct, the owner avoids a roughly 20 percent commission and may be able to offer you a discount. For more information and tips on hotel rates and deals, making reservations, finding a short-term rental, and chain hotels, see the Practicalities chapter.

AIRBNB AND OTHER RENTAL SITES

I've intentionally listed fewer hotels and guesthouses than I normally would for a city of Reykjavík's size. That's because here, even more than elsewhere, I find Airbnb and other short-term rentals to be a much better value than hotels. The bottom line: Iceland is expensive, and staying in nontraditional accommodations can have the single biggest impact on your travel budget.

Airbnb lists plenty of options in the downtown core, and is handy for finding less-expensive suburban accommodations (easier for drivers), while providing a more authentic look at Icelandic life. A search for "Reykjavík" may turn up some of these, but for more options, search for the name of the separate town: Hafnarfjörður, Garðabær, Kópavogur, Mosfellsbær, or Seltjarnarnes.

EXPENSIVE DOWNTOWN HOTELS

If you're going to spend a lot of money, you might as well do it with class. These hotels each offer something special.

$$$$ **The Reykjavík Residence Hotel** rents out studios,

suites, and apartments in five buildings located within minutes of each other along or near Hverfisgata (a block off Laugavegur). The most notable building, next to the National Theater, was once a private home built in 1912 by a local bigwig who later became prime minister. When the king of Denmark visited in 1926, this is where he stayed. It's been converted into 10 top-end suites, each with a kitchenette. For the best value, ask for the "economy studio," which costs the least, comes with a kitchenette, and is more spacious than most standard doubles you'll find in Reykjavík (includes breakfast, laundry service, Hverfisgata 45, tel. 561-1200, www.reykjavikresidence.is, info@rrhotel.is).

$$$$ Hótel Kvosin, across the street from parliament and the cathedral in a building from 1900, has 24 big suites with full kitchenettes and fine art on the walls (breakfast extra, Kirkjutorg 4, tel. 571-4460, www.kvosinhotel.is, desk@kvosinhotel.is).

$$$$ Hótel Óðinsvé, with 50 modern, stylish rooms and 10 apartments in a blocky shell, sits in a pleasant residential area a short walk from the lively Skólavörðustígur shopping and dining street (breakfast extra, Þórsgötu 1, recommended Snaps Bistro on-site, tel. 511-6200, www.hotelodinsve.is, odinsve@hotelodinsve.is).

$$$ Hótel Reykjavík Centrum boasts a great location, in view of the parliament, in a modernized building with a period facade and 89 rooms. The Settlement Exhibition on Reykjavík's early history is in the basement, centered on archaeological ruins found when the hotel was built in 2001 (breakfast extra, Aðalstræti 16, tel. 514-6000, www.hotelcentrum.is, info@hotelcentrum.is).

$$$ Icelandair Hótel Marina is at the Old Harbor in a long, skinny building that spent many years as the post office's sorting facility. This hotel's location is more interesting and convenient than the other Icelandair hotel, the Natura, and it's also home to the recommended Slippbarinn cocktail bar (includes breakfast, Mýrargata 2, tel. 560-8002, www.icelandairhotels.com, marina@icehotels.is).

GUESTHOUSES AND SMALL HOTELS

These smaller, less expensive properties are generally in converted residential buildings without elevators. Most of these listings give you the option of sharing a bathroom, which brings down the price substantially. When comparing prices, remember to factor in breakfast and parking costs.

Closer In

$$$ Guesthouse Galtafell offers 11 rooms on a quiet street in a handsome neighborhood close to the Pond—and is a convenient five-minute walk from both downtown and the BSÍ bus terminal.

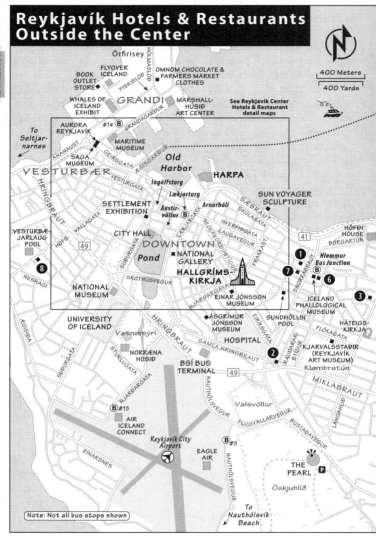

Reykjavík Hotels & Restaurants Outside the Center

One of Iceland's richest merchants and fishing magnates built this attractive house with its crenellated roof in 1916. Breakfast, which costs extra, is served in a cozy, art-filled dining room in the main house (free parking, Laufásvegur 46, mobile 699-2525, www. galtafell.com, info@galtafell.com).

$$$ **Guesthouse Sunna,** just down the street from the big Hallgrímskirkja church, is big and feels more like a hotel than a guesthouse. It offers a range of rooms with shared or private bath—some with kitchens—and some with lots of stairs. There's limited

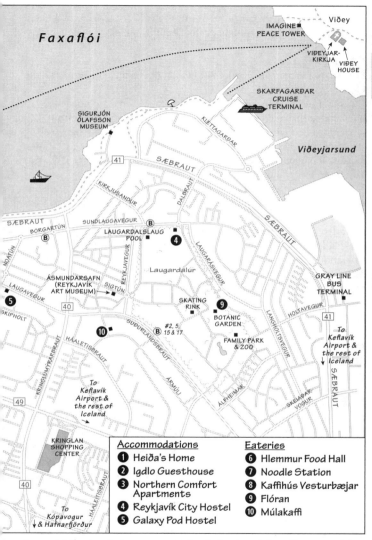

Faxaflói

IMAGINE
PEACE TOWER

Viðey

VIÐEYJAR-
KIRKJA   VIÐEY
          HOUSE

SKARFAGARÐAR
CRUISE
TERMINAL

Viðeyjarsund

SIGURJÓN
ÓLAFSSON
MUSEUM

KLETTAGARÐAR

41   SÆBRAUT

KIRKJUSANDUR

DALBRAUT

SÆBRAUT

SÆBRAUT

BORGARTÚN

SUNDLAUGAVEGUR

B

LAUGARDALSLAUG
POOL   4

REYKJAVEGUR

LAUGARÁSVEGUR

NÓATÚN

Laugardalur

B

LAUGAVEGUR

5

ÁSMUNDARSAFN
(REYKJAVÍK
ART MUSEUM)

SIGTÚN

GRAY LINE
BUS
TERMINAL

SKIPHOLT

40

SKATING
RINK

9

BOTANIC
GARDEN

HOLTAVEGUR

LANGHOLTSVEGUR

41

To
Keflavík
Airport &
the rest of
Iceland

HÁALETISBRAUT

10

SUÐURLANDSBRAUT

B 2, 5,
15 & 17

FAMILY PARK
& ZOO

KRINGLUMÝRARBRAUT

ÁRMÚLI

ÁLFHEIMAR

SÆBJAÐAR-
VOGUR

SKEIÐAR-
VOGUR

49

To
Keflavík
Airport &
the rest of
Iceland

KRINGLAN
SHOPPING
CENTER

HÁALEITISBRAUT

40

To
Kópavogur
& Hafnarfjörður

Accommodations
1 Heiða's Home
2 Igdlo Guesthouse
3 Northern Comfort
   Apartments
4 Reykjavík City Hostel
5 Galaxy Pod Hostel

Eateries
6 Hlemmur Food Hall
7 Noodle Station
8 Kaffihús Vesturbæjar
9 Flóran
10 Múlakaffi

REYKJAVÍK

free parking in their courtyard (includes breakfast, Þórsgata 26 at the corner of Njarðargata, tel. 511-5570, www.sunna.is, sunna@ sunna.is).

$$$ Hótel Hilda, a lesser value, has 15 rooms, many quite small and tight—but all with private baths. Upper rooms can be stuffy, so ask for one on the first two floors. It's in a pleasant, fairly quiet residential neighborhood just a five-minute walk west of downtown. Pay for street parking in front, or look for free spots

REYKJAVÍK

a block or two away (includes skimpy breakfast, Bárugata 11, tel. 552-3020, www.hotelhilda.is, info@hotelhilda.is).

Farther Out

For locations, see the "Reykjavík Hotels & Restaurants Outside the Center" map.

$$ Heiða's Home rents 14 tight double rooms (no sinks), all but one with shared bathrooms. It's close to the Hlemmur bus junction, occupying an older building along a busy urban-feeling street at the east end of downtown (no breakfast, shared kitchen facilities, pay on-street parking, lots of stairs, Hverfisgata 102, mobile 692-7654, heidashome@gmail.com).

$ Igdlo Guesthouse (the name is Greenlandic for "igloo") is on the outskirts of downtown, about a 5- to 10-minute walk from the BSÍ bus terminal, in a converted small apartment building on a dead-end street near a busy road. It's a bit hostel-like—all rooms share a bathroom, and most rooms have multiple beds. The exterior and location are ho-hum, but prices are low, downtown is a 15-minute walk away, and there's usually plenty of free on-street parking (kitchen, laundry facilities, rental bikes, family rooms, Gunnarsbraut 46, tel. 511-4646, www.igdlo.com, booking@igdlo.com).

APARTMENTS

These apartments are good for a longer stay, or if you want your own kitchen.

$$ Castle House Apartments at Skálholtsstígur 2a and **Embassy Luxury Apartments** at Garðastræti 40 offer a dozen well-appointed, mostly one-bedroom apartments with kitchenettes in two super downtown locations well-described on their shared website. They also have cheaper studio apartments dubbed **Northern Comfort** in a lesser location at Skipholt 15, a bit outside downtown (pay on-street parking, tel. 511-2166, www.hotelsiceland.net, 4@4.is, see map on page 82).

$$ Nest Apartments rents four units in a three-story building in a quiet spot not far from Laugavegur. The basement is generously called the "ground" floor (2-night minimum, cheaper if you stay a week, pay on-street parking, Bergþórugata 15, mobile 893-0280, www.nestapartments.is, nest@nestapartments.is).

HOSTELS

¢ Kex Hostel ("Cookie")—filling an old cookie factory—is a popular choice for backpackers. While a bit pricey, it's big, close to downtown, and has a popular café that's frequented even by nonguests (lots of stairs, pay on-street parking, Skúlagata 28, a 7-minute walk from the Hlemmur bus junction—see map on page 79, tel. 561-6060, www.kexhostel.is, info@kexhostel.is).

"**Official**" **HI Hostels:** These three **¢** listings belong to the Hostelling International network (website for all: www.hostel. is). **Reykjavík City Hostel** is a 45-minute walk or easy bus ride from downtown, conveniently next to the Laugardalslaug swimming pool and close to the Family Park and Zoo (private rooms available, bike rental, playground, free parking, Sundlaugavegur 34—see map on page 82, bus #14 to Laugarásvegur stop, tel. 553-8110, reykjavikcity@hostel.is). **Downtown Hostel** is better suited to travelers without a car (private rooms available, Vesturgata 17—see map on page 79, bus #14 to the Mýrargata stop, tel. 553-8120, reykjavikdowntown@hostel.is). **Loft Hostel** is even more urban, occupying a couple of floors in a downtown building just uphill from the prime minister's office (recommended rooftop bar, elevator, Bankastræti 7—see map on page 79, near the Lækjartorg bus stop, tel. 553-8140, loft@hostel.is).

¢ The Galaxy Pod Hostel offers something different: Guests sleep in individual capsules, which give a little privacy and space to lock up valuables. The capsules are a good value for solo travelers, but two people traveling together will do better in a two-bed room at one of the HI hostels listed earlier. It's in an uninteresting neighborhood above a Mitsubishi Motors showroom, a half-hour's walk or short drive from Parliament (elevator, breakfast optional, free parking, Laugavegur 172—see map on page 82; bus #2, #5, #14, #15, or #17 to Gamla Sjónvarpshúsið; tel. 511-0505, www. galaxypodhostel.is, bookings@galaxypodhostel.is).

OUTSIDE REYKJAVÍK, IN HAFNARFJÖRÐUR

If you're renting a car and using Reykjavík as a base for day trips to sights in the countryside, you may find it easier to stay out-side downtown in the southern suburb of Haf-narfjörður (HAHP-nar-FYUR-thur). While calling this area "charming" is a stretch, it does get you into a car-friendly zone away from the crowds (parking is easy), and gives you a glimpse of an  authentic Icelandic neighborhood, with restaurants and services in walking distance. And it's strategically located between downtown Reykjavík and points south: the airport, the Blue Lagoon, and the Golden Circle and South Coast.

While I've listed a few traditional accommodations (hotel,

REYKJAVÍK

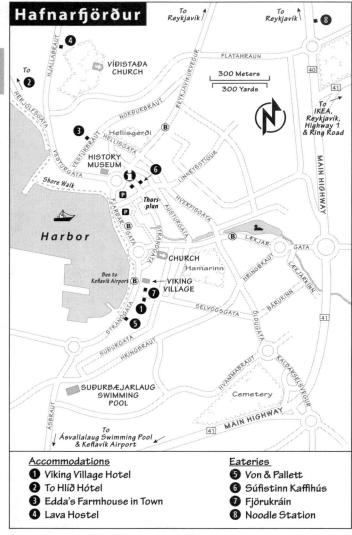

Hafnarfjörður

To Reykjavík
To Reykjavík
FLATAHRAUN
VÍDISTADA CHURCH
To
HJALLABRAUT
NORÐURBRAUT
REYKJAVÍKURVEGUR
300 Meters
300 Yards
N
To IKEA, Reykjavík, Highway 1 & Ring Road
MAIN HIGHWAY
Hellisgerði
HELLISGATA
VESTURBRAUT
HISTORY MUSEUM
VESTURGATA
Shore Walk
LINNETSSTIGUR
HVERFISGATA
AUSTURGATA
Thors-plan
STRANDGATA
FJARÐAR GATA
Harbor
LÆKJAR GATA
LÆKJARKINN
CHURCH
Hamarinn
HRINGBRAUT
ÓLDUGATA
BÁRUKINN
Bus to Keflavik Airport
VIKING VILLAGE
SELVOGSGATA
STRANDGATA
SUÐURGATA
HRINGBRAUT
HVAMMABRAUT
KALDAKSELSVEGUR
SUÐURBÆJARLAUG SWIMMING POOL
ÁSBRAUT
Cemetery
MAIN HIGHWAY
To Ásvallalaug Swimming Pool & Keflavík Airport

Accommodations
1 Viking Village Hotel
2 To Hlíð Hótel
3 Edda's Farmhouse in Town
4 Lava Hostel

Eateries
5 Von & Pallett
6 Súfistinn Kaffihús
7 Fjörukráin
8 Noodle Station

B&B, and hostel), you'll often get a better value via Airbnb. Before booking anything with a Hafnarfjörður address, check a map to make sure it's near downtown, rather than in the industrial zone to the east.

Getting There: Downtown Reykjavík is a 15-minute drive away, or a 25-minute ride on bus #1; airport buses stop in the center, but don't offer door-to-door pickup.

If you stay here and drive the Golden Circle or South Coast

day trips, Breiðholtsbraut (highway 413) is a useful shortcut from Reykjanesbraut (highway 41) over to highway 1 in the direction of Selfoss. Your GPS or map app will guide you; otherwise, from highway 41, follow the signs for highway 413 toward highway 1.

$$ Viking Village Hótel, part of the cheesy Viking-themed Fjörukráin restaurant complex, has Viking-esque common areas, but most of its 41 rooms are straightforward, on the small side, and full of heavily varnished wooden furniture; some feel a bit tired. They also have bunk-bedded cabins that sleep up to six (with private baths)—potentially cost-effective for families or small groups. There's a free sauna and hot pots, and the airport bus stops nearby (Strandgata 55, tel. 565-1213, www.fjorukrain.is, booking@vikingvillage.is). Their "Fishermen's Village" annex, called **$$$ Hlíð Hótel,** is a little compound of woody, waterfront cabins on a rustic, sparsely populated point just north of Hafnarfjörður (a 15-minute drive from the main hotel; 20 minutes from downtown Reykjavík). It feels remote, yet is still close to the city (same contact information).

$ Edda's Farmhouse in Town, in a charming and historic residential zone a short walk from town, has three simple, tidy rooms with a shared bathroom, and includes homemade breakfast. It's a "farmhouse" because Edda has cats, dogs, and rabbits (Vesturbraut 15, tel. 565-1480, mobile 897-1393, ekaritas@simnet.is).

¢ Lava Hostel, a 15-minute walk north of town, is smaller and more intimate than the hostels in Reykjavík. This nonprofit hostel raises funds for the local Boy Scout troop; they also manage the adjacent campsite. As the name suggests, it's in the midst of an old lava flow (free parking, Hjallabraut 51, tel. 565-0900, www.lavahostel.is, info@lavahostel.is).

HOTELS NEAR THE AIRPORT

It usually makes better sense to stay in Reykjavík (even when arriving or departing at odd hours). Still, given the 45-minute distance between the city and the airport, staying out here does make arrival and departure quicker: Late-night arrivals won't have to blearily pick up a rental car, or wait for an airport bus to slowly fill and rumble into town. Hotels and Airbnb lodgings in Keflavík and Njarðvík, the towns near the airport, are also a bit cheaper than in Reykjavík. But basing yourself out here makes for a much longer drive to the sights on your full days in Iceland, and drastically reduces your choice of bus tours if you're not using your own wheels. A taxi from the airport into Keflavík town can cost as much as 5,000 ISK, so figure that into your budget. For locations, see the "Keflavík Airport Area" map near the end of this chapter.

$$$ Hótel Aurora Star, a hundred yards from the terminal, is the only hotel right at the airport, with 72 rooms. It's undistinguished but gets the job done; has family rooms, free parking, and a restaurant...and starts serving breakfast at 5:00. Prices are less expensive than downtown Reykjavík hotels, but still pricey by international standards (Blikavöllur 2, Keflavík, tel. 595-1900, www. hotelairport.is, airport@hotelairport.is).

$$$ Hótel Keflavík, near the harbor in the center of the town of Keflavík, also offers breakfast from 5:00 and free transport to (but not from) the airport. They have in-house laundry that even nonguests can use. If you arrive on an early-morning transatlantic flight and get a rental car, you could have breakfast here and watch the town wake up (Vatnsnesvegi 12, Keflavík, tel. 420-7000, www. kef.is, stay@kef.is).

Eating in Reykjavík

Iceland's tourist boom has equipped Reykjavík with a surprisingly good range of dining options. You'll dine well here—and it's easier than you might think to eat out without emptying your wallet. My best budget tip is to have your main meal at lunch: If you stick to free drinking water (that's the accepted default), you can come away from a near-gourmet seafood lunch downtown only about $25 poorer. Then, for dinner, save by picnicking, having a light meal at a café, grabbing a cheap takeout or fast-food meal, or finding a restaurant that doesn't increase its prices in the evening—they do exist. For a few specific leads on cheap eats, see the "Budget Bites" sidebar in this section.

I rank restaurants from **$** budget to **$$$$** splurge, based on average main-course dinner prices; many restaurants also offer a few cheaper items (like burgers or pizza). That said, you get what you pay for—in my experience, a $40 dinner is substantially better than a basic $25 dinner. For a memorable meal, consider splurging on a fixed-price, multicourse dinner (8,000-10,000 ISK). For more advice on eating in Reykjavík, including ordering, tipping, and Icelandic cuisine, see the "Eating" section of the Practicalities chapter.

DOWNTOWN RESTAURANTS

Reykjavík's restaurants—from mom-and-pops to swanky splurges—serve weekday lunch specials for about 2,000-3,000 ISK (this may be a fixed "fish of the day," but sometimes you can choose among several options). Many places close for lunch on weekends—or, if open, have a pricier menu. Fancier restaurants become more expensive (sometimes *much* more expensive) at dinnertime.

Given the large tourist crowds, virtually any downtown restaurant (particularly in the **$$$** or **$$$$** price range) can book up during the busy summer months. In peak season, it's always smart to book ahead; in shoulder season, it's a good idea on weekends.

Fine Dining in Central Reykjavík

These are my favorite places for a classy splurge in the town center. Make reservations if you're going for dinner (all are more affordable at lunch).

$$$$ Dill is one of Iceland's finest restaurants (and its only Michelin-star recipient). They serve up high-end, New Nordic-inspired dishes at prices that aren't drastically higher than many other "upper-midrange" places in this pricey town. They often book up weeks or months ahead—reserve as early as possible (Wed-Sat 18:00-22:00, closed Sun-Tue, Laugavegur 59, second floor—above Bónus supermarket, tel. 552-1522, www.dillrestaurant.is).

$$$$ Grillmarkaðurinn (The Grill Market) has a rustic-mod, two-story setting, with big split-log counters and a lively energy. The architecture, furnishings, and food sing a chorus of Iceland; the action at their busy charcoal grill mixes with the smart clientele to create a winning conviviality. Creative dishes allow curious travelers to sample traditional Icelandic "nov-

elty foods" in a modern, palatable way. The slider trio features a few bites each of puffin, minke whale, and Icelandic lobster *(humar)*, and the grilled minke whale steak comes on its own little hibachi. The service is helpful and without pretense (enticing tasting menus worth the high price, Sun-Thu 17:30-22:30, Fri-Sat until 23:00, Lækjargata 2a, tel. 571-7777, www.grillmarkadurinn.is).

$$$$ Fiskmarkaðurinn (The Fish Market) is a stylish adventure in Icelandic cuisine, with inventive and artful takes on traditional fare such as fish, shellfish, whale, puffin, lamb, and beef. Or, venture something from their fine selection of sushi. The upstairs and downstairs dining rooms, in an elegant old wooden building, ooze a subtle Asian ambience and have a friendly, attentive staff. This is justifiably a hot spot with locals and travelers, so reservations are smart (Sun-Thu 17:30-22:30, Fri-Sat until 23:00, Aðalstræti 12, tel. 578-8877, www.fiskmarkadurinn.is).

$$$ Fiskfélagið (The Fish Company) is a classy splurge,

REYKJAVÍK

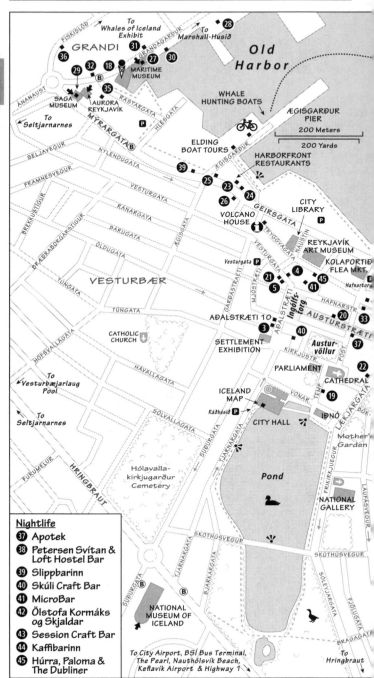

Old Harbor

FISKISLÓD
GRANDI
To Whales of Iceland Exhibit
To Marshall-Húsið
28
31
27
30
36
29 32 18
B
Maritime Museum
ÁNANAUST
35
SAGA MUSEUM
AURORA REYKJAVÍK
WHALE HUNTING BOATS
ÆGISGARÐUR PIER
To Seltjarnarnes
MÝRARGATA
RÁSTARGATA
HLÉSGATA
B
P
200 Meters
200 Yards
SELJAVEGUR
NÝLENDUGATA
ELDING BOAT TOURS
ÆGISGARÐUR
HARBORFRONT RESTAURANTS
FRAMNESVEGUR
VESTURGATA
39
BREKKUSTÍGUR
RÁNARGATA
25
23
24
CITY LIBRARY
P
BÁRUGATA
ÆGISGATA
26
GEIRSGATA
VOLCANO HOUSE
TRYGGVAGATA
REYKJAVÍK ART MUSEUM
BRÆÐRABORGARSTÍGUR
ÖLDUGATA
VESTURBÆR
VESTURGATA
VESTURGÖTU
P
KOLAPORTIÐ FLEA MKT.
TÚNGATA
Vesturgata P
4
45
Hafnartorg
GARÐASTRÆTI
MJÓSTRÆTI
21
5
41
HAFNARST.
TÚNGATA
CATHOLIC CHURCH
AÐALSTRÆTI 10
AÐALSTRÆTI
Ingólfstorg
AUSTURSTRÆTI
20
33
HOFSVALLAGATA
3
40
Austurvöllur
37
HÁVALLAGATA
SETTLEMENT EXHIBITION
KIRKJUSTR.
POST
To Vesturbæjarlaug Pool
PARLIAMENT
CATHEDRAL
22
SÓLVALLAGATA
TEMP.
19
LÆKJARGATA
To Seltjarnarnes
ICELAND MAP
VONAR
BÓK.
Ráðhúsið P
IÐNÓ
FURUMELUR
HRINGBRAUT
CITY HALL
Mother's Garden
Hólavalla- kirkjugarður Cemetery
Pond
FRÍKIRKJUVEGUR
LAUFÁSVEGUR
NATIONAL GALLERY
SÓLEYJARGATA
SUÐURGATA
TJARNARGATA
SKOTHÚSVEGUR
SKOTHÚSVEGUR
B
B
BJARKARGATA
FJÖLUGATA
NATIONAL MUSEUM OF ICELAND
BRAGAGATA
To City Airport, BSÍ Bus Terminal, The Pearl, Nauthólsvík Beach, Keflavík Airport & Highway 1
To Hringbraut

Nightlife

37 Apotek
38 Petersen Svítan & Loft Hostel Bar
39 Slippbarinn
40 Skúli Craft Bar
41 MicroBar
42 Ölstofa Kormáks og Skjaldar
43 Session Craft Bar
44 Kaffibarinn
45 Húrra, Paloma & The Dubliner

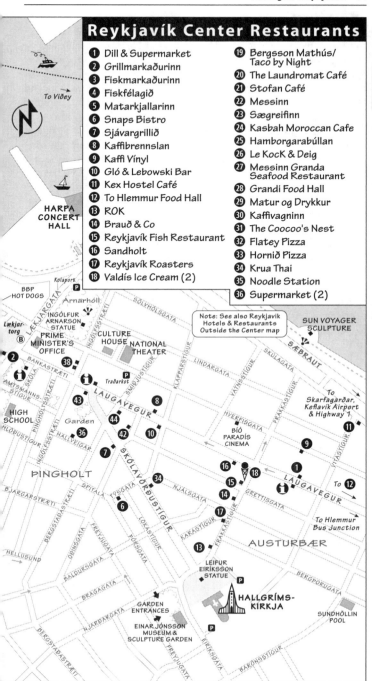

Reykjavík Center Restaurants

1. Dill & Supermarket
2. Grillmarkaðurinn
3. Fiskmarkaðurinn
4. Fiskfélagið
5. Matarkjallarinn
6. Snaps Bistro
7. Sjávargrillið
8. Kaffibrennslan
9. Kaffi Vínyl
10. Gló & Lebowski Bar
11. Kex Hostel Café
12. To Hlemmur Food Hall
13. ROK
14. Brauð & Co
15. Reykjavík Fish Restaurant
16. Sandholt
17. Reykjavík Roasters
18. Valdís Ice Cream (2)
19. Bergsson Mathús/Taco by Night
20. The Laundromat Café
21. Stofan Café
22. Messinn
23. Sægreifinn
24. Kasbah Moroccan Cafe
25. Hamborgarabúllan
26. Le KocK & Deig
27. Messinn Grandi Seafood Restaurant
28. Grandi Food Hall
29. Matur og Drykkur
30. Kaffivagninn
31. The Coocoo's Nest
32. Flatey Pizza
33. Hornið Pizza
34. Krua Thai
35. Noodle Station
36. Supermarket (2)

REYKJAVÍK

To Viðey

HARPA CONCERT HALL

Note: See also Reykjavik Hotels & Restaurants Outside the Center map

BBP HOT DOGS
Kolaport
Arnarhóll
INGÓLFUR ARNARSON STATUE
Lækjartorg
PRIME MINISTER'S OFFICE
CULTURE HOUSE
NATIONAL THEATER
Traðarkot
BANKASTRÆTI
LAUGAVEGUR
HIGH SCHOOL
Garden
PINGHOLT
BÍÓ PARADÍS CINEMA
SUN VOYAGER SCULPTURE
SÆBRAUT
To Skarfagarðar, Keflavík Airport & Highway 1
To Hlemmur Bus Junction
AUSTURBÆR
LEIFUR EIRÍKSSON STATUE
HALLGRÍMS-KIRKJA
SUNDHÖLLIN POOL
GARDEN ENTRANCES
EINAR JÓNSSON MUSEUM & SCULPTURE GARDEN

REYKJAVÍK

elegantly filling the dark, stony cellar of a historic house and serv-ing beautifully presented dishes. This is a rare place with outdoor seating for the rare day when it's warm enough to enjoy. Their French-trained chefs meld a variety of cuisines—including Medi-terranean and Asian—with a respect for Icelandic ingredients and traditions (generally Mon-Fri 11:30-14:30 & 17:30-22:30, Sat-Sun 17:00-22:30, Vesturgata 2a, tel. 552-5300, www.fiskfelagid.is).

$$$ **Matarkjallarinn** (The Food Cellar) manages to be one of Reykjavík's most popular restaurants despite being in a nearly win-dowless cellar. It's nicely decorated and feels more contemporary than its neighbor Fiskfélagið—with live piano adding to the ro-mance each evening. They serve Icelandic and international dishes (good-value fixed-priced meals and daily fish combo, open Mon-Fri 11:30-14:30 & 17:00-23:00, Sat-Sun 17:00-23:00, Aðalstræti 2, enter from Vesturgata, tel. 558-0000, www.matarkjallarinn.is).

$$$ **Snaps Bistro** is Parisian-posh, with a menu of mostly French-inspired dishes. The lively, sophisticated, glassed-in setting is just far enough off the main drag to attract locals alongside tour-ists. Their filling and artfully prepared 2,000-ISK fish-of-the-day special may be the best deal in town. They accept reservations only until 18:30, and it's busy at dinner—reserve to eat early, or plan to wait a bit (jazz club downstairs, Sun-Thu 11:30-23:00, Fri-Sat until 24:00, Þórsgata 1, in the recommended Hótel Óðinsvé, tel. 511-6677, www.snaps.is).

$$$$ **Sjávargrillið** (The Seafood Grill) is a respected seafood house with a corner location right along Skólavörðustígur where Chef Gústav Axel Gunnlaugsson grills up delicious fish, lobster, puffin, and lamb. They have a nice selection of lighter main courses and sushi for smaller appetites...and budgets. The cozy, tight inte-rior is decorated with Icelandic driftwood gathered during Chef Gústav's culinary travels (blowout fixed-price dinners, Mon-Thu 11:30-14:30 & 17:00-22:30, Fri-Sat until 23:00, Sun 17:00-22:30, Skólavörðustígur 14, tel. 571-1100, www.sjavargrillid.is).

Simpler Meals in the Center

$ **Kaffibrennslan,** a café and bar owning a prime spot on Laugavegur, offers a tasty selection of sandwiches, baked goods, coffee drinks, Icelandic beer, and wine. Eat in or grab a seat on their streetside patio for prime people-watching (Mon-Fri 8:00-late, Sat 9:00-13:00, Sun 9:00-21:00, Laugavegur 21, tel. 511-5888).

$ **Kaffi Vínyl** has a hipster-chic ambience, with mismatched furniture, old record players, and an extensive record collection (live DJs spin mostly mellow tunes Wed-Sat after 20:00). The chalkboard menu lists an eclectic selection of flavorful meat and fish dishes, plus vegan options. They also have a full bar with beer and creative cocktails, making this a cozy spot for an evening drink (order food at the bar, Mon-Fri 15:00-23:00, Sat-Sun from 11:00, Hverfisgata 76, tel. 537-1332).

$ Gló, a local vegan favorite, is a smart choice for a quick, inexpensive, healthy meal in the center. It's a cafeteria with an inviting space filling the upstairs of a characteristic old Reykjavík house just off the main street (daily 11:00-22:00, Laugavegur 20b).

$$ Kex Hostel runs a big café open to all, serving breakfast, burgers, lunch specials, and reasonably priced dinners, plus beer, wine, and cocktails in an ex-industrial space with lots of couches and a water view (daily 7:00-10:30 & 11:30-23:00, close to Hlemmur and the *Sun Voyager* sculpture at Skúlagata 28, tel. 561-6060).

$$ Hlemmur Food Hall (Hlemmur Mathöll): This food hall—with 10 trendy eateries filling a former bus depot—is worth the short walk to the end of Laugavegur. You'll find a variety of food stands, a *smørrebrød*-and-aquavit bar, and a branch of the delectable bakery Brauð & Co. Anchoring the scene is Skál!, a cocktail bar serving small plates of delicately prepared modern Scandinavian fare (a good choice if you just can't decide). There's ample shared seating, or pull up a stool at one of the bars. It feels urban and urbane, yet affordable and easy (daily 8:00-23:00, at the Hlemmur bus junction, Laugavegur 107, www.hlemmurmatholl.is).

Frakkastígur Street

For a small-plates lunch or dinner, or a pastry-and-coffee break, head to hip Frakkastígur street. Between Hallgrímskirkja and Laugavegur you'll find some of Reykjavík's most appealing little eateries separated by a grungy but colorful square, with my favorite fish-and-chips joint close by.

$$ ROK, filling a black house with a grass roof across from Hallgrímskirkja, is a hip, lively joint buzzing with energy. Serving small, stylishly presented plates featuring fish, meat, and vegetarian options, the menu lets you try a variety of imaginative dishes for a reasonable price. Dine in the two-story, wood-beamed interior or out on the cozy patio with a church view (lunch specials, daily 11:30-23:00, Frakkastígur 26A, tel. 544-4443).

$ Brauð & Co (Bread & Co.) is an artisanal bakery with a storefront slathered with a wild graffiti mural. Inside, the pastry chefs work like clockwork—churning out hot-from-the-oven cinnamon rolls *(snúðar),* danish *(vínarbrauð),* croissants, sourdough loaves, and seasonal pastries. While the to-go pastries are the hot item (literally), they also sell simple sandwiches and have two stools at the window. If you get takeaway, there's a little square with benches just up the street (daily 6:00-17:30, Sat-Sun until 17:00, Frakkastígur 16, mobile 776-0553). Understandably popular, this bakery is expanding, with locations in the Hlemmur Food Hall (described earlier), and in the suburbs. Keep an eye out.

$ Reykjavík Fish Restaurant feels like a fish restaurant in Reykjavík should—rustic with a cool young staff, cranking out basket after basket of fresh fish. It's a tough choice: the best fish-and-chips or *plokkari* (also known as *plokkfiskur*)—a traditional hash of shredded cod, potato, and onion (daily 11:30-22:00, Frakkastígur 12, tel. 578-5656).

$$ Sandholt, around the corner on Laugavegur, is a refined, upscale-feeling bakery. At the front counter they offer a fine selection of great pastries (including croissants and danish), and serve breakfast and light meals at tables in the back (daily 7:30-21:00, Laugavegur 36, tel. 551-3524).

Coffee: Reykjavík Roasters is the city's best, top-end gourmet coffee shop, where each grind of beans is weighed to ensure a perfect pull. Flip through their vintage record collection while you wait, or just hang out in the bohemian-chic interior (Mon-Fri 8:00-17:30, Sat-Sun until 17:00, intersection of Frakkastígur and Kárastígur, tel. 517-5535).

Ice Cream: Valdís, set back from the street just down from the Reykjavík Fish Restaurant, slings fresh ice cream flavors by the scoop (daily 11:30-23:00, Frakkastígur 10).

Near Ingólfstorg

$ Bergsson Mathús is a favorite with local office workers. Inviting and cozy, it has a healthy hippie feel and serves mostly vegan dishes, with some fish and vegetarian options (daily 7:00-16:00, a block off the Pond, behind the cathedral at Templarasund 3, tel. 571-1822). During the summer, Bergsson turns into a Mexican food joint—**Taco by Night**—in the evening, specializing in tacos and Mexican refreshments.

$$ The Laundromat Café is more café than launderette, and a handy place to enjoy comfort food (burgers, sandwiches, and fish) whether or not your laundry is spinning downstairs. The open-feeling space—decorated with photographs of laundromats around the world, big maps, and a bookshelf bar—is understandably popular with travelers. There's also a children's play area in the basement (Mon-Fri 8:00-23:00, Sat-Sun from 9:00, Austurstræti 9, tel. 587-7555).

$$ Stofan Café ("Living Room") is straightforward, central, and popular, with a warm living-room vibe that caters to coffee drinkers playing chess or cards. Overlooking a colorful (and touristy) slice of Reykjavík, it's a tempting place to escape the drizzle for a soup or sandwich (daily 10:00-22:00, Vesturgata 3, tel. 546-1842).

$$ Messinn, in a bright space on busy Lækjargata, has a pleasant, woody, Westfjords ambience. It features an appealing menu of fish and seafood, including "fish pans" served in sizzling skillets. You're welcome to share the large 4,400-ISK fish pan, making a budget meal for two (lunch specials, daily 11:30-14:00 & 17:00-22:00, reservations smart, Lækjargata 6b, tel. 546-0095, www.messinn.com).

IN THE HARBOR AREA

These eateries are a short walk north of downtown.

$ Sægreifinn (The Sea Baron) is a local institution beloved for its affordable lobster soup. A few decades back, commercial fisherman Kjartan Halldórsson began cooking out of his boathouse by request. His reputation grew, and his little fish joint became a harborfront fixture. Kjartan recently died, but one of his employees now runs the place, keeping the same easygoing, keep-it-simple spirit. (A wax statue of Kjartan is under the stairs in the back dining room.) There's no real menu: It's lobster soup or grilled seafood—whatever's in the display case, clearly labeled and priced (including potatoes and sample-size servings of minke whale). They also have fermented shark appetizers—just ask. Line up at the register, order your soup and/or seafood skewers, then find a seat at a shared table in the sprawling interior (squeeze past the bar to find more tables). There's a children's play area and outdoor seating with a windbreak in the back (daily 11:30-22:30, Geirsgata 8, tel. 553-1500).

$$ Kasbah Moroccan Cafe brings a slice of North Africa to the North Atlantic, serving traditional Moroccan fare such as *briouat* (stuffed pastries), *tagine* (slow-cooked meats and vegetables), couscous, *tangia* (stew), *pastilla* (meat pie), and tea. Dine in the comfy, atmospheric interior or out on the patio (daily 11:00-23:00, Geirsgata 7B, tel. 588-8484).

Burgers: $ Hamborgarabúllan is a fun little 1950s-style, street-corner hamburger joint, with a clutter of stools and service set to classic rock (daily 11:00-22:00, Geirsgata 1, tel. 511-1888). **$$ Le KocK**—just across the street—is a hipper, pricier place that regularly wins local "best burger" awards (daily 11:30-23:00, Tryggvagata 14); attached to that is **Deig** bakery, with bagel sandwiches (Sun-Fri 7:00-19:00, Sat from 12:00).

At the Far End of the Harbor, in Grandi

The peninsula called Grandi—which defines the far (western) end of the harbor area—has sprouted some good eateries that are worth the extra walk from the center.

$$ Messinn Granda Seafood Restaurant, at the Reykjavík Maritime Museum, has a big, comfortable dining hall with harbor views. They offer a quality 2,800-ISK seafood lunch buffet (11:30-14:00), with seven kinds of fish, as well as vegetables, soup, bread, and coffee (daily 11:30-17:00, Grandagarður 8, tel. 562-1215).

$ Grandi Food Hall (Grandi Mathöll) is an edible festival of Icelandic dishes filling a former fisherman's hall (Sjávarklasinn, "Ocean Cluster House") with eight small bars and restaurants. It's youthful and creative, very local, and family-friendly, with shared tables and big windows overlooking the harbor. It's easy to find something for any taste here. You could go for traditional Icelandic or choose from one of several more modern international choices (Sun-Wed 11:00-21:00, Thu-Sat until 22:00, Grandagarður 16, mobile 787-6200, www.grandimatholl.is). Hiding down a hallway is a lounge where you can peek into the actual fish processing floor where the day's catch is sorted and sold; you can even watch the fish auction take place every weekday at 13:00.

$$$ Matur og Drykkur (Food and Drink), inside the Saga Museum, prides itself on time-tested recipes that others might dismiss as old-fashioned. Here, chefs update those traditional dishes for modern tastes. For starters, give the fish-skin chips or fried cod tongues a nibble. Then consider the trademark "halibut" soup (not made with halibut—which is illegal, for complicated reasons), cod's head (more delicious than you'd  imagine), or arctic char smoked over burning sheep's dung (ditto). You'll also find lots of barley and seaweed. Despite the casual, rustic bistro ambience, the food is high-end (Wed-Sun 17:00-23:00, closed Mon-Tue, reservations smart, Grandagarður 2, tel. 571-8877, www.maturogdrykkur.is).

$$ Kaffivagninn (The Coffee Cart) perches on a pier overlooking bobbing boats. The understated nautical decor is charming, and its seaward glassed-in patio is tempting on a sunny day. The main dishes are Icelandic home-cooking classics like fish cakes, *plokkfiskur* (fish hash), and cod, plaice, and arctic char filets; on weekdays, soup and coffee are included (Mon-Fri 7:30-21:00, Sat-Sun from 9:00, Grandagarður 10, tel. 551-5932, www.kaffivagninn.is).

$ The Coocoo's Nest is a somewhat trendier-feeling café just across the street from the Reykjavík Maritime Museum, and lacks its view. But it does have a cozy, split-level, stay-awhile interior and a tempting, brief menu—ideal for escaping the elements and enjoy-

REYKJAVÍK

ing soup, salad, or sandwiches. It serves a rotating menu—tacos one night, pizza the next, then Italian (Tue-Sat 11:00-22:00, Sun until 16:00, closed Mon, Grandagarður 23, tel. 552-5454).

$$ **Flatey** fires up delicious, Neapolitan-style pizzas in a trendy modern atmosphere. If you want pizza a step above Domino's, this is the place (Mon-Fri 11:00-22:00, Sat-Sun from 12:30, Grandagarður 11, tel. 588-2666).

Ice Cream: Valdís, a couple of doors down, is a local favorite offering creative flavors. The name is a pun—it's a woman's first name, but can also be read as "Power Ice Cream" (daily 11:30-23:00, Grandagarður 21).

OUTSIDE DOWNTOWN
These places are best for drivers (all have free parking) but can also be reached by bus.

In Vesturbær, West of Downtown
$ **Kaffihús Vesturbæjar,** an inviting neighborhood café across the street from the Vesturbæjarlaug swimming pool, is the kind of place that makes you want to hang out and pretend you live here. They serve good lunches and dinners from a small menu chalked on the board. Choose a table, then order at the counter—but don't come if you're in a hurry (Mon-Fri 8:00-23:00, Sat-Sun from 9:00, hot food served 11:30-15:00 & 17:00-21:00, at Melhaga 20 at corner of Hófsvallagata, walk or take bus #11 to Melaskóli or #15 to Vesturgarður, tel. 551-0623, www.kaffihusvesturbaejar.is).

Near the Botanic Garden
For locations, see the map on page 82.

$$ **Flóran,** the relaxing café inside Reykjavík's botanic garden, has an eclectic, inventive menu, with main dishes and meal-sized salads. Eat outdoors on a nice day, or in the warm, greenhouse-like interior. They grow some of their own vegetables and herbs (daily 10:00-22:00, early May and Sept until 18:00, closed Oct-April; take bus #2, #5, #15, or #17 to the Laugardalshöll stop and walk 10 minutes downhill to the parking lot and garden entrance; tel. 553-8872).

$ **Múlakaffi** serves old-style Icelandic cuisine with all the polish of a 1970s school lunchroom. You can stuff yourself for about 2,000 ISK, even at dinnertime. Choose a main dish at the counter—it might be fish cakes, cod cheeks, or pasta with meat sauce—then help yourself to as much soup, salad, bread, and coffee as you like (dishes are listed at www.mulakaffi.is). This place has been here—in a commercial zone amidst office blocks and strip malls—for decades. You'll see tradespeople here on a midday break and older men who meet to chat and read the papers together (Mon-Fri

Budget Bites

Hot dog stands are the Icelandic "hamburger joint." They all sell the same dogs for about 600 ISK. While you can find hot-dog stands on squares just about anywhere, many make a pilgrimage to **Bæjarins Beztu Pylsur** ("The City's Best Sausages") on Pósthússtræti by the flea market (described in my "Reykjavík Walk"). It's been in the same family since 1937 and was a fixture here long before Bill Clinton made it famous with his 2004 visit. Clinton ordered his weenie with mustard only, creating his own menu item. Locals go with everything—especially fried onion.

Pizza is a bad value at lunch but competitive at dinner, when a 2,500-ISK one-person pizza starts to look cheap compared to a 5,000-ISK entree at a sit-down restaurant. Pizza joints downtown include **$$ Hornið** (at Hafnarstræti 15, close to Parliament and Lækjartorg), or, for a cheaper meal, locals call **$ Domino's,** with multiple outlets (including a central one at Skúlagata 17, near Hlemmur; easy ordering in English online or call 581-2345, locations and offers at www.dominos.is).

Just like back home, Reykjavík's suburban **IKEA** store has a handy and very cheap **$ cafeteria.** Local families pack in for inexpensive (if small) main dishes, including Swedish meatballs and Icelandic *plokkfiskur* (fish gratin or hash). Downstairs by the cash registers are Reykjavík's least-expensive hot dogs and soft-serve ice cream. IKEA is just off the main route from Reykjavík to the airport, the Blue Lagoon, and the Ásvallalaug swimming pool (daily 9:00-20:30, Kauptún 4 in the suburb of Garðabær, bus #21 to the IKEA stop—catch it at Mjódd or in Hafnarfjörður).

As in other expensive European cities, **international food** can be a good value here. **$ Krua Thai,** a couple of blocks downhill from Hallgrímskirkja church, has a wide selection and a bright upstairs dining room (daily 11:30-21:30, Skólavörðustígur 21a—see map on page 91, tel. 551-0833). **$ Noodle Station,** a small local chain, serves just one dish: big portions of a vaguely Vietnamese noodle soup, with your choice of beef, chicken, or vegetables. There's a location close to the Hlemmur bus junction (Laugavegur 103—see map on page 82), another near the Old Harbor (next to Aurora Reykjavík), and another in a strip mall on the main road through Hafnarfjörður.

Of course, the absolute cheapest option is to assemble a picnic at a **supermarket.** Discount supermarket **Bónus** has a downtown branch at Laugavegur 59 and one in Grandi at Fiskislóð 2 (daily, at least 10:00-18:00). Bónus is much less expensive than the various 7-Eleven-type convenience stores. There's also a **Super 1** grocery at Hallveigarstígur 1, a block off Skólavörðustígur (daily 10:00-22:00).

7:30-20:00, Sat 10:00-14:00, closed Sun, Hallarmúli 1, bus #2, #5, #15, or #17 to Nordica stop, tel. 553-7737).

Farther Out, in Hafnarfjörður

This bedroom community, about a 15 minutes' drive south of Reykjavík, isn't worth going out of your way for a meal. However, if you're sleeping in Hafnarfjörður—or passing through on your way to the airport or back from a day trip—it can be easier to grab a bite here than to look for parking downtown. See the "Hafnarfjörður" map, earlier, for locations.

$$ Von (Hope) is the top choice. This small, ambitious restaurant serves modern fish and meat dishes and is proud of their seafood and ox cheek. Local office workers come for the good-value weekday lunch specials, listed on the chalkboard as you enter (reservations recommended for dinner, Mon-Fri 11:30-14:00 & 17:30-21:00, Sat 16:00-22:00, closed Sun, Strandgata 75, along the water at the south end of downtown, past the fake stave church, tel. 583-6000, www.vonmathus.is).

$ Pallett, an inviting hangout café in the same building as Von, is run by an Icelandic-British couple. They serve great coffee, affordable soups and sandwiches, and—on weekends—a full traditional English breakfast at midday (Mon-Thu 8:00-23:00, Fri until 18:00, Sat 10:00-18:00, Sun 11:00-23:00, Strandgata 75, tel. 571-4144).

$ Súfistinn Kaffihús is a simple, two-story coffeehouse and café offering soups, salads, sandwiches, cakes, and a short list of hot dishes for dinner. It's on the old main street, close to the town library (Mon-Fri 8:00-23:30, Sat from 10:00, Sun from 11:00, Strandgata 9, tel. 563-3740).

$$$ Fjörukráin (The Waterside Tavern) is a Viking-themed dinner-only restaurant, often busy with groups (you can't miss it—look for the Norwegian stave-church-like roof). It's kitschy and the prices are high for what you get, but the interior is a work of art and there's occasional live Viking-style entertainment, so a visit can be fun (daily 18:00-22:00, Strandgata 55, tel. 565-1213).

Reykjavík Connections

BY PLANE
Keflavík Airport (International Flights)

Keflavík Airport (pron. KEP-la-VEEK, code: KEF, www. kefairport.is) is Iceland's only real international airport and the center of Icelandair's hub-and-spoke operation that carries thousands of passengers a day between North America and Europe. Keflavík is a particularly reliable airport thanks to its star-shaped design. (It originated as a US military airbase in World War II, and its various runways allow planes to land against any wind. Given its windy and remote location, so far from any alternative airport, it needed this flexibility...a blessing for approaching pilots to this day.)

The airport's status as a transfer point gives Icelanders a much broader range of flight options, all year long, than they would otherwise have in this small country. During summer months, the airport gets very crowded.

Arrival and departure areas are both on the ground floor, on opposite sides of the main terminal building. You'll find a café and a convenience store, car rental offices, a tax-refund desk (facing the car-rental desks), and ATMs, but no TI. A 24-hour bank is located inside (after security) where you can change any leftover Icelandic crowns when you leave the country—they're hard to exchange outside Iceland. The airport has free Wi-Fi.

If you're flying Icelandair or another budget carrier, you'll have to buy (measly and overpriced) meals on board; savvy travelers buy something more enticing ahead of time and bring their meal onto the plane.

Nearby Gas Stations: When returning a rental car be aware that the airport has only a couple of teeny self-serve pumps hidden near the car-rental return. It's smarter to fill up at the handy **ÓB gas station** just outside the airport entrance, on the corner of Aðalgata and highway 41 (self-service, accepts US credit cards with chip). Or fill up in downtown Keflavík.

Breakfast Near the Airport: Many flights from the US arrive early in the morning. Hótel Keflavík, near the harbor in the town of Keflavík, offers a buffet open to nonguests (no reservations needed, 2,800 ISK, daily 5:00-10:00, Vatnsnesvegi 12, tel. 420-7000). The Viking World museum on the Reykjanes Peninsula also does a breakfast buffet that includes admission (see page 127).

Getting Between Reykjavík and Keflavík Airport

The airport is about a 45-minute drive from downtown Reykjavík (30 minutes from Hafnarfjörður). For details on renting a car, see the Practicalities chapter. Without a rental car, your options are

Keflavík Airport Area

To Sandgerði — 459

To Garður

DUUS MUSEUM

VESTURBRAUT

Faxaflói

GAS STATION — 41

45

AÐALGATA

MAIN TERMINAL

41

KEFLAVÍK

❷

RENTAL CARS

P   Ⓑ Strætó Bus #55

DEPARTURES Ⓑ   Ⓑ ARRIVALS

❶

HANDY ÓB GAS STN.

ICELANDIC ROCK & ROLL MUSEUM

NJARÐARBRAUT

RUNWAYS

REYKJANESBRAUT

R E Y K J A N E S B Æ R

GRÆNÁS- VEGUR

Lava Fields

VIKING WORLD MUSEUM

NJARÐVÍK

SETTLEMENT AGE ZOO

Lava Fields

ÁSBRÚ (FORMER US BASE)

SUPERMARKET

41

To → Reykjavík & Blue Lagoon (via Highway 43)

N

1 Kilometer   44

1 Mile

To Hafnir & Grindavík (via Highway 425)

Not all gas stations shown

❶ Hotel Aurora Star
❷ Hótel Keflavík

private airport buses, door-to-door van service, taxis, or an infrequent public bus.

Don't worry about making an early flight: The whole system is designed for people to get from Reykjavík with plenty of time to make a 7:00 or 8:00 departure. Buses, shuttles, and taxis are ready to go by 3:00 or 4:00 in the morning.

By Airport Bus: Three companies—Reykjavík Excursions, Gray Line, and Airport Direct—run buses between Reykjavík and the airport. Buses run whenever there are flights, even at odd hours. From the airport, buses typically depart when full, which can mean a wait. From Reykjavík, buses depart according to a schedule that varies depending on the flight density.

Reykjavík Excursions runs the **Flybus** (tel. 580-5400, www. flybus.is) between the airport and the company's terminal in Reykjavík (called BSÍ, at Vatnsmýrarvegur 10, about a 10- to 15-minute walk from downtown).

Gray Line runs **Airport Express** buses (tel. 540-1313, www. airportexpress.is) to and from their terminal at Holtavegur 10, next to a Bónus supermarket in a distant part of Reykjavík.

Airport Direct has a similar service, departing from their "Reykjavík Terminal" a few blocks behind the Hallgrímskirkja (Skógarhlíð 10, tel. 497-8000, www.airportdirect.is).

Taking these buses makes good financial sense for solo travelers and for families, as children ride free or at a sizable discount. But the buses can be slow, disorganized, and stressful. The companies try to fill every seat. At busy times, the aisle will be crowded with hand bags, the luggage compartment will be jammed full, and boarding may be a mob scene.

All three companies have desks in the airport arrivals hall where you can buy tickets (about 3,000 ISK); you can also book and pay in advance online. A round-trip ticket (ranging from 5,400 to 6,300 ISK) sometimes saves you a little over two one-ways.

Gray Line's regular price is a tad cheaper, but Reykjavík Excursions tickets are discounted if you buy them from the flight attendant on board Icelandair. (Icelandair mostly promotes Reykjavík Excursions, with which they have a longstanding business alliance.)

In Reykjavík, the buses stop primarily at each company's main transfer point, but Gray Line also picks up and drops off at a few downtown locations for no extra charge. En route between Reykjavík and the airport, both companies' buses stop on request at the bus shelter across from the Viking Village Hótel in downtown Hafnarfjörður (at Strandgata 55). If you need to be picked up there, pay in advance and reconfirm with the company, as buses bypass this stop if there are no requests.

Door-to-(almost)-Door Service: For about an extra 1,000 ISK each way, each company will tack on the transportation between their transfer point and stops at or near major hotels and hostels in central Reykjavík. This usually involves a separate minibus trip between the transfer point and a drop-off point close to your hotel or Airbnb, and takes about 30 extra minutes. It's cheaper than a taxi, and easier than taking the city bus. The transfer procedures can be confusing (you'll need to carry your luggage from one bus to the other). If you're staying in an Airbnb, put in a nearby hotel or bus stop as your pickup and drop-off point, then walk between that point and your lodgings. If you're staying way out in the suburbs, the transfer service may not serve any point near you.

By Shared Shuttle: To pay a little bit more for door-to-door service, but without having to transfer between a bus and a van, you can use **Airport Direct**'s "premium" service. A smaller shuttle van will take you directly to (or from) your hotel without the intermediate transfer—though they will spend a little extra time circling the city to drop off and pick up other passengers (5,990 ISK one-way, 10,990 ISK round-trip, see contact information earlier).

By Private Shuttle: A more expensive option is **Back To Ice-**

land Travel's private door-to-door minibus service (or to the bus stop nearest your accommodation) for 20,000 ISK (up to 4 passengers). You can tack on a visit to the Blue Lagoon for an extra 2,000 ISK—lagoon admission not included (mobile 846-3837, www. btitravel.is).

By Taxi: Groups of at least four adults (who can split the cost) save time and pay only a little more to take a taxi to or from the airport. Reykjavík's two main taxi companies both offer fixed-price service to and from the airport for about 15,500-16,500 ISK (1-4 passengers) or 19,500-22,000 ISK (5-8 passengers). If you reserve in advance, they'll wait for you at the airport with a sign. When reserving, tell them your destination and ask their advice; if your starting or ending point is in the southern part of the capital area (for example, in Hafnarfjörður), using the meter may be cheaper than these fixed rates. Contact **Hreyfill** (tel. 588-5522, www. hreyfill.is) and **BSR** (tel. 561-0000, www.taxireykjavik.is). Other smaller taxi and transfer companies may offer slightly lower rates.

By Public Bus: Strætó, the public bus company, runs buses (#55) between downtown Reykjavík and Keflavík Airport every 1-2 hours, taking about 70 minutes. At some times of the day and on weekends, they run only between the airport and the Fjörður stop in Hafnarfjörður, where you change to bus #1. The public bus is meant more for commuters than for international travelers and goes infrequently, but it's the cheapest way into town and has space for luggage. As it's considered a long-distance route, you can pay the bus driver with a credit card (1,880 ISK one-way; connecting city buses are free if you ask the driver for a transfer slip). For schedules, see www.straeto.is (enter the airport as "KEF" in the journey planner).

The Strætó bus stop is out in the open air along row A of the car-rental lot. To find it, walk out from the arrivals side of the terminal under the roofed walkway, then hang a left and look for the tiny "S" sign (it's not signposted from inside the arrivals hall).

Reykjavík City Airport

Reykjavík's domestic airport (code: RKV) is just south of downtown. Planes landing from the north fly directly over Parliament at a height of only a few hundred feet. While the runways are long enough to land an Icelandair 757, the airport is only used for smaller planes flying domestic routes and to the Faroe Islands and east Greenland. Check-in at the pint-sized terminals feels informal; arriving even an hour early feels like overkill, and there's no security checkpoint for domestic flights.

It's important to know that the airport has two terminals on *opposite* sides of the runway. If you go to the wrong terminal, you'll have to take a taxi to get to the other (you can't walk). Air Iceland Connect uses the larger main terminal on the *west* side of the runways (take bus #15 to the Reykjavíkurflugvöllur stop). If you're flying on Eagle Air—for example, to the Westman Islands—you'll go from a separate, smaller terminal on the *east* side of the runways (take bus #5 to the Nauthólsvegur stop; the terminal is behind the Icelandair Hótel Reykjavík Natura and the control tower). Parking is free at both terminals.

To make an early-morning domestic flight, before buses start running, call a taxi (reserve the night before; see the taxi recommendations earlier, under Keflavík Airport). Figure about 2,000 ISK for a taxi between downtown and either terminal (or between terminals). When you get in the taxi, remember to specify which airline/terminal you're heading to.

BY BUS

Reykjavík has several bus stations. Buses run by **Reykjavík Excursions,** including all of their excursion buses and the scheduled FlyBus to the airport, use the old **BSÍ** bus terminal at Vatnsmýrarvegur 10, about a 10- to 15-minute walk from downtown (or take bus #1, #3, #5, #6, or #15 to BSÍ). Two smaller companies, Sterna Travel and TREX, also use BSÍ for their scheduled and excursion buses.

Buses run by **Gray Line** use their terminal at **Holtavegur 10,** in the Reykjavík suburbs near the container-ship harbor. Gray Line runs minibuses to hotels around town to pick travelers up and shuttle them to the terminal. You can get within a five-minute walk of the terminal by public bus (#12 or #16 to the Sund or Holtagarðar stops), but it's easier to use their shuttles.

Long-distance buses run by **Strætó,** Iceland's public bus service, depart from the Mjódd bus terminal in the eastern Reykjavík suburbs. It's next to a small indoor shopping mall, also called Mjódd (MEE-ohd). Many city bus routes stop at Mjódd, including #2, #3, #4, #11, #12, #17, #21, and #24 (no extra charge for transfer ticket).

Strætó's downtown city bus junction at **Hlemmur** doesn't serve long-distance routes, but is a good place to catch a bus to the long-distance terminal at Mjódd.

BY CRUISE SHIP

There's no scheduled boat service from Reykjavík, but cruise ships frequently stop here in summer. The cruise-ship terminal is at Skarfagarðar, a five-minute drive east of downtown; by bus, take #16 to the Klettagarðar/Skarfagarðar stop. Smaller cruise ships occasionally use a berth in the Old Harbor, just steps from downtown. The weekly ferry from Iceland to Denmark leaves from Seyðisfjörður, in eastern Iceland.

BEYOND REYKJAVÍK

BEYOND REYKJAVÍK

Reykjavík is a great city, but most visitors to Iceland want to get out into the countryside. Fortunately, some of the most beautiful places in Iceland are within striking distance of downtown. Many of the destinations in the following chapters are doable as day trips from Reykjavík, either with a rental car or with an excursion.

Two of the best side trips for experiencing Iceland's dramatic landscape are the Golden Circle, a classic loop trip featuring an impressive gorge, waterfalls, and an active geyser; and the volcano-rich South Coast, where you can hike up to the face of a glacier, stroll along black sand beaches, and walk behind a thundering waterfall.

There's also the famous Blue Lagoon spa—a serene, milky-blue oasis in a volcanic landscape—and the eclectic region around Borgarnes. The Snæfellsnes Peninsula, beyond Borgarnes, offers a little bit of everything that's made Iceland famous.

My favorite "Back Door" destination is the Westman Islands, just off Iceland's South Coast. There you can see the effects of a recent volcanic eruption and enjoy front-row views of the country's cutest bird, the puffin. The Westfjords, far to the northwest, are another relatively untouristed Back Door, but they're too distant for day-tripping (unless you fly into and out of Ísafjörður).

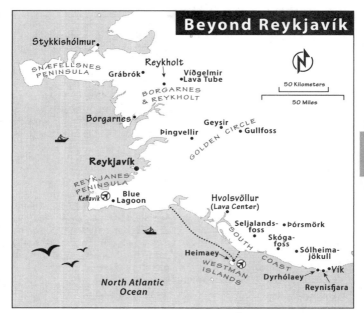

My advice here skews toward either driving yourself or joining an excursion. Public transportation—a godsend for budget travelers in most places—is sparse in Iceland. While suburban buses can help you reach points very close to Reykjavík, there's no practical way, for example, to use cheap public transit to link up the sights of the Golden Circle or South Coast on your own.

While most of this chapter (and the chapters that follow) focus on day trips from Reykjavík, travelers wanting to delve into a scenic slice of Iceland without committing to the full Ring Road can choose from several appealing multiday itineraries. See later in this chapter for suggestions.

DAY-TRIP PLANNING TIPS

For visitors, Iceland is a bit like a giant cruise ship, with thousands of passengers overwhelmed by the choices about what they can do on shore. Take the time to sort through your options (group tour, private tour, do-it-yourself with a rental car) and make the right choice for your interests, time, budget, and appetite for adventure and travel challenges.

These tips will help maximize your Icelandic experience:

Summer Daylight Bonus: In summer you'll enjoy very long hours of daylight; from early June to mid-July it never really gets dark. You can pack a day full by sightseeing close to your home base in the morning, then set out on a side trip in the late afternoon. In

Decoding Icelandic Place Names

Most Icelandic place names are simply a pileup of geographical features. For example, the word for the famous tongue-twister volcano Eyjafjallajökull can be broken down into three smaller words meaning "Island-Mountain Glacier." You can learn a lot about a place simply by decoding its name (and often just its suffix). For example, if you see *fjörður,* expect a dramatic seaside setting; *vík* is on the water, but less thrilling; *fjall* is mountainous; and *hver* means things could get steamy.

These place-name elements recur throughout the country, and in a few cases entire names are recycled (for instance, there's a Reykholt near Borgarnes in western Iceland, and another near Geysir along the Golden Circle). When that happens, the place name might get an add-on modifier for clarity. The town of Vík ("Bay"), on the South Coast, is called Vík í Mýrdal (Bay in Marshy Valley) to distinguish it from other less-visited Víks around the country. And if you're heading for Borgarfjörður Eystri (literally the "more eastern Borgarfjörður"), don't follow your GPS to plain old Borgarfjörður...nearly 400 miles to the west.

Here are the basic building blocks:

á: river, stream	*braut:* avenue
akur: field	*brú:* bridge
ár: river, stream	*bú:* estate, farm
austur: east	*dalur:* valley
bær: town, farm	*eldfjall:* volcano
bjarg: cliff	(fire mountain)
borg: outcrop, fortification	*ey:* island

the peak of summer, for example, it's possible to leave Reykjavík for the Golden Circle as late as 16:00, see most of the sights along that route, and be back in town before the sun goes down.

Winter Wake-Up: Winter is a rotten time to explore Iceland's countryside. Daylight is brief (as few as four hours), and it can be dreary and icy. Weather permitting, though, you can still join organized bus trips from Reykjavík to a few outdoor attractions; this makes good use of the few hours of light and leaves winter driving to pros. One popular way to get into the countryside in the winter is to join a northern lights tour—turning the darkness into an asset. If you do decide to drive in Iceland in winter, be alert to weather conditions, as roads may close due to snow, high winds, or ice. If roads are clear, it's smart to leave Reykjavík in the dark and time your arrival at the first attraction for sunrise.

Cost Considerations: Although a car rental may seem pricey (roughly $350 for a one-week rental in summer, plus insurance, fuel, tolls, and parking), consider this: Per person, the bus transfer

eyja: island
eyri: point, spit
fell: hill, mountain
fjall: mountain
fjara: beach, shore
fjörður: fjord
fljót: large river
flói: gulf, bay
flúðir: rapids
foss: waterfall
gata: street
gerði: fence, hedge
gígur: crater
gljúfur: canyon, gorge
grænn: green
heiði: treeless highland, heath, sometimes "pass"
hellir: cave
hlíð: mountainside, slope
holt: hill
höfn: harbor
hraun: lava
hús: house
hver: hot spring
hvítur: white

jökull: glacier
krókur: hook, river bend
laugar: hot spring, pool
lækur: creek
lón: lagoon
mýri: swamp, marsh
nes: promontory, headland
norður: north
reykur: steam, smoke
sandur: sandy area
skagi: peninsula
skarð: mountain pass
skógur: forest
staður: place, farm, town
stígur: trail
stræti: street
strönd: coast, sandy beach
suður: south
svartur: black
tún: hay field
vatn: lake (also "water")
vegur: road
vestur: west
vík: bay, inlet
völlur: field, plain (plural vellir)

to and from the airport is $50, you'll pay at least $60 for a basic Golden Circle excursion, and $90 for the South Coast. If you're in Iceland for three nights, and take two day-trip excursions, you'll spend close to $200 (double that for a couple). Suddenly that "expensive" rental car seems reasonable, considering the freedom it affords.

DAY-TRIPPING WITH A CAR

More than any other country I can think of, road-tripping is a big part of the joy of exploring Iceland. For one thing, it's hard to get lost: Even on little branch roads, you'll find signs showing what's out there. And at most points of interest, a handy pullout with an information board explains all the upcoming roadside attractions.

For travelers day-tripping on their own by car, the following chapters outline detailed self-guided driving tours with suggested schedules and opinionated descriptions to help you assess your options and plan your drive.

My driving directions assume you're starting from Reykjavík. But if you're staying outside the city, you can drive to these day-trip destinations from a home base anywhere in the southwestern part of the country—for example, from along the South Coast; from the Reykjavík suburb of Hafnarfjörður; or from Keflavík, near the international airport.

Before heading out, be sure to read the tips on driving in Iceland in the Practicalities chapter.

DAY-TRIPPING WITH AN EXCURSION

A variety of companies offer excursions around Iceland. These are great if you want to sit back, enjoy the scenery, and learn from a knowledgeable guide (or, in a few cases, a well-produced recorded commentary). With careful planning, you can cobble together several half- and full-day excursions that will get you to many of Iceland's top sights.

Excursion Destinations

The most popular excursion destinations are the Golden Circle, the Blue Lagoon, the South Coast, and the Snæfellsnes Peninsula.

In winter, you'll find evening trips in search of the northern lights. Some tours run all year, but winter offerings are generally sparser.

Most excursions start in Reykjavík, but there are also options from Ísafjörður in the Westfjords, and Akureyri, Mývatn, and other small towns around the Ring Road (see Westfjords details, later in this chapter for specific recommendations).

You may see tours advertised for the glacier lagoons and Skaftafell National Park in Southeast Iceland; while these are amazing sights, they're too far from Reykjavík for a reasonable day trip (at least 10 hours round-trip)—you'll spend far more time on the bus than at your destination. Save these for a drive around the Ring Road or add an overnight or two in the southeast and do it right.

Choosing an Excursion Company

Sorting through the numerous excursion options can be overwhelming. For starters, look at each company's brochure and website. As the offerings are constantly in flux, check reviews on TripAdvisor (in the "Things to Do" section) for recent firsthand accounts. All branches of Reykjavík's TI (called What's On, www.

whatson.is) have a booking desk for excursions that can help you
find and book a tour.

You can also turn to one of Iceland's travel-company consor-
tiums, such as Guide to Iceland (www.guidetoiceland.is), which
can be a good online
source. You'll pay the
same whether you book
direct or use a booking
service—they get their
commission from the tour
companies.

Tour Companies:
The two biggest players
are Reykjavík Excursions
(www.re.is, owned by Icelandair and promoted on their flights)
and Gray Line (www.grayline.is). Their offerings are slick and
consistent, but the 50-seat buses are typically jam-packed (though
Gray Line offers some minibus departures). An advantage, though,
is predictability and price; what these tours lack in intimacy they
make up for in efficiency and lower ticket costs.

Several smaller outfits are more personal, generally use smaller
vehicles, and can be pricier. Well-established and respected companies include family-run Nicetravel (www.nicetravel.is); environ-
mentally focused Geo Iceland (www.geoiceland.com); small-bus,
small-group Iceland Horizon (www.icelandhorizon.is); and pricey,
boutique Season Tours (www.seasontours.is).

Add-On Options: Beyond the standard sightseeing loops, excursion companies offer a wide variety of optional activities such as
hiking, caving, horseback riding, snorkeling, glacier walking, and
snowmobiling. Among the possibilities: You can do the Blue Lagoon on the way to the airport; add the Fontana baths in Laugarvatn, snorkeling, or an ATV ride to a Golden Circle trip; or visit
Game of Thrones shooting locations.

Prices: Excursions run from about $60 to $250 (more for boutique experiences). For example, an express, seven-hour Golden
Circle tour starts at around $60; a 10-hour South Coast tour starts
at around $90; and a bus trip to the Blue Lagoon, including admis-
sion, runs about $125.

When to Book: For standard tours—such as the Golden Circle or South Coast—you generally don't need to book a seat more
than a day or two in advance, so you may want to wait until you
arrive in Iceland and know what the weather will be doing. One
exception is the Blue Lagoon, which can fill up faster than other
excursions. Your hotel may be happy to book these tours for you (be
aware that they get a commission).

More specialized tours (ice caving, glacier hikes) can book up;

for these, keep an eye on online booking calendars, which typically count down the number of slots available for each tour. If it looks like they're selling fast, book yours before it's too late.

Unguided Excursions to More Remote Destinations

A number of private companies run regularly scheduled buses throughout Iceland's countryside—offering transportation to otherwise difficult-to-reach, remote areas, but without any guiding. Developed primarily to get hikers to trailheads, some of these buses can also work for independent travelers who want to put together day trips on their own.

For example, the worthwhile but difficult-to-reach Icelandic **Highlands** in the center of the country are served by specially equipped excursion buses. Two rough dirt roads (the Kjölur and Sprengisandur routes) cross the Highlands, but can only be driven in a sturdy four-wheel drive vehicle, and only from roughly the end of June to the first snows. You can take a bus from Reykjavík into the Highlands to the geothermally active Landmannalaugar, a base for hikers a short detour off the Sprengisandur route (see page 180). Similar buses cross the island from Reykjavík to Akureyri via the Highland route (see the "Transportation" section of the Practicalities chapter).

MULTIDAY ITINERARIES

The recommended itineraries in this book's introduction focus on two types of travelers: short-timers ("layover" visitors squeezing in a day trip or two) and long-haul road-trippers (devoting a week or more to the entire Ring Road). But for those whose available time falls somewhere in between, it is possible to get beyond the capital region without driving the full 800 miles of the Ring Road. Thinking creatively about domestic flights and one-way car rentals can help you make the most of your time.

Air Iceland Connect has fast and affordable flights from Reykjavík's small and easy downtown airport to Akureyri (in the north), Ísafjörður (the Westfjords' main town), Egilsstaðir (on the Eastfjords), and more (www.airicelandconnect.com). Flights run in the $100 range (if you book ahead) and tend to be quick (an hour or less), easy (there's no security checkpoint), and outrageously scenic.

Most car rental companies let you drop off a car elsewhere in Iceland. This usually comes with an extra fee, but it's often worth the time and money you'll save by not retracing your drive back to Reykjavík.

Intermediate-Length Itineraries

Here are some suggested itineraries that get you farther afield in just two to five days.

Snæfellsnes in 2 Days: Of all the day trips in this book, Snæfellsnes is the one most deserving of an overnight, which lets you spread the driving and sightseeing over two days.

The North in 2-3 Days: The Mývatn area is one of Iceland's natural treasures. Unfortunately, it's a tedious six-hour drive from the capital. To be efficient, you could fly from Reykjavík to Akureyri, pick up a rental car, and drive around a bit (including Mývatn and/or the scenic Tröllaskagi Peninsula, with the lovely town of Siglufjörður). From there, you could drop off your car and fly or take the bus back to Reykjavík—or keep your car (and pay the one-way fee) to drive the Akureyri-Reykjavík segment of the Ring Road.

The South in 2-4 Days: Simply drive down to the South Coast and find a countryside hotel to settle into before taking in the sights. You could spend a day hiking in Þórsmörk (meeting the monster-truck bus in Hvolsvöllur); do a side trip to the Westman Islands; or visit the Golden Circle as a loop from here instead of from Reykjavík (each of these takes about a day). If you'd like to linger in glacier country and have time for Skaftafell National Park, you could drive a couple of hours farther east, adding an overnight in Southeast Iceland.

The Westfjords in 2 Days: The remote and rustic Westfjords are the best place in Iceland to get away from the crowds. For a targeted visit, fly in and out of Ísafjörður, doing a day or two of excursions (either with tour companies or on your own with a rental car). Better yet...

Snæfellsnes Plus the Westfjords in 5 Days: These two areas in northwestern Iceland pair perfectly for several wonderful days of sightseeing. Do the Snæfellsnes loop (ideally with an overnight), then take the ferry to the southern Westfjords. From there, you can loop around the Látrabjarg Peninsula and head north (via Dynjandi Waterfall) to the Ísafjörður area. From Ísafjörður, you can drive six tedious hours back to Reykjavik...or, for maximum efficiency, drop your car and fly back to the capital.

BLUE LAGOON & REYKJANES PENINSULA

The Blue Lagoon—arguably Iceland's most famous attraction—is tucked into a jagged volcanic landscape in the middle of nowhere, about a 45-minute drive south of downtown Reykjavík and not far from the international airport. People flock here from around the globe to soak, splash, and bob in the lagoon's thermal and, yes, milky-blue waters. While many visitors consider the Blue Lagoon a must, it's not everyone's cup of tea—it's pricey, time-consuming, and not ideal for small kids.

The Blue Lagoon and Keflavík Airport both sit on the Reykjanes (RAYK-yah-NESS) Peninsula, which extends into the sea south of Reykjavík. A few low-impact sights are scattered around the volcanic terrain beyond the Blue Lagoon—including Kleifarvatn lake; the thermal fields at Seltún; Grindavík, a humdrum town with some good lunch options; and Keflavík, the peninsula's main town. While the scenery is more impressive in other parts of the country, a quick drive around Reykjanes provides those on a tight timeframe with an efficient glimpse of the Icelandic landscape.

PLANNING YOUR TIME

The Blue Lagoon requires reservations—you can't just show up and hope to slip in. Day-of openings are rare. To have your choice of slots, book several days ahead.

Blue Lagoon Strategic Strike: Given the Blue Lagoon's proximity to the international airport, a smart, time-saving strategy

Blue Lagoon: To Visit or Not to Visit?

Travelers are split on the Blue Lagoon. For some, a visit to this iconic thermal pool is the highlight of their time in Iceland. For others, it's outrageously expensive and overrated.

Pros: The Blue Lagoon is a unique and memorable travel experience, thanks to its stunning volcanic setting, silky-blue water, and luxury-spa class. While you can splash in hot water at any municipal swimming pool in Iceland, the Blue Lagoon is as refined as those are functional—it is, in a sense, the ultimate expression of Icelandic thermal bathing. And it's simply fun: sipping a drink, smearing fancy mud on your face, and feeling pebbles under your feet as 100°F water ebbs your stress away. As a bonus, it's easy to reach on the way to or from the airport.

Cons: The Blue Lagoon is expensive (absurdly so to Icelanders), crowded with an almost exclusively touristic clientele, grossly commercial, not great for young kids, and inconveniently located for those staying in Reykjavík. The reservation requirement is cumbersome, and minerals in the water can wreak havoc on your hair. If you believe that one big pool of hot water is pretty much the same as any other, you can pay one-tenth of the price to enjoy one of Reykjavík's many municipal swimming pools—and enjoy a far more authentic cultural experience.

is to schedule your visit to coincide with your flight: If arriving on a morning flight, hit the Blue Lagoon on your way into Reykjavík. Or if you're flying out in the afternoon, soak in the Blue Lagoon on your way to the airport. With a several-hour layover, it may not be worth the trouble to go all the way into Reykjavík—but a visit to the Blue Lagoon (or sights in the town of Keflavík) makes a far better alternative to hanging out at the airport. Luggage storage is available at the lagoon parking lot.

Blue Lagoon and Reykjanes Peninsula Loop: If you're staying longer in Reykjavík and want to make a day of it, book your Blue Lagoon reservation for 13:00 and follow this plan. For details, see page 121.

10:00	Leave Reykjavík for Kleifarvatn lake (45 minutes)
11:00	Visit Kleifarvatn and Seltún geothermal field
11:30	Drive to Grindavík (30 minutes) and have lunch
12:45	Drive to the Blue Lagoon (10 minutes)
13:00	Soak in the Blue Lagoon—*aaah*
16:00	Return to Reykjavík—or, before heading home, take in one of the museums in the town of Keflavík

Blue Lagoon

While Iceland has a wide variety of thermal baths, the Blue Lagoon's setting amid rocky, moss-covered lava fields makes it unique.
Bathing at the wildly popular Blue Lagoon is, for some travelers,
the ultimate Icelandic experience, and worth ▲▲▲.

The Blue Lagoon (Bláa Lónið) has a don't-miss-it reputation
and prices to match. Over 3,000 people visit each day. Reservations are required, and some slots sell out days in advance. (The
bottleneck isn't the lagoon itself, but the number of lockers.) The
reservation requirement keeps the lagoon from getting too congested—even on the busiest days, you can find pockets of hot water
where you can escape the tour groups.

The Blue Lagoon is a steamy oasis—a sprawling hot-water
playground for grown-ups. Chunky rocks disappear beneath the

opaque water, where they're
coated with white silica slime.
The naturally heated water is
thoroughly relaxing. You'll
smear mineral deposits on your
face, while giggling at your fellow silica-masked bathers. The
hardest "work" you'll do is keeping your Icelandic microbrew or
skyr smoothie above the water, as
you behold the surrounding rocks hissing like teakettles.

GETTING THERE

With a Car: The Blue Lagoon is very easy by car. It's about 45 minutes from downtown Reykjavík, and only 15 minutes from Keflavík
Airport, off highway 43, on the way to the town of Grindavík.
Some highway signs use only the Icelandic name: *Bláa Lónið*. It's
free to park in the lagoon's huge parking lot.

By Excursion Bus: The lagoon runs its own hourly bus service,
Destination Blue Lagoon, from Reykjavík and Keflavík Airport
(5,500 ISK round-trip; each leg 2,750 ISK one-way, i.e., airport to
lagoon or lagoon to Reykjavík; sold separately or as an add-on to
lagoon admission, www.bluelagoon.com).

Reykjavík Excursions sells packages that include standard
"comfort" admission and round-trip travel between Reykjavík and
the Blue Lagoon for about 15,000 ISK. You can use your return
ticket to continue to Keflavík Airport instead of going back to
Reykjavík. Buses run hourly between Reykjavík and the lagoon,
but less frequently between the lagoon and airport—check schedules carefully and plan ahead (tel. 580-5400, www.re.is).

Gray Line offers a pricey, four-hour private round-trip shuttle

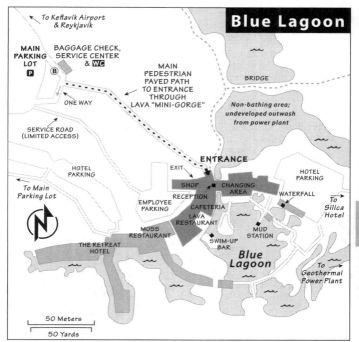

from Reykjavík starting around 27,000 ISK, including "comfort" admission (longer, more expensive packages also available; tel. 540-1313, www.grayline.is).

Note that excursion companies have access to the same time slots for the Blue Lagoon as individuals—if the lagoon is sold out in one place, it'll be sold out everywhere.

ORIENTATION TO THE BLUE LAGOON

Cost: The basic "comfort" package costs 7,000 to 12,000 ISK (depending mostly on how far in advance you buy your ticket) and includes entry, locker, towel, a drink from the lagoon bar, and a dollop of silica white mud for your face. The lagoon's website explains fancier packages that get you slippers, Champagne, in-water massage, and access to the luxury Retreat Spa. Bring your own suit or rent one there (700 ISK).

Hours: Daily 8:00-22:00, June-Aug 7:00-23:00 or 24:00, Oct-Dec 8:00-21:00, last entry one hour before closing. You need to leave the water at closing time, but have another 30 minutes after that to dress.

Information: Tel. 420-8800, www.bluelagoon.com.

Reservations: Book far in advance for the widest selection of times. Evening entries are often cheaper and less likely to be sold out.

BLUE LAGOON & REYKJANES

The Origin of the Blue Lagoon

The Blue Lagoon dates only from the early 1970s, when the local power authority drilled for hot water to heat homes on the Reykjanes Peninsula. They hit a good high-temperature source, but as often happens, the water wasn't suitable for piping directly into home radiators—it was salty (due to sea-water intrusions) and had a high mineral and clay content. Instead, they set up a heat-exchange system where the geothermal water was used to heat fresh, cold water that could then be piped to homes. After running through the system, the partly cooled geothermal water was simply dumped into the lava field near the plant.

Within a few years, locals realized this was a great place for a free dip and started to bathe in the water. Silica clay gives the water its milky texture, and sunlight gives it a blue appearance. (The name "Blue Lagoon"—borrowed from the notori-

ous 1980 Brooke Shields movie—was originally used in jest.) Authorities caught on, fenced off the lagoon, built a changing shed, and started to charge admission, which at first was no more than at a local swimming pool. Word spread, and within a few years the lagoon had become a major tourist attraction. The power authority privatized the lagoon, controversially selling it to a group of local politicians. They raised capital and did an admirable job developing and marketing the lagoon, adding cosmetics lines, a gift shop, a hotel, and a fancy restaurant.

Today, almost all the Blue Lagoon's guests are tourists; only a small percentage are Icelanders, who now find the facility too expensive. Meanwhile, more premium pools have sprung up across Iceland: **Fontana** (at Laugarvatn, on the Golden Circle); **Krauma** (at Deildartunguhver, in West Iceland), and **Geosea** and the **Mývatn Nature Baths** (along the Ring Road, in the north).

If your preferred date is sold out, check back closer to that day: Big excursion companies may release a block of unsold tickets. The website explains cancellation and change fees.

Arrival and Luggage Storage: You must enter within an hour of your selected entry time. You may be let in early depending on the locker availability—just ask; a half-hour early is often no problem.

The lagoon's parking lot is connected to the main building

by a 100-yard path cut through the lava field. A small building near the parking lot has a WC, pay luggage storage, and a waiting room for those taking buses from the lagoon.

Eyewear and Jewelry: Avoid wearing eyeglasses if you can—they fog up, and you won't find them in the opaque water if they fall off (a strap can help). Clay can scratch delicate lenses; rinse glasses in fresh water when you leave the pool. On a bright day, cheap sunglasses can make the lagoon more pleasant. Because the water is opaque, there's no need for goggles. Leave jewelry in your locker to avoid tarnishing or losing a ring in the pool.

Hair Concerns: The minerals in the Blue Lagoon can leave hair dry and brittle. The effect goes away within a day or two. Don't stress about this too much—the lagoon is more fun if you relax and let your hair get wet. Still, especially for those with long hair, it's smart to slather on the free conditioner (from dispensers in the shower stalls) before and after you bathe, or keep long hair tied up and out of the water. A bathing cap offers the best protection. In addition to conditioner, the lagoon provides free body wash and the use of hair dryers.

Kids: Children under age two are not allowed in the Blue Lagoon, and the facility is not designed for kids (no slides, kiddie pools, or play areas). The water is opaque, so if a child goes under, you won't be able to see him or her. The same goes for toys, glasses, goggles...and anything else that might slip out of little hands.

Eating: The main building has an appealing **$ self-service cafeteria** (with prepackaged sandwiches), plus the expensive, sit-down **$$$$ Lava Restaurant** (reservations recommended, same contact info as lagoon). In the luxury Retreat Hotel next door, the **$$$$ Moss Restaurant** offers elegant dining with a view (reservations recommended, tel. 420-8700). Better-value eateries are in Grindavík, a 10-minute drive away (described later in this chapter).

Sleeping: The lagoon runs the nearby **$$$$ Silica Hotel** and the preposterously expensive **Retreat Hotel.** You'll find lower prices in Keflavík and Grindavík (see "Hotels near the Airport" in the Reykjavík chapter).

Free Peek: If you just want a glimpse at the dreamy setting, you can park, enter the main building, and visit the Blue Lagoon's gift shop, cafeteria, and restaurant without a ticket. There's a good view of the pools from the cafeteria and the open deck between the cafeteria and the restaurant. A path from just outside the main entry leads through the non-bathing section of the lagoon. Also, as you drive toward the complex, there's a point where water from the power plant comes right up to the road; you could get out for a photo—if you can pull over without blocking traffic.

VISITING THE BLUE LAGOON

The procedures for a visit to the Blue Lagoon are basically the same as at other Icelandic pools (see the "Pool Rules" sidebar on page 168). Watch the helpful video on the website (www.bluelagoon.com), which walks you through a visit.

Entry Procedure: When you pay, you'll get an electronic **wristband** that serves as your locker key (and lets you charge drinks, face mud, and other extras—pay when you leave).

Once in the **changing area,** find an available locker. To lock the locker, touch your wristband to the light-up panel (if you forget, your locker will pop open after you leave—oops!). You can use your wristband to reopen your locker as often as you like (making it easy to enjoy the experience without your camera, then get a few shots when you're finished soaking). If you forget your locker number, touch your wristband to the panel and it will remind you.

Once you've changed and showered (in a private cabin, if you prefer), head out to the **lagoon.** Review the chart above the main door as you leave the indoor area. It locates everything (bar, mud shack, waterfall, sauna, steam rooms, etc.) and shows the temperature of various hot spots. If you get turned around, bath attendants are standing by to answer questions and point you in the right direction.

In the Pools: The lagoon is *big.* The towel situation is chaotic. I don't even bother tracking mine: It's easy to just ask for another.

Once you're in, be aware that the water ranges from waist to chest deep. The temperature varies more than in a regular swimming pool, with hot and cool spots—the average is around 100°F. For safety, the original scalding hot springs are contained in **"hot boxes"** (never over 105°F). While the water is not chlorinated, new water continually circulates into the lagoon—refilling the entire pool about every 40 hours. Bathers congregate by the warm spots where the hot water enters. Lifeguards love to talk and are full of fun facts.

Splish and splash around, exploring the hidden nooks and crannies of the interconnected **pools,** including a little roofed grotto, and several areas with benches that resemble hot pots at the municipal baths. The farther out you go, the quieter the pool becomes. Find the hot, thundering **waterfall** and give your shoulders a pounding. From there you can access the steam room, steam cave, and sauna.

Don't forget to find the **swim-up bar**—everyone gets

one free drink. Water fountains under the bridges help you stay hydrated.

At the **mud station,** there are three options. Every bather gets a free ladleful of the white silica mud that collects in the lagoon. Smear this exfoliant on your face, let it set for about 10 minutes, then wash it off. Bathers with a higher-end ticket (or who pay extra for a dollop) get a blob of greenish algae, which supposedly reduces wrinkles and rejuvenates the skin (same procedure: wear for 10 minutes, then rinse). Or try a black "lava scrub" face wash. While it adds to the experience, all that mud is really just a sales pitch for the spa products for sale inside.

Leaving the Bath: After you've showered and dressed, you'll pay for any extras you indulged in. At the exit turnstile, touch your wristband to the panel, then insert it in the slot. The machine eats it, and you're on your way. Now comes the hard part: Try to keep your relaxed body awake on the drive back to your hotel or the airport.

Reykjanes Peninsula

The Reykjanes Peninsula has enough sights to fill a day trip, and it's easy to combine with a visit to the Blue Lagoon. This is not the most scenic or historic part of Iceland—don't visit here at the expense of more dramatic scenery only a bit farther away, such as the Golden Circle or South Coast. But Reykjanes is handy for those who don't have time to venture far beyond the airport area. My plan for the drive from Reykjavík to the Blue Lagoon assumes you'll tour the peninsula first and then visit the Blue Lagoon, but it works just fine in reverse, too.

I've also listed a short yet scenic loop drive around the northern tip of the peninsula—a pleasant, less-touristed introduction to Iceland or fine way to kill time if you're picking up or returning a rental car at Keflavík Airport.

Reykjanes and Blue Lagoon Loop

This 90-mile loop route is fairly straightforward. From Reykjavík, you'll drive about 45 minutes across the Reykjanes Peninsula to the rugged Kleifarvatn lakeshore, with some interesting natural features (especially the Seltún geothermal field). Then you'll loop along the peninsula's south coast to Grindavík (about 30 minutes), a harbor town with some appealing lunch options. From there, it's a 10-minute drive to the Blue Lagoon. When you're done bathing, you can head straight back to Reykjavík (45 minutes), or consider a quick detour to some of the museums in Keflavík.

BLUE LAGOON & REYKJANES

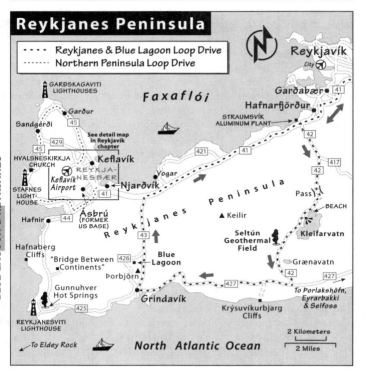

BLUE LAGOON & REYKJANES

• *Leaving the city, drive south on highway 41 through **Hafnarfjörður**—following the route toward the airport.*

Hafnarfjörður

This harborfront suburb of Reykjavík feels like a small town and has some good eateries (see page 99). It doesn't have much in the way of sights, but there are some nice places to stroll (such as its pedestrianized core and Hellisgerði, a small park off Hellisgata), and a surprisingly good little town history museum (Vesturgata 6, http://museum.hafnarfjordur.is).

As you crest the hill at the end of Hafnarfjörður, notice the red-and-white towers of the massive **aluminum plant** at Straumsvík. This was Iceland's first metal smelter, opened in 1969.

• *Before you reach the smelter, follow the signs for* Krýsuvík *and turn left on highway 42. Continue as it makes several turns through an industrial area.*

The forbidding-looking mountains ahead of you enclose your destination, the lake called Kleifarvatn. A low pass winds through the mountains to the lake; for these few miles, the road isn't paved—drive slowly as you dodge potholes.

Kleifarvatn Lake

Kleifarvatn (CLAY-vahr-VAHT) lake offers a nice sample of Iceland's distinctive volcanic scenery. In good weather, you can walk

along the black sand beach and even dip your toes in the water. There's something peculiar about Kleifarvatn: It has no outlet (it's fed by underground springs, and the water level varies). The area around the lake is totally undeveloped, and is a good (if lonely) place to look for the northern lights on clear, dark nights. There's a small parking lot near the end of the first long stretch of sandy beach, as well as parking lots at the overlooks from the headlands a little farther on. Don't drive off-road here.

• *A little past the end of the lake, take the turnoff to the right and park to explore the...*

▲Seltún Geothermal Field

This steaming, bubbling, boiling (and very smelly) landscape hints at the geothermal power just underfoot. A boardwalk and marked

paths take you on a 15-minute circuit through the field. Stay on the path, as the water and steam here are boiling hot. Partway through the loop, you can climb steeply up to a hilltop viewpoint overlooking the entire area, with Kleifarvatn lake just beyond—but the up-close boardwalk stroll through the steam zone is plenty satisfying. The environment here is not just natural, but also the product of botched attempts to exploit the geothermal field for energy—first in the 1750s, and most recently in the 1940s. In 1999, one of the boreholes from the last attempt got plugged up and exploded violently, creating a 30-foot crater now filled with water (at the first overlook). There are picnic benches here, and a WC (in summer).

Just after leaving Seltún, watch on the left for the Grænavatn parking lot. **Grænavatn** (Green Lake), a small lake that formed inside a volcanic crater, is worth a quick stop to gaze at its vivid color (from algae) and the surrounding jagged hilltops.

• *Continue south on highway 42 until it tees at highway 427, where you'll turn right. About 10 minutes from Seltún, you'll see a dirt road*

BLUE LAGOON & REYKJANES

History of the Reykjanes Peninsula

The Reykjanes Peninsula is geologically new and active, and the extensive lava fields here have at most a thin layer of vegetation. (Looking at it from an approaching plane, or on Google Maps, you'll see lots of brown.) During Iceland's early centuries, when farming was the mainstay of the economy, few people lived here. But the peninsula was a good base for rich offshore fishing grounds. As fishing became more important, the temporary settlements on the peninsula became permanent. Villages sprang up, particularly at Keflavík and Njarðvík on the north side, and at Grindavík in the south. Many of the people who settled here were poor and landless, and today's Icelanders, perhaps wrongly, still think of the peninsula as a proletarian region with little "old money" wealth—no sheep, no fine churches.

During World War II, military planners realized that the broad, flat wastelands near the town of Keflavík were an ideal place for an air base. Planes crossing the Atlantic could refuel here efficiently, and there was space for very long runways (long enough to land a space shuttle). After the war, the US military established a base next to the airport. Until 2006, when the base was closed, up to a few thousand Americans lived there, in a mostly self-contained community. The military base and the airport became the peninsula's largest employers, and the towns of Keflavík and Njarðvík grew.

branch off to the left, signposted Krýsuvíkurbjarg. *This road (too rough for two-wheel-drive cars) leads out to a high coastal cliff with a large seabird colony. Hikers not in a hurry could park along the shoulder of the dirt road and walk out (about 2.5 miles each way).*

Highway 427 continues through attractive, moss-covered lava fields and then traverses a dark, inhospitable upland before arriving in the town of Grindavík.

Grindavík Town

Unassuming Grindavík is important for its harbor, which was improved in the 20th century and is one of the few usable ports on Iceland's southern coast. Follow *Höfnin* signposts to reach the harbor, where you'll see fishing boats moored and large fish-processing factories. If you like, spend a few minutes driving around this windswept town of 2,000; keep an eye out for the old church, the new church, the

police station, the primary school, and the municipal swimming pool.

Sights in Grindavík: The town museum, **Kvikan** (Saltfish Museum), backs up to the harbor. It has exhibitions on the town's history (including life-size dioramas of the fishing industry); the history of salted cod (once the backbone of the local economy); Icelandic geology and geothermal energy; and novelist Guðbergur Bergsson (b. 1932), who was born here but spent much of his life in Spain. The building also serves as the local TI, with maps and brochures, and a contemporary art exhibition space upstairs. While nicely presented, the museum is worth visiting only if you have time to kill before your Blue Lagoon appointment (1,500 ISK; mid-May-Sept daily 10:00-17:00, Sat-Sun only off-season, Hafnargata 12a, tel. 420-1190, www.grindavik.is/kvikan).

Eating in Grindavík: The cozy **$ Bryggjan** café at the harbor specializes in lobster soup, served with bread and butter, as well as sandwiches and cakes. Decorated with fishing gear and memorabilia from Iceland and the Faroe Islands, it attracts both locals and travelers (daily 8:00-22:00, Miðgarður 2, tel. 426-7100). **$ Hjá Höllu** (Halla's Place) is a popular local lunch joint with a small, inventive, ever-changing menu that includes vegetarian options—ask them to translate. It's on the town's main road, in the tiny mall next door to the Nettó supermarket, which also houses a liquor store, pharmacy, and hair salon—enter from inside the mall (Mon-Fri 8:00-17:00, Sat from 11:00, closed Sun, Víkurbraut 62, tel. 896-5316, www.hjahollu.is). For something more formal, try the **$$ Salthúsið** sit-down restaurant, a block behind Nettó, with a spacious, woody interior and a deck that's inviting on a nice day (daily 12:00-22:00, off-season until 21:00, Stamphólsvegur 2, tel. 426-9700, www.salthusid.is).

Onward to the Blue Lagoon

The Blue Lagoon is a 10-minute drive north of Grindavík: Hopefully you've timed things so that you arrive promptly for your reservation. Even if you're not getting wet at the Blue Lagoon, you can park for free at the complex and have a look around.

• Road signs direct you to **Bláa Lónið** along highway 426, which winds through the lava around the west side of the mountain called Þorbjörn.

Alternate Route: It's also fine to take highway 43, going north past the Svartsengi geothermal plant, which feeds the lagoon. The plant is not open to the public, but you can make an unmarked turn off highway 43 and drive up as far as the visitor parking lot, getting a view of the red-painted water pipes that deliver hot water to area communities, and the turbine halls that generate electricity. (To actually visit a geothermal power plant, plan a trip to Hellisheiði, between Reykjavík and Selfoss; see page 156.)

Skip the Southwest: From Grindavík you may be tempted to drive around the desolate southwestern tip of the Reykjanes Peninsula. Be warned that the route is much less interesting than it looks on the map. Although the Reykjanesviti lighthouse and the nearby headland would seem to promise great views, in practice the lighthouse is set on a hill far, far from the shore, and the view of the coast from it or the headland path doesn't merit the effort. The Gunnuhver geothermal area is interesting, but Seltún is better; and the bridge over a tectonic fissure, which claims to let you "walk between continents," is a lame gimmick. I'd skip this circuit.

Blue Lagoon back to Reykjavík (or Detour to Keflavík/Njarðvík)

From the Blue Lagoon, most travelers get back on the road to Reykjavík. Alternatively, you can detour to Keflavík and Njarðvík, with a few good museums.

• *Head out to highway 43 and head north. After about 10 minutes, highway 43 tees into highway 41, the main road between Keflavík and Reykjavík. Turn right to head straight back to* **Reykjavík** *(about 45 minutes from the Blue Lagoon), or left to stop in* **Keflavík** *and* **Njarðvík** *(about a 15-minute drive from the Blue Lagoon).*

Keflavík and Njarðvík (Reykjanesbær)

The peninsula's main settlement (pop. 15,000) isn't a must-see, but has some attractions that can easily fill a few hours. Once separate towns, Keflavík and Njarðvík have grown together; in the 1990s they merged governments under the new name Reykjanesbær.

In 2006, the town expanded even more when the US military left its base near the airport and turned the area over to civilian use. That neighborhood is now called **Ásbrú;** if you're curious, you can follow signs into it and drive around (turning off highway 41 at a roundabout). The streets still have English names and you can drive past the old military PX, the base's theater, and the yellow-painted housing blocks.

Keflavík and Njarðvík have several museums that can be a good end to this driving tour. To reach them, turn off highway 41 and head into town, following signs for the museums. For a map of this area, see the end of the Reykjavík chapter.

Icelandic Museum of Rock 'n' Roll: Chronicling Icelandic pop music from the 1930s to the present, this museum fills a large space in the local music school and concert-hall complex. Exhibits cover the biggies

(Björk, Sigur Rós, and Of Monsters and Men), as well as lesser-known Icelandic musicians. Visitors can sample music and video clips; visit the Sound Lab to add their own vocals to tunes and try out drums, guitars, and keyboards; and watch documentary films in a small theater. The museum sells coffee and candy, but doesn't have a real café (1,500 ISK, daily 11:00-18:00, Hjallavegur 2, Reykjanesbær, tel. 420-1030, www.rokksafn.is).

Viking World: This museum houses the *Icelander,* a replica of the medieval Scandinavian ship unearthed at Gokstad, Norway in the 1880s (the original is in Oslo). While the boat itself is worth seeing, the rest of the attraction—with a few artifacts, some conceptual exhibits, and a Viking dress-up area—lacks substance. The museum is useful though for its early opening time and breakfast buffet (museum-1,500 ISK, museum and breakfast-2,500 ISK, daily 7:00-18:00, breakfast until 10:00, Víkingabraut 1, tel. 422-2000, www.vikingworld.is). More interesting is the **Settlement Age Zoo** (Landnámsdýragarður) just across the parking lot—a cute (and free) petting farm, with animals living in miniature sod-roofed huts (early May-July daily 10:00-17:00).

BLUE LAGOON & REYKJANES

Duus Museum: At the northwestern end of Keflavík, this local history and art museum has a collection of more than 100 model boats made by a retired local sea captain (1,000 ISK, daily 12:00-17:00, Duusgata 2, tel. 420-3245, http://sofn.reykjanesbaer.is/duusmuseum). A **TI** is next to the museum (Mon-Fri 9:00-17:00, Sat-Sun from 12:00, tel. 420-3246).

• *To head back to Reykjavík, it's a straight 45-minute shot along highway 41.*

Northern Peninsula Loop Drive

For a short and sweet drive that samples an uncrowded stretch of coastal Iceland, take a spin around the northern tip of the Reykjanes Peninsula. My counterclockwise route takes you to a pair of lighthouses on a windblown point, an old church built of lava rock, and a short, pleasant walk to another scenically set lighthouse. It takes less than an hour to drive the 27 miles, but be sure to allow time to linger along the way.

• *From Keflavík Airport, take highway 45 following the coastline through the tiny town of Garður. You'll come to a pair of lighthouses and a parking lot at Garðskagi Point, the northernmost tip of the Reykjanes Peninsula.*

Garðskagi Point

The short red-and-white lighthouse on the water is the old Garðskagi lighthouse. Built in 1897, it's the second oldest lighthouse in Iceland. No longer in service, it now houses the tiny, three-table **$ Old Lighthouse Café** in the former keeper's quarters (serves coffee, cakes, sandwiches, beer, and their *ástarpungar* (love balls)—like a pair of dense doughnut holes with raisins; daily June-Aug 8:00-18:00, closes in nasty weather). You can climb the five ladder-like sets of stairs to the top of the lighthouse for breezy views of some of Iceland's most treacherous waters, and to Reykjavík in the distance (500 ISK, or spend that amount in the café for free admission).

The big lighthouse you see inland, **Garðskagaviti,** was built in 1944 and is Iceland's tallest at just over 90 feet. Because of coastal erosion, this replacement for the old lighthouse was built well away from the shoreline. Inside its doorway is a plaque presented by survivors of the US Coast Guard cutter *Alexander Hamilton*—torpedoed by a German U-boat in January 1942—to the crews of Icelandic fishing boats who came to their rescue.

In the white building beyond the lighthouse is a small **maritime museum** (1,000 ISK, includes admission to Garðskagaviti lighthouse, daily 13:00-17:00) and the **$ Röstin Restaurant** (burgers and fish and meat dishes, daily 12:00-20:30, closed Mon in winter, tel. 422-7220).

Aside from the lighthouses, Garðskagi Point is a fine spot for birdwatching and catching sunsets or the Northern Lights.

• *From the point, it's about 7 miles to our next stop. Head south on road 402 (part of it gravel) until you join up with highway 45, and turn right. Continue on this lightly traveled road through the sleepy fishing port of Sandgerði, by small hay farms and pastures, until you see a dark stone church on a rise off to the right. Turn off at the* Hvalsnes *sign and drive to the walled cemetery and park.*

Hvalsneskirkja Church

Hvalsneskirkja, standing solidly against the elements, dates to 1887. It was built of local basalt, with an interior partially finished using driftwood collected from the nearby shores. Famous Icelandic poet Hallgrímur Pétursson, who wrote 50

hymns telling the story of the Passion of Christ, served as pastor from 1644 to 1651 at a previous church that stood here (the iconic Hallgrímskirkja in Reykjavík is named after him). It's a serene setting, with the church watching peacefully over wide-open fields spreading out under even wider skies.

Before driving on, visit the sweet cemetery, with lovingly tended graves decorated in summer with pots of colorful flowers braving the breeze.

• *Continue south on highway 45 another three miles until you see a sign for* Stafnes, *where you'll turn off to the right. Drive a short distance past some farmhouses to the parking lot at the end of the road.*

Stafnes Lighthouse (Stafnesviti)

The plaque in the parking lot memorializes the 1928 wreck of the trawler *Jón Forseti*, in which 15 crewmembers perished (and 10 survived). Just past the plaque, a grassy path leads out to the orange-colored Stafnes Lighthouse. Built in 1925 of concrete, today it's automated (and not open to visitors). The lighthouse itself may not be all that remarkable, but it does strike a colorful pose. Walking past the lighthouse toward the sea (if the surf allows) you can't miss the curiously pockmarked lava rock stretching along the shore. It's quiet here, and even on a sunny day you'll likely have this place to yourself, with nothing but the North Atlantic between you and Greenland.

• *From Stafnes it's a 10-minute drive through lava fields and blue lupines (in season) to the junction with highway 44. Turn left, and follow it to highway 41 where, at the roundabout, you can go right for Reykjavík, or left for Keflavík Airport and Keflavík town.*

BLUE LAGOON & REYKJANES

GOLDEN CIRCLE

The Golden Circle is Iceland's classic day trip. If you have just one day to see the Icelandic countryside from Reykjavík, this route offers the most satisfying variety of sightseeing and scenery per miles driven. And you'll be in good company: Travelers dating back to the Danish king Christian IX, who visited Iceland in 1874, have followed the same route outlined in this chapter.

The Golden Circle loop includes this essential trio of sights: Þingvellir, a dramatic gorge marking the pulling apart of the Eurasian and North American tectonic plates (and also the site of the country's annual assembly in the Middle Ages); Geysir, a bubbling, steaming hillside that's home to Strokkur, Iceland's most active geyser; and Gullfoss, one of Iceland's most impressive waterfalls.

You can round out the trip by adding any of several minor sights, taking a dip in a thermal bath, having lunch on a dairy farm, or sipping a Bloody Mary in a tomato-filled greenhouse. This chapter explains your options and links them with driving directions. As nearly everything lies along the simple loop road, navigating is easy.

Note that the Golden Circle loop is well trod and extremely touristy. Long lines of tour buses and rental cars follow each other around the route each day, but despite the crowds the attractions hold their appeal.

On Your Own vs. Taking an Excursion: Driving the Golden Circle on your own is completely doable and offers maximum flexibility, but some find it more relaxing to join an organized bus trip. If you have the time, full-day tours are best (see the Beyond Reykjavík chapter for options). Half-day tours cost only slightly less and rush you through the sights.

Golden Circle Drive

The entire 150-mile Golden Circle circuit involves about four hours of driving, not including stops. The basic self-guided route is simple: From Reykjavík, the first leg of the drive is a scenic hour to Þingvellir. After touring Þingvellir, it's about an hour to the thermal fields at Geysir, then 10 minutes farther to the gushing Gullfoss waterfall. From there, you'll backtrack to Geysir and

circle back to Reykjavík in about two hours, passing a slew of lesser roadside attractions. My suggested route goes clockwise—starting with Þingvellir—but it can also be done in the other direction.

PLANNING YOUR DRIVE

Here's a suggested plan (with stops) for those wanting to get an early-ish start and be home in time for dinner:

9:00   Leave Reykjavík and head for Þingvellir national park, taking the scenic Nesjavallaleið route (1 hour)

10:00   Visit Þingvellir

11:30   Drive from Þingvellir to the village of Laugarvatn (30 minutes); have lunch here or nearby

13:00   Head to Geysir geothermal field (20 minutes) and watch Strokkur erupt a couple of times

14:00   Drive to Gullfoss (10 minutes) and visit the waterfall

15:00   Head in the direction of Selfoss (1 hour), stopping briefly at Skálholt Church and Kerið crater (or other sights along the way that interest you)

16:30   Return to Reykjavík (about 1 hour from Selfoss)

Golden Circle Tips

This drive is peppered with additional sights and activities; you can easily alter my suggested plan to suit your interests. Before setting out, review your options, prioritize, and make a plan that hits what you want to see in the time you have. Here are some things to consider.

Dealing with Crowds: The number of visitors to Iceland has grown in recent years, but so have facilities to handle them. You'll make the same "big three" stops (Þingvellir, Geysir, Gullfoss) as everyone else. You won't be alone in enjoying the wide-open wonders...but there's a joyful mood, and the crowds are part of the fun. Most people blitz through, seeing little more than those

three—which leaves the rest of the route fairly crowd-free. Frankly, I wouldn't worry about it. But if you're set on avoiding crowds, an early start keeps you ahead of the rush (bus tours generally go clockwise, leaving Reykjavík at 9:00 to arrive at Þingvellir at 10:00); in summer, when days are long, you could instead do this trip late in the day. Or, better yet, spend the night along the route so you can visit the top sights outside of peak tourist hours—see "Sleeping on the Golden Circle" at the end of this chapter.

Activities: Several activities along the Golden Circle require extra time—and in some cases, reservations. The Silfra fissure, at Þingvellir, provides top-notch **scuba or snorkeling** opportunities (book well in advance—see details on page 143). Several horse farms are just outside Reykjavík, making it easy to incorporate **horseback riding** into your Golden Circle spin (again, this should be prearranged—see page 176). There are also several **thermal baths** along the way (see sidebar later in this chapter). If you plan to see the geothermal exhibit at the **Hellisheiði Power Plant,** note that it closes at 17:00.

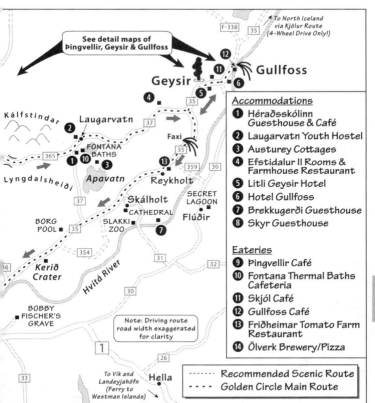

Accommodations
1. Héraðsskólinn Guesthouse & Café
2. Laugarvatn Youth Hostel
3. Austurey Cottages
4. Efstidalur II Rooms & Farmhouse Restaurant
5. Litli Geysir Hotel
6. Hotel Gullfoss
7. Brekkugerði Guesthouse
8. Skyr Guesthouse

Eateries
9. Þingvellir Café
10. Fontana Thermal Baths Cafeteria
11. Skjól Café
12. Gullfoss Café
13. Friðheimar Tomato Farm Restaurant
14. Ölverk Brewery/Pizza

Note: Driving route road width exaggerated for clarity

······· Recommended Scenic Route
- - - - Golden Circle Main Route

GOLDEN CIRCLE

Evening Options: In the summer, some intrepid travelers—determined to wring the absolute maximum travel experience out of every moment—set out on this loop in the late afternoon...making the most of the abundant daylight. And since the major Golden Circle sights (Þingvellir, Geysir, Gullfoss) don't technically "close," you can visit them anytime—plus, they're less crowded in the evening (some of the lesser sights and thermal baths do have closing times). Another fine evening activity is to have a memorable dinner in the countryside at one of my recommended restaurants—stretching your day and allowing a late return to Reykjavík.

Weather and Road Conditions: The route crosses three mountain passes (Mosfellsheiði or Nesjavallaleið, then Lyngdalsheiði, and finally Hellisheiði). These passes can be icy and slippery, especially from October to April. Check the road-conditions map at Road.is before you start off. In treacherous conditions, take a bus tour and leave the driving to pros. If you do drive the Golden Circle in winter, it's smart to set off from Reykjavík an hour before sunrise to get maximum value from the daylight hours.

Fill 'Er Up: Gas stations are few and very far between (going clockwise, the first one you hit is in Reykholt). Fill up before you start this road trip.

Name Note: Be aware that there are two Reykholts in Iceland: one here on the Golden Circle (with all the greenhouses), and the other about 100 miles away, east of Borgarnes (no vegetables).

Golden Circle Loop

Below, I've linked the main stops with driving directions. Let's get started.

REYKJAVÍK TO ÞINGVELLIR

There are two ways to get from Reykjavík to Þingvellir: the scenic Nesjavallaleið road (1 hour on highway 435) or the Mosfellsheiði road (40 minutes on highway 36). Nesjavallaleið is my preferred route—but, because of its high elevation, it's open only from May to September. If it's closed, it will appear in red on the road-conditions map at Road.is. The Mosfellsheiði route stays open all year.

Scenic Route via Nesjavallaleið

This rugged one-hour route climbs high up (to about 1,500 feet) over a craggy mountain range, descends steeply past the Nesjavel-

lir geothermal plant, and then hugs the shore of Þingvallavatn lake. Most of Nesjavallaleið (NESS-ya-VAHT-la-layth) was built as a service road for a giant hot-water pipe that feeds Reykjavík's heating system.

Start out by leaving Reykjavík south on highway 1 toward Selfoss and the South Coast. As the town thins out into countryside, turn left, following small signs for highways 431 *(Hafravatn)* and 435 *(Nesjavellir);* highway 431 becomes 435 on the way. Just after leaving the main road, you'll pass a maximum-security prison. (In a country with, on average, fewer than two murders a year, it's small—only about 40 cells.)

The road crosses the giant **hot-water pipe,** then curves around to follow straight along it. You'll drive (through a lava field from an eruption a thousand years ago) parallel to the pipe—and some high-tension wires—for quite some time. The road rises and eventually hits a ridge, part of a volcanic system called Hengill; from here the road climbs in a series of bends. Before the crest, you can stop at a pullout in the small, mountain-ringed **Dyradalur valley,** with signboards and picnic benches; an important path for travelers once led through the gully you see at the end of the valley (called Dyrnar, The Doors).

As you come over the ridge, you'll see the **Nesjavellir geothermal power station** far below you. This plant, built in the early 1990s, sends 250 gallons of boiling water through the pipe to Reykjavík every second, and also generates electricity. For a better look, take the lane to the right; it dead-ends at a tiny viewpoint parking lot. The igloo-like structures mark places where a borehole was drilled. Each little pipe feeds into a bigger pipe. Steam marks little hot springs. (Another power plant, on the Hellisheiði heath near the end of this tour, has a real visitors center.)

From here the road descends steeply into the valley. At the T-junction with highway 360, turn left toward *Þingvellir*. (Note that if you're doing the Golden Circle in reverse, highway 435 is signposted here only as *Hengilssvæði*.)

Now the road winds tightly along the shore of **Þingvallavatn** lake, with fine views, no guardrails, and several narrow, blind summits. You'll pass some nice summer homes, built before construction was banned here. Eventually, the road leaves the lake, passes a lone farm (sheep, potatoes, hay, and horses) and ends at a junction with highway 36. Turn right. From here, it's 4 miles to Þingvellir.

Alternative Route via Mosfellsheiði

If Nesjavallaleið is closed due to bad weather (typically Oct-April), take the main Mosfellsheiði route instead. While less scenic and less interesting, it's more direct.

Start this 40-minute route heading north out of Reykjavík on highway 1 toward Borgarnes and Akureyri, then turn right on highway 36 just past the town of Mosfellsbær, following the *Þingvellir* signs. This leads up through Mosfellsdalur (Moss Mountain Valley) and over a low, broad pass (900 feet above sea level) to Þingvellir.

The Mosfellsdalur valley is still rural, with several horse farms. As you drive through, look left up the hillside (or turn up the side road called Mosfellsvegur) to see the unusual church called **Mosfellskirkja,** designed

GOLDEN CIRCLE

Thermal Bathing Along the Golden Circle

To pack the maximum Icelandic experience into your Golden Circle day, add a visit to a thermal bath. This loop drive passes near four extremely different options (all described in this chapter). Skim these options before you depart, to strategize where you might squeeze in a dip...and remember to bring your swimsuit and towel (or rent one—available at all listed here except Reykjadalur).

Fontana Thermal Bath, in Laugarvatn, is the upscale choice. While not nearly as ritzy as the Blue Lagoon, it's a "premium" option that feels a notch up from standard municipal swimming pools.

The Secret Lagoon, in Flúðir (a 10-minute detour from the main Golden Circle route, near Reykholt), is a big, rustic outdoor pool packed with young travelers unwinding after a busy day of sightseeing. This is the only bathing experience on this route where it's smart to reserve ahead.

Borg swimming pool is a municipal facility right along the main road between Reykholt and Selfoss—nothing fancy, but cheap, handy, and the most authentically Icelandic of the options on the Golden Circle.

Reykjadalur—the "Smoky Valley" above the town of Hveragerði—is the adventurous choice: It's a remote, steaming, natural thermal river that requires a one-hour hike each way.

Of course, if you're heading home to Reykjavík at the end of your Golden Circle day, you can have your pick of the capital area's many **public swimming pools** (options described on page 64); two good suburban pools, Lágafellslaug and Árbæjarlaug, are convenient to the Golden Circle route.

Before visiting any of these, get up to speed by reading the "Pool Rules" sidebar on page 168.

by architect Ragnar Emilsson in the 1960s. It's full of triangular shapes—including the bell tower and roof—as a reference to the Trinity.

Note that this route passes by the former home of Iceland's most famous author, **Halldór Laxness** (open to tourists; for details see page 63). Otherwise, it's a (fairly dull) straight shot to Þingvellir. When you begin to see **Þingvallavatn lake**—Iceland's largest—on your right, you know you're getting close.

▲▲▲Þingvellir

The gorge at Þingvellir (THING-VET-leer), dear to all Icelanders, is both dramatic and historic. It's dramatic because you can readily see the slow separation of the North American and Eur-

asian tectonic plates—the earth's crust is literally being torn apart. And it's historic because, about a thousand years ago, it was here at "Assembly Plains" (as its name means) that chieftains from the different parts of Iceland began gathering annually to govern themselves (at a meeting called the Alþingi). Today the area has been preserved as a national park. Visitors can walk along the rifts created by the separating plates, stand at the place where the original Icelanders made big decisions, hike to a picturesque waterfall, see a scant few historic buildings, and even go for a snorkel or scuba dive into a flooded gorge.

Orientation to Þingvellir

Cost and Hours: The natural site is always open and free, but you'll pay 750 ISK to park. The visitors center features a skippable high-tech interactive exhibit explaining the geology, history, and nature of Þingvellir, and has free WCs and a gift shop/café (exhibit-1,000 ISK, visitors center open daily 9:00-18:00, tel. 482-3613, www. thingvellir.is). Free one-hour guided tours in English depart daily at 10:00 and 15:00 from the Þingvellir church.

Arrival at Þingvellir: You can park on either the upper (west) or the lower (east) side of the Öxará river. The two sides are no more than a half-mile apart if you use the footbridges over the river, but it's a five-mile drive by car.

The first turnoff you'll reach is for the main lot, **P1** (sometimes called *Hakið* on maps). I prefer to park here because this is where the facilities are clustered. Farther along (on road 361, beyond the intersection with the park offices/café) are several **smaller parking lots** on the lower side: P2, P4, P5, and Silfra. These parking lots can be handy for hikers, divers, and picnics. If P1 is full and you're with a group, consider having the driver drop everyone off at P1; the driver can park at one of the lower lots and hike back up to meet you.

A camera records your license-plate number as you drive in; at **pay machines** (P1's is in the visitors center), punch in your license-plate number, then insert your credit card.

Length of This Visit: For a quick visit, you can enjoy the overview, hike the gorge, and see the Law Rock in less than an hour. Add a half-hour to hike up to the waterfall (about a mile one-way from P1), and a half-hour to cross the river to the church (least interesting and skippable).

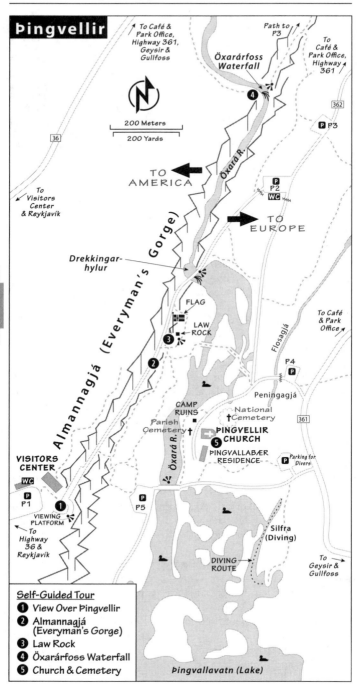

GOLDEN CIRCLE

Þingvellir

To Café &
Park Office,
Highway 361,
Geysir &
Gullfoss

Path to
P3

Öxarárfoss
Waterfall

To Café &
Park Office,
Highway
361

N

200 Meters
200 Yards

362

P3

36

TO
AMERICA

Öxará R.

P2
WC

TO
EUROPE

To
Visitors
Center &
Reykjavík

Almannagjá (Everyman's Gorge)

Drekkingar-
hylur

FLAG

LAW
ROCK

To Café
& Park
Office

Flosagjá

P4

Peningagjá

CAMP
RUINS

National
Cemetery

Parish
Cemetery

Öxará R.

ÞINGVELLIR
CHURCH

361

ÞINGVALLABÆR
RESIDENCE

Parking for
Divers

VISITORS
CENTER

WC

P1

VIEWING
PLATFORM

P5

To
Highway 36 &
Reykjavík

Silfra
(Diving)

To
Geysir &
Gullfoss

DIVING
ROUTE

Þingvallavatn (Lake)

Self-Guided Tour
1 View Over Þingvellir
2 Almannagjá
  (Everyman's Gorge)
3 Law Rock
4 Öxarárfoss Waterfall
5 Church & Cemetery

Eating: In good weather, Þingvellir is a nice place for a picnic. There are benches, wooded areas, and free portable WCs near P2. The visitors center (at P1) has a basic **$ café** selling premade sandwiches, ice cream, snacks, and hot and cold drinks. Otherwise, the only eatery nearby is the small **$ café** at the national park office a couple of miles away, at the junction of highways 36, 361, and 550 (daily 9:00-22:00, Sept-May until 18:00).

Self-Guided Tour

This plan assumes that you're parking at the upper P1 lot. The visitors center is helpful for geological and historical context, but is skippable.

• *From P1 and the visitors center, walk a few steps to the overlook with the railing.*

❶ **View Over Þingvellir:** Look down at the lake and the land that's subsided to its north. You can see how the Öxará (Ax River)

empties into the lake. Þingvellir's church (and some ruins of the old chieftains' encampments) lies just across the river below you. The five-gabled farm building dates from 1930.

Directly below you is Þingvellir's **great fissure;** look at how the North American and Eurasian tectonic plates are moving apart. Imagine pulling a big, chewy cookie apart very slowly; you'd start to see cracks in the dough, and eventually crumbs would start to slide into the gap. Here, you can see long, narrow fissures in the earth, running roughly north-south. The lake itself sits in the largest fissure of all. The lake bed (and the land to the north and south) basically has slid into the gap between the plates. It's deep. In fact, the deepest parts of the lake bed are actually below sea level.

• *Follow the boardwalk as it switchbacks down between the cliffs, descending through the little side channel that leads into...*

❷ **Almannagjá** (Everyman's Gorge): As you walk, you're tracing the boundaries of continents. To your left is America. To your right is Europe. (A geologist might say it's not quite that simple, but would agree that Iceland is half in Europe and half in America—and this is where they meet.)

On the left, the vertical cliff face is original

rock as it was laid down by volcanic eruptions and compressed over the eons. On the right, you can see how the rock—once even with the cliff on your left—has fallen away into the gap due to the subsidence that also created the lake. On the right (fallen) side of the gorge, you can scramble out to various walkways and viewpoints.

• *As you approach the valley floor, follow the boardwalks to the right to stand in the area just below the flagpole. This marks the likely location of...*

❸ The Law Rock (Lögberg): Within about 60 years of the first settlements, Iceland was home to roughly 15,000 people—almost

all of them farmers, scattered across the island on isolated homesteads. In about AD 930, local chieftains began to gather at an annual meeting called the Alþingi ("all-thing"), which took place more or less where you're standing. For this reason, Þingvellir can be thought of as Iceland's first capital. Today, this site remains important for Icelanders—it's their Ancient Agora, their Roman Forum, their Independence Hall.

Gaze over the marshy delta below you, and time-travel back a thousand years. It's the middle of June, and you're surrounded by fellow chieftains, some having traveled on horseback more than two weeks, over challenging terrain, just to be here. Each chieftain has brought along an entourage of *þingmenn* (assemblymen). The field below you is dotted with temporary turf huts—like a festival grounds, set up only in summer.

The meeting is about to begin, and you're immersed in a hairy mosh pit of hundreds—maybe thousands—of unwashed Norsemen (and Norsewomen). The collective body odor is overwhelming. But for two weeks, you've all agreed to set aside your grudges and work together to find consensus on critical issues of the day. This is your one chance all year to learn the latest news and gossip. And while everyone's here, there are sure to be some big parties, business wheeling and dealing, marriages arranged...and, quite likely, some duels. Merchants, tradesmen, and panhandlers are milling about, trying to drum up a little business. The whole event has a carnival-like bustle.

GOLDEN CIRCLE

Iceland's Conversion to Christianity

In AD 1000, the Alþingi had its most important session. Iceland's longtime ally Norway—whose king had recently converted to Christianity—was exerting tremendous pressure on Iceland to follow suit. When Norwegian missionaries failed to convert the entire island, the impatient king took several Icelandic traders hostage. Losing its primary trade partner would have been devastating to Iceland, and at the next summer's Alþingi, all hell broke loose between the pro- and anti-conversion factions. Civil war was in the air.

Eventually, both sides agreed to let the law speaker, a pagan named Þorgeir Ljósvetningagoði, make the decision for all of Iceland. According to the sagas, Þorgeir covered himself with a fur pelt and slept on it (literally) for one night and one day. Upon emerging, he addressed the assembly with his decision: Iceland was now Christian, but Icelanders could still worship their pagan gods privately, and continue a few key pagan practices (including the consumption of horse meat, the infanticide of unwanted children, and animal sacrifices to the old gods). And so, in one fell swoop, Þorgeir brought Iceland into the Christian fold, and averted a conflict with Norway that could well have wiped out the island's still-fragile civilization. This stands as one of the most peaceful mass religious conversions in history.

GOLDEN CIRCLE

The crowd quiets with the appearance of the *allsherjargoði* (grand chieftain)—a direct descendant of Ingólfur Arnarson (who was, according to the sagas, the first Icelandic settler of Reykjavík). As the high priest of the Norse pantheon, the *allsherjargoði* calls the assembly to order, and sanctifies the proceedings before the gods. Then the "law speaker" *(lögsögumaður)* takes his position at the Law Rock and recites the guidelines for the assembly, outlines the broad strokes of Icelandic law, and recaps the highlights of last year's session. The acoustics created by the cliff behind him help bounce his voice across the throngs; other speakers, strategically located at the back of the crowd, carefully listen to, then repeat, whatever the law speaker says.

As the Alþingi continues, the law speaker also presides over the Law Council *(Lögrétta)*, on the opposite riverbank. A more select group of chieftains reviews and debates existing legislation, and weighs in on legal disputes, and the law speaker is responsible for memorizing whatever is decided. Eventually, Christianity brings literacy and the Latin alphabet, and the law speaker's role gives way to that of a sort of "high attorney"—*lögmaður*.

The Alþingi gatherings took place as long as Iceland was independent. But things changed after 1262, when the chieftains entered into union with Norway—pledging fealty to the Norwegian king under an agreement called the Old Covenant. The Alþingi still convened annually at Þingvellir, but morphed into an appeals court; it continued this way until 1798.

Þingvellir became a national park in 1930, to celebrate the millennial anniversary of the first Alþingi. And in 1944, the modern, independent Republic of Iceland was proclaimed right here. The stands below the flag are for official ceremonies; one of the information boards at the railing displays photographs of some of these ceremonies.

By the way, those original settlers couldn't possibly have known that the place they selected for their gathering also happened to straddle America and Europe. They chose this site mainly because Þingvellir is fairly central (relatively accessible in summer from every corner of Iceland) and had ample water, grazing lands, and firewood to supply the sprawling gatherings. Its location along the cusp of continents is just one of those serendipities of history.

• *Follow the wide, gravel path straight ahead, and cross the river on a small bridge over a waterfall (the bottom end of Öxarárfoss, which we'll visit next). To your left is Drekkingarhylur (Drowning Pool), where women accused of witchcraft were drowned between the late 16th and mid-18th centuries.*

If you're short on time, you could turn back here. Otherwise, continue along the path. After about 300 yards, just before reaching parking lot P2, branch off on the small path to your left. Follow it for a few minutes as it crests the rise to your left. Then, a hundred yards to your left is the large waterfall called...

❹ **Öxarárfoss:** This is where the river—which rises up on the plateau—plunges over the cliff face into the valley. Old sagas say that the early settlers changed the course of the river to improve the water supply at Þingvellir, but no one is exactly sure whether this is true and how that might have been done.

• *You've already seen the most interesting parts of Þingvellir—you can head back the way you came (past the P2 lot). With more time, cross the footbridges on your left (below the Law Rock) to reach the...*

❺ **Church and Cemetery:** The current **church** was built in 1859, but churches have stood here for centuries. The original church was supposedly built using timbers sent to Iceland by Norway's St. Olaf (King Olav II, 995-1030). If the church is open, step inside to see the humble, painted interior (generally closed Sept-May). Local parishioners lie in the small cemetery in front of the church. The multi-gabled house just beyond it, called **Þingvallabær,** was built in 1930 as a residence for the local priest, who was also the park warden. It's now used for ceremonial functions.

Behind the church, the round, elevated area up the stairs is a **cemetery** lot. This was planned as a resting place for national heroes, but the idea never took off, and only two people (well-known writers) were ever buried there.

Along the riverbank near the church, the **mounds** contain the remains of the temporary dwellings that were set up here each year for the annual assembly. From here, looking back the way you came, enjoy great views of the sheer cliff that defines the fissure.

• *Between the church and the river, a waterside path allows further exploration. Following this path takes you to the P5 lot, where a steep shortcut (on a rocky path through the woods) leads back up to the P1 lot and the high viewpoint where you started. Also nearby is Silfra, a favorite destination of divers—described next. For an easier route back to P1, backtrack along the river, take the bridge on your left to reach the Law Rock, and then hike back up through Everyman's Gorge.*

Silfra Snorkel or Dive Trip

One of the many fissures at Þingvellir, Silfra is renowned among snorkelers and scuba divers for its water clarity. Thanks to the purity of the glacial water that fills it, you can see underwater for more than a hundred yards.

To snorkel or dive in Silfra, you'll need to join a tour (such as those offered by Dive.is, the largest operator—book well in advance). Snorkelers must be relatively fit and comfortable in the water, while divers need to be certified and experienced. There have been a few fatal accidents at Silfra in recent years (even involving snorkelers)—don't overestimate your abilities.

The water is a constant 35-39°F, so you'll be outfitted with some serious gear: a neoprene dry suit, hood, gloves, fins, mask, and snorkel. (Some companies have basic changing cabins in the parking lot; otherwise, there's limited privacy.) The suit keeps your body warm enough, but expect your face to go numb and your hands to get cold. After changing into your gear, you'll walk a few minutes to the entry stairs and descend into the fissure with your guide. A gentle drift current slowly takes you along the fissure and into a lagoon, where you'll need to kick against the current to U-turn to the metal exit stairs. You'll be in the water for about 30-40 minutes.

Cost: 20,000 ISK for guided snorkeling, extra 5,000 ISK for pickup in Reykjavík; 35,000 ISK for package that includes pickup, Silfra, and bus tour of Golden Circle; more for divers; tel. 578-6200, www.dive.is.

Getting There: Silfra is at the lakeshore near the east bank of the river. The entry point to Silfra is between parking lots P4 and P5. Follow the directions to Þingvellir and turn off onto road 361 to reach this area; look for the designated parking lot.

ÞINGVELLIR TO GEYSIR AND GULLFOSS

This section of the drive circles around the far end of the lake, where you can clearly see the intercontinental rift—as if a giant dropped his hoe and dredged out a tidy furrow between America and Europe.

• *Leaving Þingvellir, return to highway 36 and continue east for about 10 minutes around the lake's north shore, crossing smaller fissures, and passing fishermen hoping to hook one of the lake's famously big trout. Soon you'll pass the intersection with road 361 (a right turn here takes you back to Þingvellir's lower parking lots) and, immediately after that, the national park office, with a café.*

Continuing along the east side of the lake, you'll reach a point where highway 36 turns off to the right. Stay straight toward Laugarvatn on highway 365. This road crosses an upland heath called Lyngdalsheiði (altitude: about 700 feet; if it's closed, use highways 35 and 36).

On your left, enjoy some otherworldly, craggy mountain scenery—the Kálfstindar ridge. A half-hour after leaving Þingvellir, you leave the heath, and descend to a village on a lake. At the roundabout, follow signs onto route 37 toward Geysir (not Selfoss) and enter sleepy, unassuming Laugarvatn.

Laugarvatn

Set by a small lake of the same name, Laugarvatn was long the home of Iceland's college for sports teachers (the program has now been moved to Reykjavík), and it's in a region popular with local vacationers. As you drive you'll see many summer cottages owned by the country's labor unions for member use. Driving into the village, take the exit (right) by the recommended Héraðsskólinn Guesthouse and head down to the fancy, thatched Fontana Thermal Baths. There are hot springs in and around the lake, and Fontana, a nicely designed premium bath, makes good use of them.

▲Fontana Thermal Baths

Sitting right along the Laugarvatn lakeshore and built atop a natural hot springs, Fontana is one of Iceland's handful of premium baths—a step up in comfort (and price) from municipal swimming pools, and a bit more tourist-oriented. For some, Fontana may be a good alternative to the Blue Lagoon—it's cheaper, smaller (easier to navigate), less pretentious, much less crowded, and

doesn't require reservations. But it's also more functional than spa-like, and lacks the Blue Lagoon's romantic, volcanic setting.

Beyond the visitors center—with ticket desk, changing rooms, and a good cafeteria—is the outdoor bathing area, overlooking the lake. The complex has three modern, tiled pools, artfully landscaped with natural boulders, as well as a steam room (where you can hear the natural hot spring bubble beneath your feet) and a dry sauna. To cool off or for a change of pace, bathers are encouraged to take a dip in the lake.

Cost and Hours: 3,800 ISK, daily 10:00-22:00, Sept-May from 11:00, tel. 486-1400, www.fontana.is.

Thermal Bread Experience: Fontana follows the Icelandic tradition of baking sweet, dense rye bread right in the thermal

sands at its doorstep. Twice daily, you can pay to join the baker as they dig up a pot of bread, then taste it straight out of the ground (1,500 ISK, daily at 11:30 and 14:30). But note that you can eat the very same bread as part of their regular lunch buffet.

Nearby Thermal Beach: The lake in front of Fontana—heated by natural hot springs—is free to bathe in. Facing the lake, head right to find a small, black sand beach next to the fenced-off geothermal area (keep well clear of this area of boiling-hot water). The water near the springs is warm, but it gets colder as you go deeper. At a minimum, consider rolling up your pants and dipping your feet. On the wooden walkway between the geothermal plant and the lakeshore, notice—but don't touch—little boiling pools in the mud.

Eating in Fontana

In addition to three very good lunch options listed here, there's an "art café" at the far end of town and a grocery store next to the N1 gas station.

$$ Fontana Thermal Baths cafeteria is in the bath's entrance lobby, and open to the public (no bath entry required). You can order from the menu or spring for their full 2,900-ISK lunch buffet or 3,900-ISK dinner buffet (daily from 12:00, last lunch served at 13:45, dinner 18:00-21:00).

$$ Héraðsskólinn Café, at the recommended Héraðsskólinn Guesthouse, serves an inexpensive lunch of soups, salads, and sandwiches, and dishes up fish, meat, pizza, and vegetarian plates for dinner. The spacious dining room is filled with light and fun mid-century furniture (daily 11:00-16:00 & 18:30-21:30, breakfast available, Laugarbraut 2, tel. 537-8060).

$$ Efstidalur II Farmhouse Restaurant, 10 minutes beyond Laugarvatn, is on a large family-run dairy farm (with a recommended hotel) just off highway 37. Downstairs, a counter serves homemade ice cream. The upstairs restaurant, with windows overlooking the cows in the barn, specializes in burgers and pricier main courses. It's a popular, bustling place—family-friendly and often crowded with groups. Their 2,000-ISK special of soup, bread, fancy spreads, and coffee is fast, affordable, and delicious (daily 11:30-21:00, mid-Sept-mid-May until 20:00, well-signposted up a gravel driveway, tel. 486-1186, www.efstidalur.is). Even if you're not hungry, Efstidalur II is worth a stop for a peek at an Icelandic farm.

• *From Laugarvatn, highway 37 leads 20 minutes onward to the geothermal field at Geysir. On the right, just past Efstidalur II, notice the small farm that's augmenting its income by harnessing geothermal power (just as wind turbines generate electricity on US farms). Soon, the road changes numbers to highway 35.*

▲▲Geysir Geothermal Field

When people around the world talk about geysers, most don't realize they're referencing a place in Iceland: Geysir (GAY-seer), which literally means "the gusher." While the original Geysir geyser is no longer very active, the geothermal field around it still steams, boils, and bubbles nonstop, regularly punctuated by a dramatic eruption of scalding water from the one predictably active geyser, Strokkur.

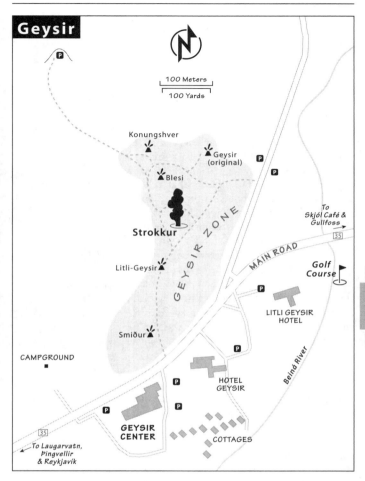

This stop is pretty simple: Watch Strokkur erupt a couple of times, look at the rest of the field, and then continue on.

Cost and Hours: Free and always open.

Safety Warning: Make sure to keep young children close. Impress upon them that they should not touch any of the water, which is boiling hot, and that they must stay behind the ropes. At Strokkur, standing upwind will keep you out of any spray.

Arrival at Geysir: Approaching Geysir, you'll see the geothermal field on your left, and a visitors complex with parking lots on your right. Park as close to the geothermal field as you can (if you drive 100 yards past the hotel and take the lane to the left, you'll find the spots closest to the geyser action).

Services and Eating: Across the road from the geothermal area is a strip mall with a clothing and souvenir store, free WCs, a golf course, a hotel, and a handful of restaurants. (I'd opt for one of the Laugarvatn eating options described earlier, or wait for Skjól Café, about 2 miles farther down the road.)

Visiting Geysir: The geothermal field lacks the boardwalks and other maintenance you would normally expect at a sight this popular. Outdoor signboards explain the geology.

The area's centerpiece is a geyser called **Strokkur** (Butter Churn), which erupts about every 5-10 minutes. The eruptions,

which shoot about 50 feet in the air, are relatively short—in every sense—and won't wow anyone who has seen Old Faithful at Yellowstone. What's nice about Strokkur, though, is the short wait between gushes and how close you can get. Each eruption is a little different. It's surreal to stand around in a field with people who have come from the far reaches of the globe, just to share this experience...of staring at a water-filled hole in the ground. Everyone huddles in a big circle around Strokkur, cameras aimed and focused, trigger fingers twitching, waiting for the spurt. When it finally happens, it's over in a couple of seconds, as abruptly as it started. After each show, the crowd thins out, and new arrivals shuffle in to take their place, shoulder-to-shoulder, cameras cocked, waiting...waiting...waiting. (To record the entire spurt on video, stand on the high end and watch for the dome-shaped bubble that shows a second before it blows.)

Just a few yards up the hill above Strokkur, check out the other **fumaroles and hot pools,** including Konungshver and the colorful Blesi. The miniature Litli-Geysir, along the path from the main parking lot, bubbles and boils but doesn't erupt.

Steaming uneasily off to the side is the **original "great" Gey-**

sir. This was the only one known to medieval Europeans, and is the origin of the word geyser. It was dormant for most of the 20th century, but after a nearby earthquake in 2000 it started erupting occasionally. It blows higher and longer than Strokkur, but rarely and unpredictably, so don't expect to see anything.

For a commanding view over the Geysir area, continue past Konungshver, climb over the stile, and make your way 10 minutes up to the top of one of the rocky outcroppings that overlook the geothermal field and surrounding terrain. Snowy glaciers loom to the east.

• *From Geysir, continue to the Gullfoss waterfall, a straight shot 10 minutes onward along highway 35. Along the way you'll pass $ Skjól Café (connected to a hostel and campground, serving good, affordable, splittable pizzas, burgers, and fish-and-chips; June-Aug daily 10:00-15:00 & 18:00-23:00, shorter hours off-season; mobile 899-4541, www.skjolcamping.com).*

▲▲Gullfoss Waterfall

The thundering waterfall called Gullfoss (GUTL-foss) sits on the wide, glacial Hvítá river, which drains Iceland's interior. The name means "Golden Falls" and gives this "Golden Circle" its name. The waterfall has two stages: a rocky upper cascade with a drop of about 35 feet, and a lower falls where the water plummets 70 feet straight down into a narrow gorge. Somewhat unusually for a

waterfall, the gorge runs transverse to the fall line, effectively carrying the water off to the side. Dress warmly: Cold winds blow down the valley, and the spray from the falls can soak you. Winter visitors should watch for slippery areas. If you have ice cleats, this is a good place to put them on.

Cost and Hours: Free and always open, tel. 486-6500, www.gullfoss.is.

Arrival at Gullfoss: Two viewing areas—connected by a metal staircase—let you admire the falls; each has its own free parking lot and viewpoints. Both are equally worth seeing, but if you're short on time, focus on the lower one, where you can get up close and feel the spray. To park there, watch for a blue *P* sign as you approach, and take the right turn to the lower parking lot. With more time, continue to the upper parking lot, with a huge tourist complex housing a pay WC, café, and massive gift shop (with free WCs for customers).

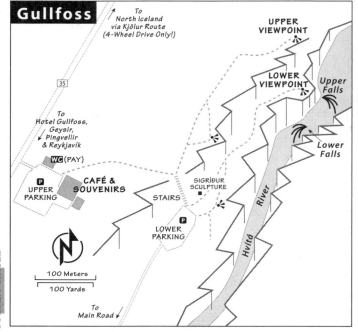

Gullfoss

To North Iceland via Kjölur Route (4-Wheel Drive Only!)

35

To Hotel Gullfoss, Geysir, Þingvellir & Reykjavík

WC (PAY)

P UPPER PARKING

CAFÉ & SOUVENIRS

STAIRS

P LOWER PARKING

SIGRÍÐUR SCULPTURE

UPPER VIEWPOINT

LOWER VIEWPOINT

Upper Falls

Lower Falls

Hvítá River

100 Meters
100 Yards

To Main Road

Eating: The large **$ café** at the upper parking lot serves soup, salad, and sandwiches (daily 9:00-21:30, Sept-May 10:00-18:00).

Visiting the Waterfall: From the upper parking lot, boardwalks lead along the edge of the plateau, high above the falls, to two good **upper viewpoint** spots. On a clear day, you can see glaciers in the distance. The view upriver gives a sense of Iceland's vast and lonely interior Highlands.

From here, stairs lead down to the **lower viewpoint.** This area gets you close to the falls. It's closed in winter, when ice can make it dangerous (don't try it). A narrow trail leads through the spray from the falls to a level area between the upper and lower stages of the waterfall.

It would be easy to dam or divert the river above the falls for electricity generation. In the early 1900s, British investors tried to buy the waterfall and do just that, but their plans fell through. The government acquired the land and the falls have been left in their natural state. Near the base of the staircase, look for the relief sculpture of **Sigríður Tómasdóttir,** a local farmer who helped thwart plans for the dam.

Near Gullfoss: Leaving Gull-foss, look to your right, where you'll see the **Langjökull glacier** in the distance and get a sense of Iceland's vast interior. This no-man's-land, uninhab-ited and without roads, stretches over a hundred miles to Iceland's north coast. After a couple of minutes (just past the Skjól Café), a farmer has cre-ated a little **horse-petting experience** (complete with a shack that sells "horse candy"—corn goodies to feed as you make friends with young Icelandic horses).

GULLFOSS BACK TO REYKJAVÍK

You've seen the main three sights on the Golden Circle. This last stretch features a grab bag of interesting stops to consider on the way back to Reyjavík—waterfall, thermal pool, tomato farm, church, petting zoo, crater, and thermal river—but if you're in a hurry, these are all skippable. It's about two hours back to Reyk-javík (direct) but, even on a quick trip, I'd give it four hours with stops of your choice.

• *The following sights are all on (or are short detours from) highway 35/ highway 1 and the main Golden Circle route. From Gullfoss, return to highway 35 and pass by Geysir again. Shortly after Geysir, make a left turn to stay on highway 35 toward Reykholt and Selfoss.*

The first sight, the Secret Lagoon, is a 10-minute drive off the main Golden Circle route. From highway 35, just before the village of Reyk-holt, turn left at highway 359, signed Flúðir. *Follow this about 5 miles into the small village of Flúðir, watching on your left for the turnoff to* Hvammur *and* Gamla Laugin. *The Secret Lagoon is tucked amid the big greenhouses, on your right.*

Secret Lagoon (Gamla Laugin)

Claiming to be the oldest swimming pool in Iceland (from 1891), the Secret Lagoon is a big, rustic, three-foot-deep, 100°F pool in front of a dilapidated old house (with a modern entrance/changing facility; 3,000 ISK, daily 10:00-22:00, Oct-April 11:00-20:00, last entry one hour before closing, tel. 555-3351, www.secretlagoon. is). The pool is surrounded by an evocative thermal landscape; a boardwalk leads around the pool, past steaming and simmering crevasses. Greenhouses stand nearby. Compared to the over-the-top-romantic Blue Lagoon, or even Reykjavík's municipal swim-ming pools, this is a very straightforward experience: Its proximity to the Golden Circle and clever marketing make it more popular than it probably should be. On the other hand, the bathers here seem very happy— sipping drinks, bobbing on colorful pool noodles, happy to enjoy this après-Golden Circle hangout. Far from "secret" (it's included on several day tours

from Reykjavík), the pool can get quite crowded with a younger clientele. It's smart to reserve ahead online—when it's full, it's full.
• *Return to highway 35 heading southwest toward Reykholt.*

Faxi Waterfall

Just before Reykholt you'll see a tiny sign for *Faxi Camping and Restaurant* on the left. Exit and enter the upper parking lot, where you'll pay 700 ISK (park in the lower lot closer to the falls). Faxi is a lovely waterfall, but nothing on the scale of Gullfoss. Notice the fish ladder built alongside it for the convenience of spawning salmon. A small café with a view deck perches along the road from the upper lot.

Reykholt—the Greenhouse Town

With Iceland's long dark winters and lack of fertile topsoil, the only way to grow anything well (other than hay) is in greenhouses. Reykholt is known for its man-made fertility. Greenhouses here grow strawberries, cucumbers, peppers, herbs, flowers—and at the Friðheimar farm (described next, open to non-diners) it's all about tomatoes.

$$ The Friðheimar Tomato Farm Restaurant, a very popular, borderline-pretentious tomato farm and eatery, offers lunch daily (12:00-16:00). You'll dine right in the greenhouse, with a muggy warmth, surrounded by rows of tomato plants, with pots of fresh basil on each table. The brief menu is all tomato: tomato soup with bread, fresh pasta with tomato sauce, and tomato ice cream or cheesecake with green tomato sauce. If you want just a quick bite or drink (or don't have a reservation), you can enjoy the bar, which serves a creative array of Bloody Marys and more. As the farm is popular with big bus groups, reservations are smart (along highway 35, in the village of Reykholt, tel. 486-8894, www.fridheimar.is).

Even if not eating at the farm restaurant, you're welcome to read their info boards and wander into the tomato-filled greenhouse. The Friðheimar farm has been in the family, growing tomatoes in greenhouses, since 1946. Today they claim to produce about a fifth of all tomatoes in Iceland, shipping a ton of tomatoes to

Reykjavík each day. Taking advantage of a hot spring above town, the greenhouse walls are lined with heat-radiating water pipes. This off-the-grid farm uses geothermal energy to produce electricity to power its lights, providing a kind of synthetic sunshine in the darkness of winter. And the greenhouse cleverly corrals all that goodness, nursing its sweet vegetables.

• *To reach the next two sights a few minutes southwest of Reyhkolt, detour left onto highway 31, following* Skálholt *signs. The church is just over the hill, overlooking a lake-and-mountain panorama.*

Skálholt Church

This church was the old seat of the bishopric of southern Iceland. The current church was built in the 1960s and is flanked by a retreat center run by Iceland's Evangelical Lutheran state church. This low-key site is worth a few minutes if you want to mix something nongeological into your day.

Cost and Hours: Church entry—free, crypt—500-ISK donation requested; daily 9:00-18:00, pay WC in complex next to church.

Visiting the Church: As you drive up, you can see how the rich farmland around the church was able to support a medieval religious community and imagine how, in the 1700s, this was one of the most densely populated—and most powerful—places in Iceland.

It's peaceful here, with no tourist crowds. Almost nothing is left of the original buildings, many of which were destroyed by earthquakes in the late 18th century. The **church** is simple, with locally designed stained-glass windows and a thousand years of bishops listed on the back wall.

Downstairs, the **crypt** has a small exhibit of historical and archaeological artifacts, including a bishop's stone coffin dating to at least the 14th century. There's also a period sketch of the 18th-century church, which survived the earthquakes but was torn down soon after. From the crypt, you can exit directly outdoors (open the door in the right-hand corner) through the only original part of the building, a short tunnel. An old-style, turf-roofed wooden chapel on the grounds is usually open (often with temporary exhibits).

Slakki Zoo

Slakki (about a mile past Skálholt Church along highway 31) is designed for little kids. It's a combination petting zoo and indoor mini-golf complex, housed partly in cute buildings meant to look like a typical old-style Icelandic farm. There's a decent café, tiny playground, and good photo ops, and kids can get to know a big, noisy green parrot.

Cost and Hours: 1,300 ISK, kids-700 ISK, daily 11:00-18:00 in summer, May and Sept Sat-Sun only, closed Oct-April, off Skálholtsvegur in the hamlet of Laugarás, tel. 486-8783.

• *Backtrack to highway 35 and continue southwest to the town of Borg.*

Borg Public Swimming Pool

In the tiny town of Borg (at the junction of highways 35 and 354), a simple community pool offers about the least touristy and most basic Icelandic swimming opportunity available. Look for the water slide just past the main turnoff into Borg (1,000 ISK; Mon-Fri 10:00-22:00, Sat-Sun until 19:00; late Aug-May Mon-Thu 14:00-22:00, Sat-Sun 11:00-18:00, closed Fri; tel. 480-5530, www.gogg.is).

• *After passing Borg, watch for the little* Kerið *sign, which comes up very quickly (look for an Icelandic flag and people hiking along a ridge on your left as you approach).*

▲Kerið Crater

The Kerið (KEH-reethe) crater is a volcanic cone from an eruption about 6,500 years ago that collapsed and filled with water—creating a tiny crater lake. It's right next to highway 35, but you'll see nothing without paying to climb the little hill. The crater is vividly colorful: red walls draped with green vegetation, overlooking deep aquamarine-blue water. You can see it in a single glance, take a half-hour to walk around the rim, or de-

scend 150 feet down a set of stairs to the surface of the lake (400 ISK when staffed, not staffed at night or in darkness, mobile tel. 823-1336, www.kerid.is).

• *Continue southwest from Kerið crater toward Selfoss on highway 35.*

Kerið Crater to Highway 1

Just before crossing a river, there's a popular pizza joint on the right. After the river, you'll drive past a dramatic slope on your right. Look at the mountainside to see the huge boulders that have tumbled down the slope over the ages—and see if you can spot the one lonely summer house taking its chances among them.

• *When you finally reach highway 1, turn right for Reykjavík. (You're skirting the town of Selfoss, known for having the grave of chess master Bobby Fischer (see map on page 133). It's about an hour's drive from here back to Reykjavík.*

Road safety is an issue here. Notice the road sign with wind direction and speed along with temperature. After that is a speed-camera warning...then the camera. On the left you'll see 52 white crosses at the base of a conical hill. These commemorate motorists and pedestrians killed on this busy, poorly lit road—statistically one of Iceland's most dangerous—between 1972 and 2006. Consider this a sobering reminder to drive with extra caution. (Farther along you'll see two smashed cars with an indication of how many deaths there have been on Icelandic roads so far this year.)

▲Reykjadalur Thermal River

At the town of Hveragerði is the exit for this aptly named natural thermal area—literally "Steamy Valley." For outdoorsy hiker/bathers, Reykjadalur (RAYK-yah-dah-lrr) is worth ▲▲. The hike to the river is just over two miles one way along a well-maintained

path, with a 600-foot elevation gain (allow at least three hours total for this experience).

Stepping out of your car at the end-of-the-road parking lot, you're surrounded by steaming hillsides. From here, cross the bridge, then hike approximately one hour up the valley. Eventually you'll reach some basic changing cabins next to a hot stream. The water is shallow—you'll need to lie down to be submerged—but wonderfully warm. Reykjadalur is far from undiscovered, so you'll likely have plenty of company. Relax and enjoy the experience...but remember it's an hour's hike back down to your car.

Warning: Stay on marked paths at all times. This entire area is very geologically active, and anyone wandering off the path could end up stepping into a hidden, underground pool of boiling water.

Eating in Hveragerði: Other than the river, the main reason to visit nearby Hveragerði is to eat at **$$ Ölverk** (Beerworks), a friendly little microbrewery/pizzeria tucked in a dreary strip mall a couple of blocks into town. In addition to a chalkboard menu of their own beers, and others by local brewers, they dish up decent pizzas from a brick oven. Casual and family-friendly, it works well for an easygoing dinner on your way back to Reykjavík (lunch specials, daily 11:30-23:00, take the main road through Hveragerði and watch for the pizzeria on your right at Breiðumörk 2b, tel. 483-3030, www.olverk.is).

• *Past the small town of Hveragerði, the road climbs steeply in a series of wide bends to a high upland plateau (1,200 feet above sea level) called Hellisheiði. This plateau separates southern Iceland from the Reykjavík area. About halfway across the plateau (the turnoff is clearly marked* Hellisheiðarvirkjun*), you'll see pipes and steam from a geothermal plant that welcomes visitors.*

Hellisheiði Power Plant (Hellisheiðarvirkjun)
This is the only one of Iceland's seven geothermal energy plants where visitors can get a good look at the powerful turbine machinery at work. The hot water from the ground (which is piped to homes for heating) drives the turbines that generate electricity.

In the geothermal exhibit, you can see turbine rooms through big windows, read posters on how geothermal energy works, and watch a couple of films. Included guided tours run several times a day (last tour at 15:00, see details at their website).

Cost and Hours: 1,750 ISK, Mon-Fri 8:00-17:00, Sat-Sun from 9:00, confirm hours in advance, tel. 591-2880, www.geothermalexhibition.com.

• *From the power plant, it's less than 30 minutes—across a lunar landscape—to Reykjavík. Your Golden Circle loop is finished.*

Sleeping on the Golden Circle

For locations, see the map near the beginning of this chapter.

In Laugarvatn: $$ Héraðsskólinn Guesthouse is hard to miss as you drive into Laugarvatn from Þingvellir, with its green gables and prominent location on a bluff above the lake (just above the Fontana Thermal Baths). This historic 1928 schoolhouse, designed by Guðjón Samúelsson of Hallgrímskirkja fame, is filled with light and offers generous, warmly decorated public areas and a recommended in-house café. Its bright, clean rooms come with views (breakfast extra, family rooms, cheaper rooms with shared baths, hostel-style dorm in the basement, laundry, elevator; Laugarbraut 2, 25 minutes to Geysir, 35 minutes to Gullfoss; tel. 537-8060, www.heradsskolinn.is, booking@heradskolinn.is).

¢ **Laugarvatn Youth Hostel,** on the main drag, offers basic, economical accommodations (breakfast extra, family rooms,

GOLDEN CIRCLE

private rooms with baths available, laundry facilities, Dalbraut 10, tel. 486-1215, www.laugarvatnhostel.is, laugarvatn@hostel.is).

Near Laugarvatn: $$ Austurey Cottages are six modern, one-bedroom cabins plopped on a sheep farm owned by the same family since 1926. Here you'll find peace and quiet (except for the occasional bleating sheep) and floor-to-ceiling windows offering wide-open vistas that, on a clear day, include volcanoes Hekla and Eyjafjallajökull (indoor kitchenettes, gas grills outside; located at Austurey 1, south of Laugarvatn near the shore of lake Apavatn in Bláskógabyggð; 5 minutes to Laugarvatn town and grocery store, 30 minutes to Geysir, 40 minutes to Gullfoss; tel. 773-0378, www.austurey.is, austureycottages@gmail.com).

$$$ Efstidalur II, home to the recommended Farmhouse Restaurant, is a fine place to get a hint of what life is like on a real Icelandic farm—with horses, cows, and dogs. They rent 15 rooms in two buildings with either private or shared baths; several rooms come with views over the valley (family room, farm scents, horse rental, free parking, 10 minutes east of Laugarvatn on highway 37; 15 minutes to Geysir, 25 minutes to Gullfoss; tel. 486-1186, www.efstidalur.is, info@efstidalur.is).

In Geysir: $ Litli Geysir Hotel, tucked away from the Geysir tourist hubbub, is a straightforward one-story hotel offering 22 tidy, modern rooms a short walk from the geothermal action. When booking, don't mistake the good-value Litli for its big sister, the brash and pricey new Hotel Geysir by the shopping center (well-regarded restaurant, look for parking lot on the right after you pass the shopping zone, 10 minutes to Gullfoss, tel. 480-6800, www.hotelgeysir.is—choose Litli Geysir, geysir@geysircenter.is).

Near Gullfoss: $$ Hotel Gullfoss offers comfortable, good-size, modern rooms just minutes from its namesake falls. From the outside this family-run hotel doesn't exude a ton of charm, but inside everything's bright and fresh (off highway 35 a few minutes past Skjól Café, tel. 486-8979, www.hotelgullfoss.is, info@hotelgullfoss.is).

Near Skálholt: $ Brekkugerði Guesthouse offers nine simple yet modern rooms in a quiet, woodsy setting amid pastures above the Hvítá river (flowing from Gullfoss upstream). Helpful and friendly host Haraldur is happy to answer questions and offer tips (cheaper rooms with shared bath, shared kitchen, garden area in back, free parking; at Austurbyggð 26—from highway 35 take the Skálholt exit to highway 31, pass the Skálholt Church, turn left onto Skúlagata, then right onto Brekkugerðisvegur, which leads straight onto Austurbyggð; 30 minutes from Geysir, tel. 779-7762, www.brekkugerdi.is, brekkugerdi@brekkugerdi.is).

In Hveragerði: $$ Skyr Guesthouse, charmingly occupying a former *skyr* factory, is convenient to the Reykjadalur thermal river. The decor of its 13 warm rooms swings between vintage and modern; some come with a private bath and all share a shower (cozy dining room and café, Breiðamörk 25, just up the street from the recommended Ölverk microbrewery, tel. 481-1010, www.skyrgerdin.is, info@skyrgerdin.is).

ICELANDIC EXPERIENCES

Iceland is a small land that packs in a lot of experiences. From gazing into a volcanic crater lake to descending into the underground magma chamber of a dormant volcano, from exploring glaciers and geysers to luxuriating in an outdoor pool filled with earth-warmed water, Iceland offers adventures and activities that you can't do anywhere else (not easily, at least).

Many of these experiences require going through a tour operator (even if you have a car). I've listed some established outfits. A good one-stop resource is Guide to Iceland, a for-profit consolidator of travel providers (www.guidetoiceland.is). They charge no additional commission and will match a better price if you find one. They work with some, but not all, tour providers in Iceland, so it's smart to also do your own research (for instance, the "Things to Do" reviews on TripAdvisor can offer a helpful roundup of tour companies and the latest experiences).

Note that while Reykjavík is generally a good home base, many excursions head to farther away destinations involving higher prices and long hours in a bus. Consider booking tours that are closer to where you're staying, even if it means home-basing outside of Reykjavík. For example, if you're interested in glacier activities, consider spending a night or two on the South Coast or in Southeast Iceland.

As you join the hordes of international visitors who treat Iceland as a newly discovered playground, do so considerately. Respect the land. The nature on display may seem raw and powerful, but it's also extremely fragile. Nobody yet knows precisely what long-term impact the recent influx of tourism will have on this special place. To be part of a sustainable long-term prosperity, treat Iceland as a precious treasure...because that's what it is.

ICELANDIC EXPERIENCES

The Many Ways Iceland Can Kill You

Several times a year, Iceland is captivated by a full-scale land and helicopter search for travelers sucked out to sea by a wave, separated from their snowmobile tour group, or lost in the wilderness. More so than in any other country in Europe, in Iceland nature can threaten your very survival.

To encourage safe travel, Iceland operates the SafeTravel.is website with detailed advice and up-to-the-minute alerts. Their "112 Iceland" app is free; they also staff a counter at the What's On TI in Reykjavík at Bankastræti 2. For help in English, dial 112, the national emergency number.

Travel smart and keep the following risks in mind. For specific driving hazards, see page 187.

Wind: The signature feature of Icelandic weather is wind. For Icelanders, good weather means no wind or a light breeze; bad weather means it's blowing hard. Even in summer, you'll likely encounter winds that are uncomfortable or dangerous to walk or drive in. On a recent trip, when picking up my rental car, I was talked into a $20-a-day insurance supplement for "wind damage and sandstorms." And later, while I was standing on a rock to snap a photo, a freakish gust nearly blew me into the sea. Check the forecast at the Icelandic weather service's website (https://en.vedur.is). If it's windy and icy at the same time, take extra care.

Slips and Falls: In winter, Reykjavík's sidewalks generally aren't cleared or salted, and are very slippery and icy. Falls are common. Paths in the countryside ice over, too. Cautious travelers visiting from December through February can pack a pair of ice cleats to strap over their shoes.

Exposure and Getting Lost: When traveling in less inhabited parts of the country, be prepared for the unexpected. Your car could break down or run out of gas, or you could take a wrong turn. Travel with extra clothing (even summer days can turn cold and windy, especially at higher elevations) and keep your phone charged (bring a portable charger; reception is good all around the Ring Road). Carry a paper map as a backup. Before heading into wilderness areas, upload your itinerary to SafeTravel.is.

Glaciers

More than one-tenth of Iceland's surface is covered with glaciers *(jökull)*—mainly along the southern coastline and in the desolate interior. Glaciers are most accessible at so-called tongues, where a slow-motion river of ice flows down a valley.

Below are several glacier-related experiences you can do on your own. For more options, join a guided excursion. If you won't be venturing beyond Reykjavík, the Wonders of Iceland exhibit at

Sneaker Waves: Iceland's South Coast has some very dangerous beaches with strong waves that regularly pull unsuspecting tourists out to sea. Those breathtaking black sand beaches can suddenly become dangerous. Obey all signs, and stay *much* farther from the water than you think is safe.

Trail Hazards: There are very few ropes, guardrails, or warning signs in Iceland—but if you see any, take them seriously. Step carefully, and watch out for loose stones, crevices, and sharp lava rocks.

Scalding Thermal Water: The water in Iceland's geothermally active area can be boiling hot, and the danger is often unmarked. Every year or two a tourist falls in and gets severely burned, typically in a less-visited geothermal area without ropes or walkways.

Avalanches: Icelanders have taken this danger more seriously since 1995, when two avalanches in the Westfjords killed 34 people. Wintertime travelers may encounter avalanche warnings in any settled area close to a steep mountain slope.

Volcanoes: On average, a volcano erupts in Iceland every five years. Some eruptions can be viewed from a safe distance, but others melt glaciers, let loose streams of boiling lava, give off poisonous gases, or spew ash and boulders that will damage you or your car. Volcanic eruptions and their consequences can and regularly do interfere with travel plans. The Icelandic weather service website posts regular updates on eruptions (and earthquakes).

Angry Birds: While not life-threatening, angry birds can be a nuisance. In late spring and early summer, Arctic terns *(kríur)* will dive-bomb your head if you get too close to their breeding grounds. Obey any closure signs near major nesting areas.

the Pearl has a simulated ice cave and glacier, and exhibits that focus on Iceland's glacial geology.

Glacier Sightseeing

There are several accessible glacier tongues along Iceland's southern coast, from near Skógar in the west to near Höfn in the east. If traveling on your own, you can **hike close to the tongue of a glacier** in two places: at the Skaftafell wilderness area, where you can walk to a branch of Iceland's largest glacier, Vatnajökull, or

at Sólheimajökull, along the
southern coast closer to Reykjavík.

In Southeast Iceland,
Jökulsárlón and Fjallsárlón are
two **glacier lagoons** within
minutes of each other, where a
glacier tongue terminates in a
beautiful pool of water, and icebergs calve off and float around.
At either, you can pull over to view the lagoon, or take a boat trip
between bobbing icebergs. Near Jökulsárlón is another enchant-
ing glacial sight, the so-called **Diamond Beach,** where chunks of
shimmering ice from the nearby lagoon wash up on a black sand
beach. This is a grand look at the final stage of glacial ice's very
long, very slow journey to the open ocean.

Guided Glacier Tours

For more extreme glacier adventures, you'll need to go with a guided tour.

Glacier Walks: Equipped with cold-weather gear, cram-
pons, and ice axes, you and your group will be tied together for
an amble across the ice. The
most popular places for this
are Sólheimajökull and Skaftafell in Southeast Iceland, and
Snæfellsjökull on the Snæfellsnes Peninsula. Companies offering glacier walks include the
big Reykjavík Excursions and
Gray Line, along with smaller,
more specialized operators, such

as Icelandic Mountain Guides (www.mountainguides.is), Arctic
Adventures (www.adventures.is), Troll Expeditions (www.troll.
is), Glacier Guides (www.glacierguides.is), Glacier Journey (www.
glacierjourney.is), and Extreme Iceland (www.extremeiceland.is).

Snowmobiling: The Mountaineers of Iceland offers a variety
of snowmobile trips across Langjökull, near the Golden Circle
($250-450, www.mountaineers.is; or try Glacier Journey). At the
Snæfellsjökull glacier (at the tip of the Snæfellsnes Peninsula), you
can join a **snowcat tour** (essentially a big van on tank treads). You
can even go on a **dogsled trip** across a glacier (consider Extreme
Iceland).

Ice Caves: Visitors can explore three ice caves burrowed into
glaciers ($160-250, 3-4 hours). Into the Glacier takes visitors to

an artificial cave in Langjökull in West Iceland—the only ice cave open year-round (www.intotheglacier.is). The glacier atop the Katla volcano in southern Iceland has a natural cave that's open from June to December—but it's melting quickly, so could close soon (tours depart from Vík; try Katlatrack, www.katlatrack.is). In the winter (Nov-March), Vatnajökull has a natural cave that you can explore with a tour that departs from the Jökulsárlón glacier lagoon (companies include Arctic Adventures, Extreme Iceland, and Glacier Journey; you'll pay more for pickup in Reykjavík).

Volcanoes

Travelers come to Iceland hoping for a glimpse of a volcano. When the volcano called Eyjafjallajökull spewed ash into the atmosphere in 2010—bringing European air travel to a halt—it grabbed the imagination of many. While you probably won't see any spewing ash or flowing lava while you're here, there is a variety of volcanic sights where you can learn more about the island's unique geology.

Volcanic Landscapes

Because much of Iceland is plainly shaped by volcanic activity, lava landscapes are common. Here are a few of the most dramatic and accessible (all are described in detail elsewhere in the book).

Westman Islands: This archipelago, just off the South Coast, is the most interesting volcano-related sight in Iceland, and a pilgrimage for those with serious interest. The Westman Islands saw some of Iceland's most spectacular volcanic activity in recent times. First, from 1963 to 1967, the islet of Surtsey literally rose from the Atlantic Ocean; while it can't be visited, on a clear day you can see the islet from the main island, Heimaey. Then, in 1973, the town of Vestmannaeyjar was rudely awoken in the middle of the night by a surprise eruption on the adjacent hillside. Residents were evacuated, and the flowing lava gradually swallowed the eastern part of the town. Today, streets dead-end at steep walls of volcanic rock, and a few lucky houses are surrounded on three sides by jagged cliffs. The still-warm crater hovers above it all. And the Volcano Museum in town is literally built around a house buried by lava—letting you peek into a family home forever trapped in rock.

Reykjanes Peninsula: As you'll see as you're flying into Iceland, the area around Keflavík Airport is covered with jagged lava fields. The nearby Blue Lagoon is situated in this same rocky world. Closer to Reykjavík, the suburb of Hafnarfjörður is nicknamed the "Town in the Lava" because it sits on a lava flow.

Mývatn: This North Iceland lake is ringed by a variety of otherworldly features, from the "pseudocraters" at Skútustaðir (where giant bubbles of steam burst through molten rock) to the jagged

Iceland's Volcanoes

Iceland is one of the most volcanically active places in the world, with roughly one eruption every five years. Aside from liquid lava, Iceland's volcanoes eject gas, ash, cinders, and solid rock (like pumice). The biggest rocks are sometimes called "volcanic bombs." Volcanic eruptions can last from a couple of days to several years.

Grímsvötn, a hard-to-reach volcano under the Vatnajökull glacier (in Southeast Iceland), is currently Iceland's most active; it last erupted in May 2011. Bárðarbunga, another volcano under the same glacier, began rumbling awake as recently as late 2017. The more famous Eyjafjallajökull, on the South Coast, made news in 2010—costing airlines more than $1 billion in disruptions. Other well-known Icelandic volcanoes include Hekla (once nicknamed the "Gateway to Hell"), Krafla, Askja, and Katla, which has the most potential for a damaging eruption (it threatens coastal hamlets with flooding; Katla erupts about once a century—the last time in 1918—so many think it's due).

Of the roughly 130 volcanoes in Iceland, the most common type is the stratovolcano—the classic cone-shaped peak with explosive eruptions that form a crater in the very top (such as Hekla and Katla). There are also a few dormant shield volcanoes—with low-profile, wide-spreading lava flows (one called Skjaldbreiður is near the Golden Circle). Eruptions from fissure vents (long cracks in the earth's crust) are also common in Iceland, such as the Holuhraun eruption of 2014 or the destructive Laki eruptions in the 1780s.

Iceland's entire surface is made of volcanic rock, most of it basalt—the rock that forms when lava cools. Iceland's towering cliffs and jagged islands and skerries are all made of basalt. When basalt cools in particular ways, it forms the hexagonal rock columns that you see at Reynisfjara (on the South Coast), near Dettifoss (in the north), and other places.

At the lake called Mývatn, in North Iceland, you can see pseudocraters (also called rootless cones), which form after lava flows over a pond or marsh. The water beneath the lava boils and a giant bubble breaks through the lava, leaving a crater-like depression.

New lava is shiny and oily-looking, while old lava loses its gleam. Old lava fields—recognizable by their unique, bumpy ap-

formations along the lake's eastern shore, at Dimmuborgir, and at the huge, climbable Hverfjall crater.

South Coast: All along the South Coast, you'll see plenty of volcanoes—but you may not realize it, since they're currently dormant and covered with thick glaciers. The most famous, under

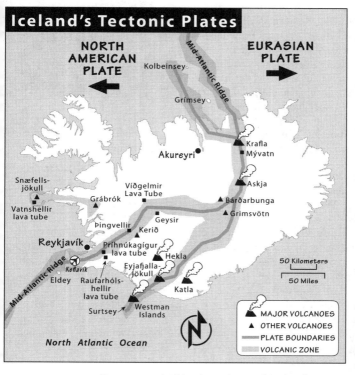

Iceland's Tectonic Plates

NORTH
AMERICAN
PLATE

EURASIAN
PLATE

Mid-Atlantic Ridge

Kolbeinsey

Grímsey

Krafla
Mývatn

Akureyri

Askja

Snæfells-
jökull

Víðgelmir
Lava Tube

Bárðarbunga

Grábrók

Grimsvötn

Vatnshellir
lava tube

Geysir

Þingvellir

Kerið

Reykjavík

Þríhnúkagígur
lava tube

Hekla

Keflavík

Eyjafjalla-
jökull

50 Kilometers

Eldey

Raufarhóls-
hellir
lava tube

Katla

50 Miles

Surtsey

Westman
Islands

North Atlantic Ocean

Mid-Atlantic Ridge

MAJOR VOLCANOES
OTHER VOLCANOES
PLATE BOUNDARIES
VOLCANIC ZONE

pearance—are often covered with a fuzzy layer of Icelandic moss.

So why does Iceland have so many volcanoes? The answer lies beneath the surface. Iceland is located on the long, mostly underwater Mid-Atlantic Ridge—the meeting point of the Eurasian and North American tectonic plates. As the two tectonic plates move apart, magma from the earth's mantle rises to the surface (we start calling it "lava" when it erupts). Iceland is located on a mantle plume, where magma is especially close to the surface, which explains why land formed here and not elsewhere along the tectonic ridge.

Eyjafjallajökull, blew its top in 2010. Several other large glaciers, such as Mýrdalsjökull and Vatnajökull, have volcanoes underneath. For a hike with the best views of glacier-topped volcanoes, head to **Þórsmörk,** where a huff up to the Valahnúkur viewpoint affords you panoramas over three volcanoes.

Climbable Craters: Several craters around Iceland invite you to climb up onto their rims for spectacular views. One of the finest, **Grábrók,** is alongside the Ring Road in West Iceland, just before the pass to the north. **Kerið,** along the Golden Circle route, requires almost no climbing and has a lovely lake inside. On Snæfellsnes Peninsula, Saxhóll crater has a staircase to the

top. Near Mývatn, in the north, you can hike to the top of **Hverfjall** or drive just over the mountains and up the Katla Valley to reach **Víti** ("Hell"), a rugged crater encircling a deep-blue lake.

Volcano Museums

To learn more about volcanoes, visit one of these museums.

Westman Islands: Iceland's best explanation of volcanic activity is here, at the Volcano Museum.

South Coast: The high-tech Lava Center in Hvolsvöllur is both entertaining and educational. A short drive up the road is the more modest Katla Geopark Visitor Center, which has exhibits and shows a dramatic video of the 2010 Fimmvörðuháls and Eyjafjallajökull eruptions.

Reykjavík: The Volcano House shows films about two of Iceland's most famous eruptions (Westman Islands and Eyjafjallajökull). At the Pearl, visitors feel and hear the power of volcanoes and earthquakes in the Wonders of Iceland exhibit.

Snæfellsnes Peninsula: Stykkishólmur's Volcano Museum collects artistic depictions of volcanoes from cultures around the world.

Volcanic Underground Tours

Iceland offers several opportunities for subterranean volcanic exploration. While pricey (especially the first option), they're definitely memorable experiences and worth at least ▲▲ for those interested in an up-close look. The first two can be done as excursions from Reykjavík.

Þríhnúkagígur ("Inside the Volcano" Tour)

At this cinder cone in the Bláfjöll mountains southeast of Reykjavík, you have the chance to descend into the magma chamber of a dormant volcano that erupted about 4,000 years ago. When the magma drained out, it left a cavity so big that it could contain the Statue of Liberty. The first explorer entered in 1972. Today, visitors can ride a lift through the opening at the volcano's top and 400 feet down into the vast chamber. At the bottom you're free to wander around a rocky floor that's the size of three basketball courts.

Cost and Hours: 44,000 ISK, includes lunch and shuttle transfer from Reykjavík hotel, tours run several times a day mid-May-Oct, 4-6 hours, 20-person max, tel. 519-5609, book ahead at www.insidethevolcano.com. Wear sturdy shoes and bring extra layers for the chilly chamber.

Visiting the Volcano: The tour starts at a ski lodge a half-hour from Reykjavík (take their shuttle from town or drive there your-

self) with a brisk 45-min-ute hike to the "base camp" hut at the foot of the vol-cano. Along the way your guide points out features of the otherworldly volca-nic terrain. At base camp you'll get a briefing on the journey, and be fitted with a hard hat and a harness (for safety when boarding the lift). From here a lift operator will take you to the top of the cone, help you board the open lift (eight people max), and—down you go.

During the seven-minute descent, your lift operator stops to describe the fascinating features of the chamber walls. Lamps illu-minate the chamber, bringing out its pastel colors. On the bottom, you have about 30 minutes to explore. No more than 16 people are on the floor at one time, so it's an intimate experience.

Once back outside, you'll head down to base camp for an in-cluded lunch, and then hike back to the lodge.

Raufarhólshellir ("The Lava Tunnel" Tour)

The fourth-longest known lava tube in Iceland, Raufarhólshellir was created 5,000 years ago during a lava flow that extended to

the South Coast and Reykjavík. The tube formed as the flow-ing river of molten rock began crusting over, causing the lava to burrow deeper. When the erup-tion ceased, the lava drained out, leaving behind an extensive tun-nel covered in colorful forma-tions. In 2017, the tunnel was closed to the public and convert-ed into a private attraction—infuriating local spelunkers, as well as partyers who were trashing the place.

Cost and Hours: Basic one-hour tour costs 6,900 ISK (11,900

Pool Rules: Visiting an Icelandic Thermal Swimming Pool

Icelanders love going to their local swimming pools, which are heated with natural thermal water. These aren't elaborate water parks, but more like municipal swimming pools back home. (Not so long ago, it was common for Icelanders to live in apartments with no shower or bathtub—instead, they had an annual pass for the pool and went daily.)

Of course, the big draw of Icelandic pools is the naturally steamy water, which is pumped right out of the ground. Even the lap pools stay at a warm temperature (around 85°F), while "hot pots" (smaller hot pools) are in the 100°F range. Bigger pools have more facilities, which can be indoors, outdoors, or both. Very windy or cold weather makes indoor bathing attractive. But if it's not too bad out, there's something cozy about submerging yourself in hot water while the wind ruffles your hair and snowflakes settle on your nose.

Iceland's public bathing culture has its own set of customs, which locals take very seriously. You'll quickly get the hang of the system. Just follow these steps.

1. Bring a swimsuit and towel (rentals are available but expensive). Also bring any other gear you need: bathing cap, goggles, flip-flops (although most Icelanders don't bother with them), or toys for children (you can bring a bag into the pool area and stow it discreetly). There's no need to bring soap or shampoo— there are liquid soap dispensers in the showers.

2. Pay. Most towns have a shareable 10-visit discount card, which can save money with as few as five adult entries. At some pools, you'll be issued a locker key or an electronic wristband that will open a locker; at others, keys are in the locks.

3. Change. Changing rooms are sex-segregated. Young children may go with a parent of either sex. Before entering the locker area, take off your shoes. (Many Icelanders leave them on public shoe racks, but I put mine in my locker.) Find an available locker, disrobe and lock your clothes inside, and carry your swimsuit and towel with you to the shower area.

ISK with Reykjavík bus transfer), tours depart daily every hour between 9:00 and 17:00—best to book ahead, 30-person max. "Adventure" tour costs 19,900 ISK (more with transfer), lasts 3-4 hours, and goes deeper into the tunnel. Tours run year-round; bring warm clothing—the temperature in the tunnel is 38 degrees. Mobile 760-1000, www.thelavatunnel.is.

4. Shower. Store your towel in one of the cubbyholes and keep your swimsuit handy. Soap down and shower thoroughly. Yes, you're expected to shower naked: Icelanders are relaxed about nudity, and showering is considered a (required) sanitary issue. (Only the touristy Blue Lagoon has some frosted-glass stalls for bashful foreigners.) Note: Iceland's water is extremely soft. You don't need much soap, and it can take a long time to wash it off.

5. Swim and soak. After showering, slip on your swimsuit and head for the pool area. Typically, people start out in the warm pools (usually a lap pool for swimmers, a shallower pool for recreation, and a wading pool for kids; these are typically around 29°C/85°F). Then they finish off with a soak in the hot tubs or a visit to the sauna. Each tub is marked in Celsius, and you'll quickly find your own comfort range. (For reference, 38°C is 100°F, 40°C is 104°F, 42°C is 108°F, and 44°C is 111°F.) Stay as long as you want; if you feel dizzy or uncomfortable, take a break outside or in a cooler pool. Drink water even if you're not thirsty—when you're in hundred-degree water, dehydration can sneak up on you.

6. Finish up. When you're done, return to the shower room, take off your swimsuit, shower again, and retrieve your towel. Towel off *before* returning to the locker area (they like to keep it as dry as possible). Many pools have a centrifuge to wick the water out of your suit—find it and use it. Back at your locker, get dressed, but don't put your shoes on until you exit the locker room. Return any keys or armbands to the counter.

7. Refuel. Most pools have tables and chairs in the entry hall where you can eat a packed lunch or snack. Most also have vending machines, snack counters, or even full-fledged cafés.

Note: At the pool, Icelanders usually just talk to the people they came with and generally leave strangers alone. Everyone is polite and helpful, but don't expect long conversation. At some times of day, groups of local "regulars" (often senior citizens) may seem to take over one of the hot pots, but you're welcome to squeeze in, too.

No Phones or Photos: Phones and cameras are strictly prohibited anywhere near the pool and dressing rooms. Just relax, and enjoy the experience.

ICELANDIC EXPERIENCES

Visiting the Tunnel: The tour starts at the visitors center about 40 minutes from downtown Reykjavík (take their shuttle or drive there yourself), roughly on the way to the South Coast. There you'll meet your guide and receive a hard hat.

After a quick briefing, you'll enter the tunnel, passing beneath several "skylights" where the tunnel's ceiling had completely collapsed. Then, it's into the intact lava tube, which is as big as a railroad tunnel in most places. There's some uneven ground, but the route is mostly easygoing on boardwalk and stairs. Subtle lighting brings out the tube's variety of colors. At the turnaround point, you'll have the chance—if the group is willing—to experience a few minutes of total darkness when the guide shuts off the lights.

Other Volcanic Caves

Víðgelmir ("The Cave" tour): Located in West Iceland, this cave is newer than Raufarhólshellir (about 1,000 years old rather than 5,000) and more extensive, but also more remote (about a 2-hour drive north of Reykjavík, or an hour east of Borgarnes). With a guide, you can walk about a half-mile into a lava tube.

Vatnshellir: This lava tube, near the tip of Snæfellsnes Peninsula in the national park, is similar to but less impressive than the ones mentioned above; still, if you're going to Snæfellsnes, it's convenient and satisfying.

Thermal Waters

Iceland's volcanic activity goes hand-in-hand with naturally heated water—which Icelanders have cleverly harnessed in a number of ways, from thermal baths to sources of electricity and heat.

Thermal Baths and Pools

Iceland has a wide range of options for enjoying its relaxing (and, yes, slightly stinky) thermal waters. Some bathing experiences cater primarily to tourists, chief among them the heavily advertised "premium baths." While those baths have big marketing budgets and attract lots of international visitors, they're rarely frequented by Icelanders—who know that you can bathe in equally luxuriant 100°F water for a fraction of the price at one of the country's many thermal swimming pools.

Touristy Baths

The most famous of these is the **Blue Lagoon** near Keflavík Airport (see the Blue Lagoon & Reykjanes Peninsula chapter); a similar (if smaller) version is **Mývatn Nature Baths** in North Iceland—a must for those doing the Ring Road. A less impressive premium bath is **Fontana,** in Laugarvatn and handy to the Golden Circle route. Smaller, more upscale baths include **Krauma** at Deildartunguhver (west of Borgarnes) and **Geosea** in Húsavík, to the north of Mývatn. Another tourist-oriented bathing experience is the **Secret Lagoon,** a simple but cleverly marketed bath a short drive from the Golden Circle route at Flúðir.

Swimming Pools

Every community of even a few hundred people seems to have scraped together the funds for their own well-maintained pool complex, often with a (warm) lap pool and at least one or two smaller hot pools (called "hot pots"). Many have a wide variety of pools, saunas and steam rooms, and colorful waterslides for kids. In addition to being affordable, these pools *(sundlaug)* provide a pleasantly authentic Icelandic experience, allowing you to rub elbows with locals who come home from work or school, grab a towel, and head to the pool. I've listed several of these in the Reykjavík area, and throughout the country—including in Borg, right along the Golden Circle; in a remote corner of West Iceland, at Húsafell; in Patreksfjörður, in the Westfjords; in tiny Hofsós, just off the Ring Road, with an infinity pool overlooking a fjord; and in Iceland's second city, Akureyri.

Up-to-date opening hours for each pool are on the website of each town, but you usually have to hunt for them a bit amid the other municipal services. These websites also won't show temporary closures (for special events, maintenance, etc.), so it's wise to confirm opening hours by telephone before making a trek to a distant pool.

For a list of Iceland's thermal pools, try https:// sundlaugar.is. Or you can simply keep a lookout for the international "pool" symbol—a swimmer's head poking out above

waves—anywhere you go. Even though the clientele is mostly Icelandic, visitors are welcome (just follow the rules—see sidebar).

Natural Thermal Springs

Iceland has a few opportunities to (carefully) bathe in natural thermal springs. Above the town of Hveragerði, near the end of the Golden Circle route, you can hike an hour to soak in the ther-

ICELANDIC EXPERIENCES

mal river of Reykjadalur (see page 155). There are a couple of these on the Westfjords—one near the town of **Tálknafjörður,** and the other on a remote road along the Reykjafjörður **between Bílduda-lur and Dynjandi waterfall.** In the Highlands, Landmannalaugar ("The People's Pools") has a famous natural thermal area, which takes quite some effort to reach (described later, under "Other Out-door Experiences"). It's important to note that tourists regularly wind up in the burn unit of Reykjavík's hospital after being scalded at natural thermal areas. Watch your step, keep on marked trails, and bathe only where you see others doing so safely.

Thermal Sights

Wandering through a steaming, bubbling, colorful, otherworldly thermal landscape is a uniquely Icelandic treat. For such a small

island, Iceland has a remarkable variety of these locations. Just watch your step—always stay on marked trails, as a thin crust can cover a boiling-hot reser-voir—and be ready for some in-tense sulfur smells.

The most visited is **Gey-sir,** on the Golden Circle. But, while it's unique in offering the chance to watch a geyser spurt high into the air, it's crowded. For more interesting and varied thermal landscapes, consider the fol-lowing options.

Perhaps the best thermal area is at **Námafjall,** just over the hills from Mývatn, in North Iceland. Much closer to Reykjavík, the **Seltún** geothermal area on the Reykjanes Peninsula is quite strik-ing. "Honorable mentions" go to the sputtering shore of **Laugar-vatn** lake, along the Golden Circle route; the bubbling spring at **Deildartunguhver,** in West Iceland; and the steaming valley of **Reykjadalur,** above the town of Hveragerði (just off the Golden Circle route). See "Thermal Bath Hikes," later.

To see how Iceland has harnessed the substantial power of its

thermal waters, stop by a geo-thermal plant. **Hellisheiðar-virkjun** sits amid a lunar land-scape just outside Reykjavík, on the way to the Golden Circle and South Coast day trips, and boasts Iceland's most extensive visitors center about its geother-mal energy industry. **Krafla,**

with a modest information center, fills a dramatic valley in the north, near Mývatn.

Whales, Birds & Horses

Whale Watching

Many come to Iceland hoping to catch a glimpse of the elusive whales of the North Atlantic. The waters here are home to 23 different varieties of gentle giants. On a typical whale-watching trip, you're most likely to see white-beaked dolphins, harbor porpoises, and mid-sized minke whales (the species also listed on local menus). With luck, you may spot a breaching  humpback whale (often seen from ports in North Iceland, such as Húsavík and Akureyri) or a black-and-white orca (Keiko, the late killer whale of *Free Willy* fame, was captured in Iceland). On very rare occasions, some get a glimpse of one of the two biggest mammals on the planet: the blue whale or the fin whale.

Whale-watching trips generally last 3-4 hours and cost about 11,000 ISK (twice that much for smaller tours in RIBs, described below). While Icelanders say that the best place to whale-watch is in North Iceland (in the tiny town of Húsavík, and Iceland's second city of Akureyri), if you don't have time, you can also do whale-watching tours in Reykjavík. (Or, at the very least, stop by the Whales of Iceland exhibit near Reykjavík's harbor; all described in the Reykjavík chapter).

Be aware that most whale sightings will be from a distance. Multiple boats often converge on the same whale, taking turns getting closer. Also, boats are only allowed to get so close with their engine on; at a certain distance they must drift, and you can only hope that the whales get curious and come to you.

When to Go: Ideally, don't book your whale-watching trip too far in advance. Track the weather and choose a summer day that's as sunny and windless as possible; like you, whales and dolphins enjoy nice weather and are most likely to surface then. The best months are May through August, when whales are attracted to the small creatures feeding near the sun-warmed surface of the water. It's best to avoid whale watching in winter (Nov-Feb) and in windy weather, when seas can be rough, seasickness can get bad, and it's unlikely you'll see much wildlife. At any time of year, dress warmly.

Types of Boats: Most companies use fairly **large boats** with a comfy, heated, indoor seating area and a simple on-board café. In bad weather, some companies offer coveralls for those who want to be out on the deck the entire time. There's typically a naturalist guide on board, who describes the types of whales in Iceland and points out wildlife.

Some outfits offer whale-watching trips in **RIBs** (rigid inflatable boats; sometimes billed as a "premium" trip). These small, open boats zip across the water in search of whales and offer no indoor cover (all passengers get coveralls). In bad weather, the trip can be pretty miserable. In good weather, you get two fun experiences in one: a high-speed RIB trip, plus whale watching.

Birds and Birding

Birders find plenty of seabird species to get excited about in Iceland. For a one-stop look at (taxidermy-style) examples of all Icelandic bird species, head north to Sigurgeir's Bird Museum near Mývatn.

Puffins

Adorable, chubby little puffins—with their black-and-white markings and cartoonish beaks—are fun to watch. They usually arrive in Iceland in April/May, then take off again at summer's end—making the window for seeing them quite short. (For more on puffins, see the sidebar.)

The biggest puffin populations are in the Westman Islands (with about half of Iceland's estimated 10 million puffins—and one-fifth of the world's puffins); along the South Coast (particularly around the Dyrhólaey promontory, and farther east, at Ingólfshöfði cape); and along the Westfjords (at Látrabjarg, Hornbjarg, Hornstrandir, and Breiðafjörður). The islet called Lundey ("Puffin Island")—with a relatively small population of about 20,000 puffins—is ideally situated just a short boat trip from downtown Reykjavík, and a handy destination for a puffin cruise from the Old Harbor.

Other Birds

Along with puffins, the auk family includes the guillemot, the murre, and the razorbill (all of which have a black body and white belly, but lack that cute orange beak). Arctic terns are sleek flyers—gray on top, white on bottom, with a black crown and a reddish beak. They're notorious for aggressively dive-bombing tourists who wander too close to their nests, then pulling up at the last second. Arctic terns have the longest migration in the animal kingdom: They spend their summers in the Arctic...and then, come fall, fly to the "southern summer" in the Antarctic (over its life, an Arctic tern

Puffins

Iceland's unofficial mascot is the Atlantic puffin *(Fratercula arctica)*—that adorably stout, tux-
edo-clad seabird with a too-big
orange beak and beady black
eyes. Some 10 million puffins summer in Iceland—the largest population of any country on earth.

Puffins live most of their lives
on the open Atlantic, coming to
land only to breed. They fly north
to Iceland in April/May and lay
their eggs (usually by June). Puffins mate for life and typically lay
just one egg each year, which the
male and female take turns caring
for. A baby puffin usually leaves
the nest by mid-August and is
called—wait for it—a puffling. Puffins return to the ocean by early September.

To feed their pufflings, puffins plunge as deep as 200
feet below the sea's surface to catch sand eels, herring, and
other small fish. Their compact bodies, stubby wings, oil-
sealed plumage, and webbed feet are ideal for navigating
underwater. Famously, puffins can stuff several small fish into
their beaks at once, thanks to their agile tongues and uniquely
hinged beaks. This evolutionary trick lets puffins stock up before returning to the nest.

Stocky, tiny-winged puffins have a distinctive way of flying. To take off, they either beat their wings like crazy (at sea)
or essentially hurl themselves off a cliff (on land). Once aloft,
they beat their wings furiously—up to 400 times per minute—
to stay airborne. Coming in for a smooth landing on a rocky
cliff is a challenge (and highly entertaining to watch): They
choose a spot, swoop in at top speed on prevailing currents,
then flutter their wings madly to brake as they try to touch
down. At the moment of truth, the puffin decides whether to
attempt to stick the landing; more often than not, it bails out
and does another big circle on the currents...and tries again...
and again...and again.

Each August, the puffins head south at night, following
the moon. On the Westman Islands, pufflings are often dis-
tracted by the town lights and crash-land on streets and rooftops. It's a tradition for local children to collect and help release them into the wild to try again.

In addition to seeing puffins along the summer coastline,
you may occasionally see them on restaurant menus. With
such abundant numbers, Iceland doesn't protect the puffin.
Considered by some Icelanders to be a delicacy, puffin tastes
like salty, smoked chicken...but cuter.

might fly as many as 1.5 million miles). Rounding out the flock are seagull-like fulmars and kittiwakes.

But there's more: Iceland is very proud of its eider ducks, which produce a down that's very useful in this frigid climate. You may also see oystercatchers and golden plovers.

Icelandic Horses

Icelandic horses are small, strong, and docile, and descend from the ponies originally brought to Iceland in the Settlement Age. (Viking Age settlers carefully selected only the strongest horses for the journey—small enough to fit on their ships, but capable of working hard once in Iceland.) After an early attempt to crossbreed these horses failed, the Alþingi (parliament) stopped horse imports to the island altogether in 982—so every Icelandic horse

you see is a purebred. Today, there are about 60,000 horses on the island.

Icelandic horses are renowned for their unique gaits: In addition to the typical walk, trot, and gallop, Icelandic horses employ the *tölt*, which is fast and extremely smooth, and the *skeið*, a high-speed "flying pace." This "five-gaited" status is their claim to fame.

Horseback Riding

Horseback riding is big business, and dozens of farms all over Iceland offer rides for travelers—including a cluster just outside Reykjavík.

Near Reykjavík: From Reykjavík, the experience takes about a half-day (either morning or afternoon). This includes a ride to and from the farm and about an hour and a half on horseback (about 12,000-19,000 ISK, includes helmet and riding gear, some tours come with lunch, check for lower prices if you drive out yourself). Browse and book on company websites: Íslenski Hesturinn (The Icelandic Horse, tel. 434-7979, http://islenskihesturinn.is), Viking Horses (mobile 660-9590, www.vikinghorses.is), Laxnes (tel. 566-6179, www.laxnes.is), and Íshestar (tel. 555-7000, www.ishestar.is).

Elsewhere in Iceland: Options include some in dramatic surroundings, including in the broad valley of Skagafjörður, through the glacial rivulets of Þórsmörk, along the beaches of the South Coast, and so on. Wherever you ride, check the weather forecast before booking.

Other Horse Sights

For just a glimpse of an Icelandic horse, watch for roadside pad-docks all around the island. Or head to the Reykjavík Family Park and Zoo (see page 61), ideally at feeding time. On weekends, the zoo lets little kids trot around the horse paddock, accompanied by a keeper.

Hiking

Iceland is a wonderland for hikers, whether you're taking an easy stroll from your car to a waterfall, or embarking on a grueling but dramatic multiday trek.
Before heading out on a challenging hike, make sure you have proper equipment, water, maps, and advice from an experi-enced local. Be aware of current weather condi-tions—and don't under-estimate the impact of

Iceland's howling winds and bone-chilling (even in summer) tem-peratures. Read "The Many Ways Iceland Can Kill You" sidebar (earlier in this chapter).

Easy Hikes

Throughout this book, I've focused on easy hikes that offer a big reward for minimal effort—mainly starting from a parking lot and looping through an accessible slice of Icelandic scenery. More de-tails on these are given in select chapters. Some of my favorite easy car hikes include the loop through Þingvellir along the Golden Circle route; the hikes up to the South Coast glaciers at Sólheima-jökull and Skaftafell; the hike up to the lighthouse at Dyrhólaey promontory, on the South Coast; and walking up to Eldfell volcano on the Westman Islands.

Along the Ring Road is a variety of enjoyable options around Mývatn lake—including the pseudocraters at Skútustaðir, the for-ested peninsula at Höfði, and the lava pillars at Dimmuborgir. Other Mývatn hikes include the Námafjall thermal field and adja-cent hill-climb just over the mountains from the lake, and the hike out to the volcanic cone at Leirhnjúkur. Also consider the crater hikes described in the "Volcanoes" section, earlier.

Each of the great **waterfalls** I've described in Iceland comes with a hike—some short, some long—and often an opportunity to climb up to a higher vantage point: Gullfoss on the Golden Circle, Seljalandsfoss (and its neighbor Gljúfrabúi) on the South

Coast, Skógafoss on the South Coast, Hraunfossar and Barnafoss in West Iceland, Dynjandi in the Westfjords, and along the Ring Road—Goðafoss and Dettifoss in North Iceland, and Svartifoss in the southeast.

Thermal Bath Hikes

To combine a hike with a natural thermal bathing experience, you can walk about an hour up the valley called **Reykjadalur,** just above the town of Hveragerði (an hour from Reykjavík and on the route of both the Golden Circle and the South Coast day trips). Your reward is a thermal river where you can recline in warm, rushing water. Less of a hike, and less rewarding, is **Seljavallalaug,** a tepid pool tucked into the side of a mountain about a 15-minute hike from the South Coast road. At both, expect minimal, grubby changing areas and plenty of adventurous hikers.

Serious Hikes

For serious hikers, Iceland offers dozens of premier hiking destinations—many in the Highlands, and inaccessible with a standard car. The two below (Þórsmörk and Landmannalaugar) are perhaps the best known; for either you'll need a high-clearance four-wheel drive vehicle, or you can ride in a specially equipped excursion bus.

Perhaps the best combination of quality hiking and accessibility is **Þórsmörk,** a volcanic landscape with glorious mountain, valley, and canyon walks; the moderately challenging hike up to Valahnúkur is spectacular. Þórsmörk is a short detour from the South Coast, but most people get there via excursion bus from Reykjavík (5 hours each way; for more on Þórsmörk, see page 113).

More remote is **Landmannalaugar,** in the Highlands, with lots of good hiking (described below, under "Other Outdoor Experiences").

Both Þórsmörk and Landmannalaugar are key stops along a variety of popular multiday hikes (with overnights in staffed huts) that traverse the glacial landscape of the south. One of the most popular routes, called **Laugavegur,** takes three to five days (34 miles over challenging terrain) and connects Þórsmörk and Landmannalaugar. Another favorite is the two-day, 14-mile **Fimmvörðuháls** hike, from Þórsmörk south, over the saddle between Eyjafjallajökull and Mýrdalsjökull, to Skógar on the South Coast—right over the site of the first stage of the 2010 Eyjafjallajökull eruption.

For something closer to the capital, you could ascend **Esja—** the big, long ridge that looms just north of Reykjavík. The most popular hike here is the four-mile round-trip to Steinn ("The Stone"), with an elevation gain of 650 feet (don't attempt this in cold weather).

For details on these, and good overall information about hiking, see the websites of FÍ (the Iceland Touring Association, www. fi.is) and NAT (Nordic Adventure Travel, www.nat.is). Companies offering guided hikes in Iceland include Icelandic Mountain Guides (www.mountainguides.is) and Trek Iceland (www.trek.is).

Other Outdoor Experiences

Land Tours

To reach spectacular scenery without the climb, you can choose from a variety of wheeled tours. Tours by **mountain bike,** by **ATV,**

or by **"Super Jeep"** (a generic term for any monster 4x4 vehicle that can go just about anywhere) give you access to some of the more remote areas mentioned earlier.

Landmannalaugar ("The People's Pools"): This remote area, 120 miles east of Reykjavík in the Highlands—and only reachable via off-road vehicle—offers vivid landscape, a famous natural thermal area, and a variety of hikes. This area is striped with volcanic hues and features a petrified lava field from 1477 that butts up against pointy peaks. Excellent hiking trails abound, and you'll encounter some natural thermal pools. You could trek to the crater lake called Ljótipollur ("Ugly Puddle"); huff your way up the extremely colorful Brennisteinsalda, with high-altitude views and an optional detour to the Stórihver thermal area near the top; or opt for an easier walk to the big lake called Frostastaðavatn.

To reach Landmannalaugar, you'll need a 4x4 vehicle, or—better—join a guided excursion (only in summer, around 25,000 ISK, offered by various outfits, includes pickup and drop-off in Reykjavík). You can also take a bus operated by Iceland On Your Own (www.ioyo.is), Trex (www.trex.is), or Iceland By Bus (www.icelandbybus.is). Much of the route is on difficult-to-traverse, gravel-and-rock roads (about 4.5 hours one-way). While you can get a glimpse of the area in a very long day trip from Reykjavík, serious hikers overnight at the Landmannalaugar hut/campground.

Water Activities

Various companies offer **rafting and kayaking tours,** either in the canyon just below Gullfoss (the thundering waterfall on the Golden Circle), or in North Iceland on two rivers that drain the Hofsjökull glacier, south of Sauðárkrókur in the Skagafjörður region. Companies include Arctic Adventures (www.adventures.com) and Viking Rafting (www.vikingrafting.is).

For divers, **scuba diving or snorkeling at Silfra**—a fissure flooded with crystal-clear glacial water, at Þingvellir on the Golden Circle—is a highlight (see the Golden Circle chapter).

Northern Lights

The northern lights are a magical, occasional, serendipitous sight on clear, crisp nights in Iceland from about the end of August to the middle of April. You can't really plan to see the northern lights—they don't always appear, and when they do, are often obscured by cloud cover. While often visible in Reykjavík, the northern lights stand out better farther from the center of town and in the countryside, where there's less light pollution. All things being equal, spending a night or two in a more remote area could increase your chances.

The dreamy northern lights images that you see are done using long exposures and sometimes Photoshop (tweaking the aurora colors to a Kermit-the-Frog green). What you'll actually see will probably be closer to the color of a Thai green curry—more coconut milk than Kermit.

With all the interesting things to do in Iceland, it would be a shame to spend your energy chasing after the northern lights every evening. I suggest planning your trip as if you won't see them, and considering it a bonus if you do. Whether you'll see the lights or not is mostly out of your control, but consider the tips below to improve your odds.

Come during aurora season. Visit Iceland in aurora season

Nature's Light Show

The northern lights arc across Iceland's wintery sky, primarily  in shades of green. The lights are caused by charged particles from the sun that collide with the earth's upper atmosphere and cause it to glow. The earth's magnetic field deflects most of these particles (which, if they hit the earth's surface, would cause catastrophic radiation), but near the poles, where the field is weakest, some can seep through, creating the northern lights. They are strongest along a ring-shaped band that crosses Iceland, Greenland, northern Canada, Alaska, Russia, and northern Scandinavia, and diminish as you move farther north toward the magnetic pole. Their intensity varies with the sunspot cycle; the last maximum was in 2013, and the next will be in 2025.

While Iceland is relatively easy to get to and a good place to see the northern lights, it's not the best because of its frequent cloudy weather. So if you're planning a trip specifically to see the lights, your best bet is places that have more reliably clear winter weather and are closer to the center of the band, such as the northern parts of Norway, Finland, and Sweden (especially spots where the weather is continental and dry).

(from a little before the fall equinox to a little after the spring equinox). Some say that September/October and February/March are the best months. At the least, they have longer days and nicer temperatures, so you can enjoy regular sightseeing more. If you're planning to rent a car, go in fall, when the road conditions are better.

Maximize your chances. It's easy to miss the northern lights simply by not bothering to look for them.

On any clear, dark night, go outside and scan the sky every half hour or so up until bedtime. You can follow the aurora and cloud-cover forecast on the Icelandic weather service's English-language website (https://en.vedur.is; click on "Weather," then "Aurora forecasts"). The American aurora forecasts at www.swpc.noaa.gov also cover Iceland.

See the lights without a car. If you're staying in Reykjavík and you don't have a car, consider taking a northern lights bus tour (4,500-9,000 ISK). Tours only run when conditions look good—call around dinnertime to find out. You'll leave town at 21:00 or 22:00 and you won't be in bed until almost four hours later. Read a few reviews before you go, and remember that even if the fore-cast is good, you may see nothing at all. (If so, the bus company will likely give you a voucher for another trip—not much help on a short visit.) For some, the trip is a nice chance to snuggle up with a travel partner on a bus and listen to an entertaining tour guide who serves hot cocoa. For others, it's a disappointing few hours of yawning and wishing they'd turned in early.

See the lights with a car. If you're staying in Reykjavík and have a car, you could put together your own northern lights tour by driving out into the suburbs or a little way into the countryside. Þingvellir (see the Golden Circle chapter) and Kleifarvatn (see the Blue Lagoon & Reykjanes Peninsula chapter) are plenty dark and within a 45-minute drive of town. If you stay within greater Reykjavík, drive out to the end of Seltjarnarnes (to the parking area facing the little island called Grótta) or to the tip of Álftanes (by Bessastaðir, the presidential residence), where city lights are a little dimmer.

"See the lights" without actually seeing the lights. Two mu-seums in Reykjavík offer the chance to "see" the aurora and learn the science behind it: the 20-minute "Áróra" planetarium show at The Pearl and Aurora Reykjavík, near the harbor in Grandi (for detailed descriptions of these exhibits, see the Reykjavík chapter). While nowhere near as thrilling as seeing the real thing, they're visual and informative.

ICELANDIC EXPERIENCES

PRACTICALITIES

This chapter covers just the basics on traveling in Iceland (for much more information, see *Rick Steves Iceland*). You'll find free advice on specific topics at Ricksteves.com/tips.

MONEY

Icelanders rarely use cash; they pay with plastic even for small purchases such as parking meters and hot dogs. In Iceland, I use my credit card nearly exclusively, for everything from hotel reservations and car rentals to everyday expenses such as meals and sightseeing.

If you need cash, Iceland uses the króna (meaning "crown"; plural krónur): 120 ISK = about $1. To very roughly convert prices in Icelandic krónur to dollars, simply lop off the last two zeros and subtract 20 percent: 2,000 ISK = about $16, 6,000 ISK = about $48. (Check Oanda.com for the latest exchange rates.)

Icelandic cash machines (labeled *Hraðbanki*) have instructions in English and work just like they do at home. Don't withdraw more Icelandic currency than you need. Most merchants prefer plastic, and you'll scramble to spend unused krónur at the end of your trip. To keep your cash, cards, and valuables safe, wear a money belt.

Before departing, call your bank or credit-card company: Confirm that your card(s) will work overseas, ask about international transaction fees, and alert them that you'll be making withdrawals in Europe. Also ask for the PIN number for your credit card—you may need it for Europe's "chip-and-PIN" payment machines. Allow time for your bank to mail your PIN to you.

European cards use chip-and-PIN technology; most chip cards issued in the US instead require a signature option. European card readers may generate a receipt for you to sign—or prompt you to enter your PIN (so it's good to know it). US credit cards may not work at some self-service payment machines (transit-ticket kiosks, parking kiosks, etc.). If your card won't work, look for a cashier who can process the transaction manually—or pay in cash.

Drivers Beware: Drivers may encounter automated pay points—such as parking meters or automated gas pumps—where US cards are not accepted. Be prepared to move on to another gas station if necessary.

At attended gas stations, if you have trouble at the pump, go inside and ask the cashier to process your card manually (or ask for a prepaid gas card, which you should be able to buy with any US card). Carry cash as a backup.

Especially in rural areas, don't let your tank get too low. You can plan gas stops in advance: Major fuel providers N1, ÓB, Orkan, and Olís list their pump locations online.

Dynamic Currency Conversion: If merchants offer to convert your purchase price into dollars (called dynamic currency conversion, or DCC), refuse this "service." You'll pay extra for the expensive convenience of seeing your charge in dollars. If an ATM offers to "lock in" or "guarantee" your conversion rate, choose "proceed without conversion." Other prompts might state, "You can be charged in dollars: Press YES for dollars, NO for krónur." Always choose the local currency.

STAYING CONNECTED

The simplest solution is to bring your own device—mobile phone, tablet, or laptop—and use it just as you would at home (following the money-saving tips below).

To call Iceland from a US or Canadian number: Whether you're phoning from a landline, your own mobile phone, or a Skype account, you're making an international call. Dial 011-354 and then the local number. (The 011 is our international access code, and 354 is Iceland's country code.) If dialing from a mobile phone, you can enter + in place of the international access code—press and hold the 0 key.

To call Iceland from a European country: Dial 00-354 followed by the local number. (The 00 is Europe's international access code.)

To call within Iceland: Just dial the seven-digit phone number.

To call from Iceland to another country: Dial 00 followed by the country code (for example, 1 for the US or Canada), then the area code and number. If you're calling European countries whose phone numbers begin with 0, omit that 0 when you dial (except when calling Italy).

Tips: If you bring your own mobile phone, consider signing up for an international plan; most providers offer a simple bundle that includes calling, messaging, and data.

Sleep Code

Hotels are classified based on the average price of a standard double room with breakfast in high season.

$$$$	**Splurge:** Most rooms over 35,000 ISK
$$$	**Pricier:** 28,000-35,000 ISK
$$	**Moderate:** 20,000-28,000 ISK
$	**Budget:** 15,000-20,000 ISK
¢	**Hostel/Backpacker:** Under 15,000 ISK

Unless otherwise noted, credit cards are accepted, hotel staff speak English, and free Wi-Fi is available. Comparison-shop by checking prices at several hotels (on each hotel's own website, on a booking site, or by email). For the best deal, *always book directly with the hotel.*

Use Wi-Fi whenever possible. Most hotels and many cafés offer free Wi-Fi, and you may also find it at tourist information offices (TIs), major museums, and public-transit hubs. With Wi-Fi you make free or low-cost calls via a calling app such as Skype, FaceTime, or Google Hangouts. When you need to get online but can't find Wi-Fi, turn on your cellular network (or turn off airplane mode) just long enough for the task at hand.

Without a mobile device, you can make calls from your hotel and get online using public computers (there's usually one in your hotel lobby or at local libraries). Most hotels charge a fee for international calls—ask for rates before you dial. Or you can use a prepaid international phone card (sold at supermarkets, convenience stores, and gas stations).

For more on phoning, see Ricksteves.com/phoning. For a one-hour talk on "Traveling with a Mobile Device," see Ricksteves. com/travel-talks.

SLEEPING

I've categorized my recommended accommodations based on price, indicated with a dollar-sign rating (see sidebar). I recommend reserving rooms as soon as your itinerary is set, particularly during the peak summer season. Check the specific price for your preferred stay at several hotels, either by comparing prices on booking sites such as Hotels.com or Booking.com, or the hotels' own websites. After you've zeroed in on your choice, book directly with the hotel itself. Some Icelandic hotels use Booking.com as their default booking engine and list prices in euros or US dollars; calling or emailing to book direct may net you a better rate, and increases the chances that the hotelier will be able to accommodate any special needs or requests (such as shifting your reservation).

For complicated requests, send an email with the following information: number and type of rooms; number of nights; arrival

PRACTICALITIES

date; departure date; and any special requests. Use the European style for writing dates: day/month/year. Hoteliers typically ask for your credit-card number as a deposit.

In Iceland, hotels are usually large (big enough for groups), impersonal, and corporate-owned. If you want a more mom-and-pop feeling, look for guesthouses and farmstays. An ample breakfast buffet is generally included.

A short-term rental—whether an apartment, house, or room in a local's home—is an increasingly popular alternative, especially in expensive Iceland. Websites such as Airbnb, FlipKey, Booking.com, and the HomeAway family of sites (HomeAway, VRBO, and VacationRentals) let you browse properties and correspond directly with Icelandic property owners or managers.

EATING

I've categorized my recommended eateries based on price, indicated with a dollar-sign rating (see sidebar).

Traditional Icelandic cuisine isn't too far removed from its Viking Age roots—relying heavily on anything hardy enough to survive the harsh landscape (lamb, potatoes), caught in or near the sea (fish, seabirds), or sturdy enough to withstand winter storage (dried and salted fish). Today's chefs have built on this heritage, introducing international flavors and new approaches to old-style dishes. Reykjavík has emerged as a foodie destination—with both high-end, experimental "New Icelandic" cuisine and a renewed appreciation for the country's traditional, nose-to-tail "hardship" cuisines. The capital offers a wide variety of dining options, but even in the countryside, you're never far from a satisfying meal.

Food and drink prices in Iceland are strikingly high, but it is possible to eat well here without going broke. There's no tipping, taxes are built into prices, and restaurants cheerfully dispense free tap water, making eating out more reasonable than the menu prices might suggest.

In Reykjavík, lunches are a particularly good value, as many eateries offer the same quality and similar selections for far less than at dinner. Make lunch your main meal, then have a lighter evening meal. Many places offer a lunch special—typically a plate of fish, vegetables, and a starch (rice or potatoes) for 2,000-3,000 ISK. An unlimited soup-and-bread buffet—typically available for less than 2,000 ISK—is another good budget lunch option, commonly offered at cafés, bakeries, touristy rest stops, and other basic eateries.

Picnicking is a good way to stretch a limited budget. Seek out the budget supermarket chains Krónan and Bónus. But be wary of grocery shopping at the omnipresent convenience stores, which are well-stocked but far more expensive.

Restaurant Price Code

Eateries in this book are categorized according to the average cost of a typical main course. Drinks, desserts, and splurge items (steak and seafood) can raise the price considerably.

$$$$ **Splurge:** Most main courses over 5,500 ISK
$$$ **Pricier:** 4,000-5,500 ISK
$$ **Moderate:** 2,500-4,000 ISK
$ **Budget:** Under 2,500 ISK

In Iceland, a takeout place or soup-and-bread buffet is **$**; a sit-down café is **$$**; a casual but more upscale restaurant is **$$$**; and a swanky splurge is **$$$$**.

If you drink alcohol, prices are high, especially for wine and spirits. If you plan to seriously imbibe during your visit, make a point of stopping at the airport duty-free store on your way into the country (check current allowances at www.dutyfree.is).

TRANSPORTATION

If you're staying in Reykjavík and plan only a few brief forays outside the city, you can get by without a car. But most visitors find that renting a car gives them maximum flexibility for getting out into the Icelandic countryside—the highlight of any visit to this country. You won't find convenient public transportation options for reaching some sights (including the Golden Circle); instead you'll likely need to rely on pricey excursions, or rent a car (often the more cost-effective choice).

By Car: Two people splitting the cost of a rental car and gas will likely save a lot over the cost of bus excursions, while enjoying the flexibility of stopping whenever and wherever they want. It's cheaper to arrange most car rentals from the US, so research car rentals before you go. For tips on your insurance options, see Ricksteves.com/cdw, and for route planning, consult Viamichelin. com. Bring your driver's license. Many tourists think of a trip to Iceland as more of an "expedition" than it really is, and shell out for a high-clearance SUV when they would do just fine with a teeny two-wheel-drive car. You won't need four-wheel drive for the destinations in this book in summer, or even for a quick winter stopover if you stick to Reykjavík. Driving is easy here—the hardest part is navigating the roundabouts of suburban Reykjavík.

Local road etiquette is similar to that in the US. The website www.drive.is has a helpful (if overlong) video with tips for safely navigating the country's many unpaved roads and one-lane bridges. The Icelandic Road Authority (Vegagerðin) website (www.road.is) shows up-to-date snow, ice, and wind conditions on all the major roads in the country. Visiting this site is a must before setting off

PRACTICALITIES

on any car trip, even in summer. Ask your car-rental company about the rules of the road or check the US State Department website (www.travel.state.gov, select "International Travel," then "Country Information," search for Iceland in the "Learn about your destination" box, then select "Travel and Transportation").

By Bus: You can select from a full menu of **guided bus tours** to get into the countryside. You'll pay a premium for a guide and a carefully designed experience, but these excursions take the guesswork out of your trip. The dominant operators are Reykjavík Excursions (www.re.is) and Gray Line (www.grayline.is), while several smaller companies offer a more intimate experience. Guide to Iceland (www.guidetoiceland.is), a consortium of several travel outlets, can be a good one-stop source for tours; they have a desk inside the Reykjavík City Hall's TI.

Iceland has a good network of scheduled **public buses** (painted yellow and blue and called *strætó*), run as a single system by city and local governments (www.straeto.is). Although the Strætó network is more geared to locals than visitors, it can be useful to those traveling from one town to another. However, these buses typically do *not* connect the big countryside sights (such as Þingvellir, Geysir, and Gullfoss on the Golden Circle). Reykjavík city buses are part of the Strætó network and use the same tickets and fare structure.

In summer months, several private companies offer direct, regularly scheduled, if still pricey **bus transport** to many popular outdoor destinations that are otherwise challenging to reach (even by car). Companies to consider include Reykjavík Excursions (under the name Iceland On Your Own, www.re.is/iceland-on-your-own), Sterna Travel (www.icelandbybus.is), and Trex (www.trex.is).

HELPFUL HINTS

Emergency Help: To summon the **police** or an **ambulance**, call 112 from a mobile phone or landline. For passport problems, call the **US Embassy in Reykjavík** (tel. 595-2200, after-hours line for emergencies only—595-2248, http://is.usembassy.gov) or the **Canadian Embassy in Reykjavík** (tel. 575-6500, www.canadainternational.gc.ca/iceland-islande).

ETIAS Registration: Beginning in late 2021, US and Canadian citizens may be required to register online with the European Travel Information and Authorization System (ETIAS) before entering certain European countries (quick and easy process, $8 fee, valid 3 years, www.etiasvisa.com).

Theft or Loss: To replace a passport, you'll need to go in person to an embassy or consulate (see above). Cancel and replace your credit and debit cards by calling these 24-hour US numbers

PRACTICALITIES

with a mobile phone: Visa (tel. +1-303-967-1096), MasterCard (tel. +1-636-722-7111), and American Express (tel. +1-336-393-1111). From a landline, you can call these US numbers collect by going through a local operator. File a police report either on the spot or within a day or two; you'll need it to submit an insurance claim for lost or stolen travel gear, and it can help with replacing your passport or credit and debit cards. For more information, see Ricksteves.com/help.

Time: Iceland doesn't observe Daylight Saving Time (due to its far-north location). In summer, Iceland is one hour behind Great Britain and four/seven hours ahead of the East/West coasts of the US. In winter, Iceland is on par with Great Britain and five/eight hours ahead of the East/West coasts of the US.

Climate: Summer or winter, be prepared to bundle up (pack gloves, sturdy boots, and a waterproof jacket). While conditions overall are surprisingly moderate for the latitude, frosty temperatures and bone-chilling wind can happen at any time of year.

Holidays and Festivals: Iceland celebrates many holidays, which can close sights and attract crowds (book hotel rooms ahead). For information on holidays and festivals, check Iceland's tourism website: InspiredbyIceland.com. For a simple list showing major—though not all—events, see Ricksteves.com/festivals.

Numbers and Stumblers: What Americans call the second floor of a building is the first floor in Europe. Europeans write dates as day/month/year, so Christmas 2021 is 25/12/21. For measurements, Iceland uses the metric system: A kilogram is 2.2 pounds; a liter is about a quart; and a kilometer is six-tenths of a mile.

RESOURCES FROM RICK STEVES

This Snapshot guide is excerpted from my latest edition of *Rick Steves Iceland,* one of many titles in my ever-expanding series of guidebooks on European travel. I also produce a public television series, *Rick Steves' Europe,* and a public radio show, *Travel with Rick Steves.* My website, Ricksteves.com, offers free travel information, a forum for travelers' comments, guidebook updates, my travel blog, an online travel store, and information on European rail passes and our tours of Europe. If you're bringing a mobile device on your trip, you can download my free Rick Steves Audio Europe app, featuring dozens of self-guided audio tours of the top sights in Europe and travel interviews about Europe. For more information, see Ricksteves.com/audioeurope.

ADDITIONAL RESOURCES
Tourist Information: www.inspiredbyiceland.com
Passports and Red Tape: www.travel.state.gov
Packing List: www.ricksteves.com/packing

Travel Insurance: www.ricksteves.com/insurance
Cheap Flights: www.kayak.com or www.google.com/flights
Airplane Carry-on Restrictions: www.tsa.gov
Updates for This Book: www.ricksteves.com/update

HOW WAS YOUR TRIP?

To share your tips, concerns, and discoveries after using this book, please fill out the survey at Ricksteves.com/feedback. Thanks in advance—it helps a lot.

Icelandic Survival Phrases

Icelandic has some unique letters, most notably Ð/ð (the voiced "th" sound in "breathe," represented by "th") and Þ/þ (the unvoiced "th" sound in "breath," also represented by "th"). The letter á sounds like "ow" (rhymes with "now"). The long i in "light" is represented by "ī."

English	Icelandic	Pronunciation
Hello (formal)	Góðan daginn	GOH-thahn DĪ-ihn
Hi / Bye (informal)	Hæ / Bæ	HĪ / bī (as in English)
Do you speak English?	Talarðu ensku?	TAHL-ar-thoo EHN-skoo?
Yes. / No.	Já / Nei.	yow / nay
I (don't) understand.	Ég skil (ekki).	yehkh skeel (EH-kee)
Please. / Thank you.	Vinsamlegast. / Takk.	VIN-sahm-lay-gahst / tahk
Excuse me.	Fyrirgefðu.	FIH-ree-GEHV-thoo
No problem.	Ekkert mál.	EHK-kert mowl
Super	Fínt	feent
OK	Allt í lagi	ahlt ee LAH-yee
Goodbye (more formal)	Bless	bless
one / two	einn / tveir	ayt / tvayr
three / four	þrír / fjórir	threer / FYOH-rir
five / six	fimm / sex	fim / sex
seven / eight	sjö / átta	syur / OWT-tah
nine / ten	níu / tíu	NEE-oo / TEE-oo
hundred	hundrað	HOON-drahth
thousand	þúsund	THOO-sund
How much is it?	Hvað kostar þetta?	kvahth KOHS-tar THEHT-tah?
Is it free?	Er þetta ókeypis?	ayr THEHT-tah OH-kay-pis?
Is it included?	Er þetta innifalið?	ayr THEHT-tah EEN-nee-fah-lith?
(Icelandic) crowns	(íslenskar) krónur	(EE-slehn-skar) KROH-nur
Where is...?	Hvar er...?	kvar ayr...?
...the toilet	....klósettið	...KLOH-seht-tith
men	karlar	KAHT-lar
women	konur	KOH-noor
left / right	vinstri / hægri	VIN-stree / HĪ-grih
straight	beint	baynt
opening hours	opnunartími	OHP-noo-nar-tee-mih
At what time?	Hvenær?	KVEH-nīr
Just a moment.	Augnablik.	OOG-nah-bleek
now / soon / later	núna / bráðum / seinna	NOO-nah / BROW-thoom / SAYT-nah
today / tomorrow	í dag / á morgun	ee dahkh / ow MOR-goon
Cheers!	skál	skowl

INDEX

Explore Europe

At ricksteves.com you can browse through thousands of articles, videos, photos and radio interviews, plus find a wealth of money-saving travel tips for planning your dream trip. And with our mobile-friendly website, you can easily access all this great travel information anywhere you go.

TV Shows

Preview the places you'll visit by watching entire half-hour episodes of *Rick Steves' Europe* (choose from all 100 shows) on-demand, for free.

your travel dreams into affordable reality

Radio Interviews

Enjoy ready access to Rick's vast library of radio interviews covering travel tips and cultural insights that relate specifically to your Europe travel plans.

Travel Forums

Learn, ask, share! Our online community of savvy travelers is a great resource for first-time travelers to Europe, as well as seasoned pros.

Travel News

Subscribe to our free Travel News e-newsletter, and get monthly updates from Rick on what's happening in Europe.

Classroom Europe

Check out our free resource for educators with 400+ short video clips from the *Rick Steves' Europe* TV show.

*Gear up for your
next adventure at
ricksteves.com*

Light Luggage

Pack light and right
with Rick Steves'
affordable, custom-
designed rolling carry-on
bags, backpacks, day
packs and shoulder bags.

Accessories

From packing cubes to
moneybelts and beyond,
Rick has personally
selected the travel
goodies that will
help your trip
go smoother.

Shop at ricksteves.com

Save time and energy

This guidebook is your independent-travel toolkit. But for all it delivers, it's still up to you to devote the time and energy it takes to manage the preparation and logistics that are essential for a happy trip. If that's a hassle, there's a solution.

Rick Steves Tours

A Rick Steves tour takes you to Europe's most interesting places with great

guides and small groups of 28 or less. We follow Rick's favorite itineraries, ride in comfy buses, stay in family-run hotels, and bring you intimately

close to the Europe you've traveled so far to see. Most importantly, we take away the logistical headaches so you can focus on the fun.

Join the fun

This year we'll take 33,000 free-spirited travelers—nearly half of them repeat customers—along with us on 50 different itineraries, from Athens to Istanbul. Is a Rick Steves tour the right fit for your travel dreams?

Find out at ricksteves.com, where you can also request Rick's latest tour catalog. Europe is best experienced with happy travel partners. We hope you can join us.

BEST OF GUIDES

Full-color guides in an easy-to-scan
format. Focused on top sights
and experiences in the most
popular European destinations

Best of England
Best of Europe
Best of France
Best of Germany
Best of Ireland
Best of Italy
Best of Scotland
Best of Spain

COMPREHENSIVE GUIDES

City, country, and regional guide
printed on Bible-thin paper. Pac
with detailed coverage for a mu
week trip exploring iconic sights
and venturing off the beaten pa

Amsterdam & the Netherlands
Barcelona
Belgium: Bruges, Brussels,
  Antwerp & Ghent
Berlin
Budapest
Croatia & Slovenia
Eastern Europe
England
Florence & Tuscany
France
Germany
Great Britain
Greece: Athens & the Peloponne
Iceland
Ireland
Istanbul
Italy
London
Paris
Portugal
Prague & the Czech Republic
Provence & the French Riviera
Rome
Scandinavia
Scotland
Sicily
Spain
Switzerland
Venice
Vienna, Salzburg & Tirol

HE BEST OF ROME

ne, Italy's capital, is studded with
an remnants and floodlit-fountain
es. From the Vatican to the Colos-
, with crazy traffic in between, Rome
nderful, huge, and exhausting. The
ds, the heat, and the weighty history

of the Eternal City where Caesars walked
can make tourists wilt. Recharge by taking siestas, gelato breaks, and after-dark
walks, strolling from one atmospheric
square to another in the refreshing evening air.

d **Pantheon**—which
st dome until the
ly 2,000 years old
ty over 1,500).

f Athens in the Vat-
dies the humanistic
ce.

gladiators fought
nother, entertaining

Rome ristorante

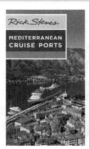

CKET GUIDES

mpact color guides for shorter trips

APSHOT GUIDES

cused single-destination coverage

CRUISE PORTS GUIDES

Reference for cruise ports of call

Mediterranean Cruise Ports
Scandinavian & Northern European
  Cruise Ports

Complete your library with...

TRAVEL SKILLS & CULTURE

*Study up on travel skills and gain
insight on history and culture*

Europe 101
Europe Through the Back Door
Europe's Top 100 Masterpieces
European Christmas
European Easter
European Festivals
For the Love of Europe
Travel as a Political Act

PHRASE BOOKS & DICTIONARIES

French
French, Italian & German
German
Italian
Portuguese
Spanish

PLANNING MAPS

Britain, Ireland & London
Europe
France & Paris
Germany, Austria & Switzerland
Iceland
Ireland
Italy
Spain & Portugal

PHOTO CREDITS

Avalon Travel
Hachette Book Group
1700 Fourth Street
Berkeley, CA 94710

Printed in Canada by Friesens.
Second Edition. First printing June 2020.

ISBN 978-1-64171-234-7

For the latest on Rick's talks, guidebooks, tours, public television series, and public
radio show, contact Rick Steves' Europe, 130 Fourth Avenue North, Edmonds, WA
98020, 425/771-8303, www.ricksteves.com, rick@ricksteves.com.

Rick Steves' Europe

Managing Editor: Jennifer Madison Davis
Assistant Managing Editor: Cathy Lu
Special Publications Manager: Risa Laib
Editors: Glenn Eriksen, Tom Griffin, Suzanne Kotz, Rosie Leutzinger, Jessica Shaw,
Carrie Shepherd
Editorial & Production Assistant: Megan Simms
Editorial Intern: Bridgette Robertson
Researchers: Jennifer Davis, Glenn Eriksen
Contributors: Cameron Hewitt, Ian Watson
Graphic Content Director: Sandra Hundacker
Maps & Graphics: David C. Hoerlein, Lauren Mills, Mary Rostad
Digital Asset Coordinator: Orin Dubrow

Avalon Travel

Senior Editor and Series Manager: Madhu Prasher
Associate Managing Editors: Jamie Andrade, Sierra Machado
Copy Editor: Maggie Ryan
Proofreader: Patrick Collins
Indexer: Stephen Callahan
Production & Typesetting: Lisi Baldwin, Christine DeLorenzo, Rue Flaherty, Jane
Musser
Cover Design: Kimberly Glyder Design
Maps & Graphics: Kat Bennett, Mike Morgenfeld

Let's Keep on Travelin'

Your trip doesn't need to end.

Follow Rick on social media!